Stigma and Sexual Orientation

PSYCHOLOGICAL PERSPECTIVES ON LESBIAN AND GAY ISSUES

editors

Beverly Greene
Gregory M. Herek

▼ 1. Lesbian and Gay Psychology:
Theory, Research, and Clinical Applications
Edited by Beverly Greene and Gregory M. Herek

▼ 2. AIDS, Identity, and Community:
The HIV Epidemic and Lesbians and Gay Men
Edited by Gregory M. Herek and Beverly Greene

▼ 3. Ethnic and Cultural Diversity Among
Lesbians and Gay Men
Edited by Beverly Greene

▼ 4. Stigma and Sexual Orientation: Understanding Prejudice
Against Lesbians, Gay Men, and Bisexuals
Edited by Gregory M. Herek

EDITORIAL BOARD

Stigma and Sexual Orientation

Understanding Prejudice Against Lesbians, Gay Men, and Bisexuals

editor

Gregory M. Herek

Psychological Perspectives on Lesbian and Gay Issues

Volume 4

*Sponsored by the Society for the Psychological Study
of Lesbian and Gay Issues, Division 44 of the
American Psychological Association*

SAGE Publications
International Educational and Professional Publisher
Thousand Oaks   London   New Delhi

For information:

 SAGE Publications, Inc.
2455 Teller Road
Thousand Oaks, California 91320
E-mail: order@sagepub.com

SAGE Publications Ltd.
6 Bonhill Street
London EC2A 4PU
United Kingdom

SAGE Publications India Pvt. Ltd.
M-32 Market
Greater Kailash I
New Delhi 110 048 India

Printed in the United States of America

Library of Congress Cataloging-in-Publication Data

Main entry under title:

Stigma and sexual orientation: Understanding prejudice against lesbians, gay men, and bisexuals/editor, Gregory M. Herek.
    p. cm.—(Psychological perspectives on lesbian and gay issues; v. 4)
    Includes bibliographical references and index.
    ISBN 0-8039-5384-4 (cloth: acid-free paper).—ISBN 0-8039-5385-2 (pbk. : acid-free paper)
    1. Heterosexiam. 2. Homophobia. 3. Gays—Public opinion. 4. Stigma (Social psychology) I. Herek, Gregory M. II. Series.
HQ76.25.S78 1998
305.9'0664—dc21   97-33909

98 99 00 01 02 03 04 10 9 8 7 6 5 4 3 2 1

Acquiring Editor:	C. Terry Hendrix
Editorial Assistant:	Dale Mary Grenfell
Production Editor:	Diana E. Axelsen
Production Assistant:	Karen Wiley
Typesetter/Designer:	Marion Warren
Indexer:	Mary Mortensen
Print Buyer:	Anna Chin

When citing a volume from **Psychological Perspectives on Lesbian and Gay Issues,** please use the following style:

Herek, Gregory M. (Ed.). *Psychological perspectives on lesbian and gay issues: Vol. 4. Stigma and sexual orientation: Understanding prejudice against lesbians, gay men, and bisexuals.* Thousand Oaks, CA: Sage.

Contents

Evelyn Hooker, Ph.D.
1907–1996

This volume is dedicated to the memory of Evelyn Hooker, a pioneering psychologist who was not afraid to use the scientific method to question the prevailing assumptions of her time. Her research helped to lay a foundation for the modern movement in psychology that is affirmative of minority sexual orientations—lesbian, gay, and bisexual. She was an inspiration, mentor, and friend to scientists, clinicians, and teachers from all over the world. Her passing leaves a gap in our lives that will not soon be filled.

Preface

This volume, the fourth in the annual series Psychological Perspectives on Lesbian and Gay Issues, is devoted to research on the phenomenon variously referred to as homophobia, heterosexism, and simply prejudice based on sexual orientation. Empirical study in this area has advanced at a rapid pace in the 1990s. Researchers increasingly are using more sophisticated theories and methods to investigate stigma and sexual orientation, and their reports are appearing more frequently in general scientific journals.

This mainstreaming of research on antigay stigma is important not only because it offers the promise of finding better ways to combat prejudice, but also because studying homophobia will enrich the study of intergroup attitudes in general. Understanding prejudice based on sexual orientation inevitably raises a wealth of important questions relevant to other forms of stigma—about the nature of concealable stigmas, the expression of prejudice through violence and discrimination, the dialectic between cultural ideologies and individual attitudes and values, and responses to stigma by its targets.

The first six chapters of the present volume address the nature of antigay stigma. The authors consider attitudes, values, and stereotypes, as well as homophobic assaults and public opinion. They also examine antigay behaviors outside the laboratory—in the courtroom, on the streets, and in the voting booth. Karen Franklin reports findings from her study of perpetrators of hate crimes. Her data highlight the importance of understanding situational factors that give rise to assaults based on sexual orientation. Drury Sherrod and Peter Nardi report data from a large-scale study of homophobia among prospective jurors in 15 different states. Mary Kite and Bernard Whitley consider the underlying sources of the frequently observed gender difference in heterosexuals' attitudes toward homosexuality and toward lesbians and gay men. Angela Simon considers the relationship between antigay stereotypes and prejudice, and whether the two are inseparably linked. Geoffrey Haddock and Mark Zanna discuss the role of personal values and authoritarian personality traits in antigay attitudes. Douglas Strand reviews national survey data to disentangle various components of heterosexuals' attitudes—his distinction between attitudes toward basic civil liberties and attitudes toward broader civil rights policies represents an important step toward improving our understanding of the multiple manifestations of cultural and psychological heterosexism.

Perhaps one of the most important conclusions that may be drawn from these six chapters is that the phenomenon we are studying is not monolithic. Verbal expressions of opinion are not necessarily predictive of verbal expressions of belief, or of behavior in situations with strong demands for antigay conduct. Moreover, the types of attitudes routinely tapped in social psychological laboratory studies appear to be different from attitudes toward policies relevant to gay rights and civil liberties for gay people.

The authors of Chapters 7, 8, and 9 consider the consequences of antigay stigma and related phenomena for the well-being of lesbians, gay men, and bisexuals. Joanne DiPlacido places this question within the broader framework of health psychology studies on coping and stress. Ilan Meyer and Laura Dean report findings from their study of gay and bisexual men in New York. Anthony D'Augelli provides a thoughtful discussion of the special challenges that cultural heterosexism creates for lesbian, gay, and bisexual youth. These chapters point us toward an attempt to understand both how so many lesbians, gay men, and bisexuals successfully face the challenges created for them by societal prejudice and what we can do to best assist those who are victimized by that prejudice.

What can psychology and science do to confront homophobia and antigay stigma? The final two chapters in this volume focus on some ways in which law and policy have been influenced by heterosexism, especially in regard to the family relations of gay, lesbian, and bisexual people. Andrew McLeod and Isiaah Crawford discuss the nexus (and frequent disjunction) between legal and scientific approaches to gay and lesbian families. My own chapter critiques a survey study conducted by

Paul Cameron and his colleagues, which, despite its serious methodological flaws and lack of scientific credibility, has been used in the legal and policy arenas.

Like the previous books in this series, the current volume is sponsored by the Society for the Psychological Study of Lesbian and Gay Issues (Division 44 of the American Psychological Association). I extend my thanks to all of the contributors, especially those who generously provided constructive feedback on chapters other than their own. From the very beginning of my work on this volume, it has been my good fortune to have the invaluable assistance of Mary Ellen Chaney and the help and patience of Dale Grenfell and Terry Hendrix of Sage Publications. I sincerely thank them. Finally, I thank Jack Dynis for his advice and unwavering support throughout this and so many other projects.

—GREGORY M. HEREK

1

Unassuming Motivations
Contextualizing the Narratives
of Antigay Assailants

KAREN FRANKLIN

B ias-related violence against homosexuals is believed to be widespread in the United States, with perpetrators typically described
by victims as young men in groups who assault targets of convenience
(Berrill, 1992).[1] Victim accounts suggest that assailants possess tremen-
dous rage and hatred; indeed, documentation of horrific levels of
brutality has led gay activists to characterize the violence as political
terrorism aimed at all gay men and lesbians (National Gay and Lesbian
Task Force, 1993). Other motives for antigay violence suggested in the
literature include male bonding, proving heterosexuality, and purging
secret homosexual desires (e.g., Goff, 1990; Harry, 1990). Due to a
dearth of empirical research with assailants, motives are largely in-
ferred from victim accounts and a handful of publicized cases. Thus,
the goal of the research discussed in this chapter was to investigate
assailants' self-described motivations for their assaults.

I present below the stories of three assailants whom I interviewed
as part of my dissertation research into the motivations and attitudes

AUTHOR'S NOTE: I gratefully acknowledge the financial support of the Harry Frank
Guggenheim Foundation, which made the writing of this chapter possible. Deepest thanks
also go to Greg Herek and Kathleen Erwin for their inspiration and thoughtful feedback.

underlying antigay violence (Franklin, 1996). For the larger study, 11 assailants were recruited through newspaper advertisements and public records of criminal convictions. People who admitted assaulting gay men or lesbians were asked to complete a 2-hour interview. They were paid $20 and were assured of confidentiality within legal limits. The semistructured interviews elicited details of the assaults; the assailants' explanations and justifications; biographical information on the assailants, as well as descriptions of their families and friendship networks; and the interviewees' beliefs about social issues such as homosexuality, AIDS, and sex roles.

The larger project also included a survey of antigay behaviors and attitudes among 484 young adults at six community colleges in the greater San Francisco Bay Area. The 137-item anonymous questionnaire consisted of a lengthy violence inventory as well as indexes of attitudes toward homosexuality, attitudes of respondents' parents and friends, and beliefs about masculinity.[2] The survey results confirmed the commonplace nature of antigay behaviors in a region known for social tolerance, with 1 in 10 students admitting to physical violence and another 23.5% to name-calling directed at gay men and lesbians.

In this chapter I explore four central components of antigay violence. Although for heuristic purposes the constructs are presented as distinct, in fact my interviews supported the thesis of *multiple determinism*, in which a variety of social, psychological, and situational forces converge to create a violent incident (Pervin, 1986). The three cases presented here illustrate how these central elements play out in the context of one particularly prevalent pattern of antigay violence: assaults by men in groups or pairs on suspected homosexual men who are strangers to the assailants.

Other than their assaults, Andrew, Brian, and Eric have little in common.[3] They span the spectrum of opinion toward homosexuality and, indeed, contemporary lifestyles more generally. Brian is a young White man with a college education; a self-described liberal, he has gay friends and argues against homophobia with family members. Andrew is an African American man in his mid-30s with a postcollege education who also espouses progressive politics and is "down with gay rights";[4] he resigned from the military after witnessing a brutal gay bashing by fellow soldiers, but he also expressed personal revulsion for male-male sex acts, saying he would rather "lick my dog's butt" than kiss a man. Eric is an economically and politically marginalized biracial (Native American and White) man who professes hatred of "faggots" and a litany of other groups, including both Jews and "rednecks," but denies committing assaults based on sexuality per se:

> Faggots are disgusting. It's sick. . . . That's why they destroyed Sodom and Gomorrah, because all these guys were butt-fucking each other. . . . But what they do is their business. Some people beat the shit out of people instead of just accepting it. And that's wrong. . . . I don't like niggers, I don't like faggots, I don't even like too many White people. But I've never assaulted anyone just because they're a fag or a Jew or a Black.

Andrew

Andrew is a soft-spoken 35-year-old "born-again pagan" from a large and "crazy" Catholic family. As a child, he was subjected to "unimaginable acts of cruelty" by his father, who tied him up and beat him for associating with the wrong crowd. Although liberal about race issues, Andrew's father is virulently homophobic and has accused Andrew of being a "fag" and effeminate. Andrew's mother is the opposite: "She doesn't care if I marry a homo as long as he's a Black one."

Andrew expressed considerable preoccupation with homosexuality. Seeking reassurance from me that he looked heterosexual, he explained that not only his father but several other relatives and acquaintances as well have insinuated that he is gay. Andrew frequents a local gay bar, where he allows men to buy him drinks and then tells them that he is not gay. "Who am I to argue with a free drink?" he explained.

Two years before the assault, Andrew was "sitting around smoking dope and drinking" with his martial arts partner and good friend of many years, when the friend tearfully confided that he was gay. Although the friend feared that Andrew "would think badly of him," Andrew said he did not in fact lose respect. "He is no less of a man for telling me he's gay. I'm prejudiced against certain types of gays, effeminate men. . . . My friend is a man's man. He'd be the last person I'd expect."

The assault took place while Andrew, his gay friend, and three other friends were "getting drunk" at a park and a man passed by smoking marijuana. When Andrew asked if he could buy a joint, the man reportedly patted Andrew's buttock and said, "Sure, if I can take you in the bushes and fuck you in the ass."

"He said it in Spanish, and at first I thought I'd mistranslated or he was joking," Andrew recalled. "I didn't give a thought to the man being gay till he opened his mouth. He sounded effeminate."

Andrew said he "snapped." He threw the man's motorcycle down an embankment, punched the man in the throat, and kicked him once before his workout partner was able to restrain him. "I would have killed him."

In line with his expressed animosity toward effeminate men, Andrew also recounted a separate incident in which he threatened an effeminate gay coworker whom he described as "lewd and obnoxious." When the man joked about Andrew's new shoes, Andrew retorted, "You drink the semen out of men's penises and you have the nerve to insult me!" The man became angry, and Andrew "told him to calm down before I kicked his ass."

Andrew's emotional intensity and preoccupation with male homosexuality seem to fit the folkloric explanation of antigay violence as a defensive reaction to internal homosexual impulses. Nor is the fact that Andrew assaulted a homosexual in front of his close gay friend probably coincidental. How better to prove his masculinity and heterosexuality than by demonstrating it to his gay friend?

Reaction formation is probably the most popular explanation for antigay assaults. In this classic psychoanalytic defense mechanism, individuals replace anxiety-producing same-sex attractions with hostility and disgust (Ferenczi, 1914/1952). Particularly for young men reaching sexual maturity, same-sex attractions or difficulties forming intimate relationships with girls often combine with societally induced fear of homosexuality to cause insecurities about sexuality. Because young men feel they cannot discuss these concerns, their worries may lead to confusion, anxiety, shame, and—in some cases—public denigration of homosexuals in order to prove masculinity (Goff, 1990).

This defensive explanation is alluring both in its simplicity and in its location of the problem within the individual, thus psychologizing the phenomenon of heterosexism. However, my own research and that of Herek (e.g., 1987) suggest that negative attitudes and behaviors toward homosexuals are more commonly based on social affiliation needs and value conflicts than on exclusively defensive factors. Furthermore, because same-sex attractions do not engender defensiveness in cultures where homosexuality is not constructed as problematic, the defensive explanation is somewhat circular in that it does not explain why homosexuality is perceived as threatening in our particular culture in the first place. Although a minority of individuals like Andrew may indeed be attempting to exorcise forbidden homosexual desires, this interpretation fails to explain the behaviors of the majority of people who assault gay men and lesbians.

Brian

Brian is a trim, athletic 27-year-old who sported a Malcolm X cap during our meeting. Raised in a White, middle-class Protestant family with "the '50s paradigm, father-knows-best and all," he rebelled against his parents' conservative religious and political values and became a Libertarian and Jesse Jackson supporter. He prides himself on being an independent thinker who opposes male "tribalism" and "groupthink."

At age 21, Brian committed a series of four late-night assaults on gay men. All were committed with friends in a secluded area known locally for gay male cruising. The first assault occurred when Brian and a friend went to the location to "check it out." To prove to his doubting friend that a man loitering nearby was looking for sex, Brian approached the man and, "in a gay voice, with a lisp," said, "We're looking for some action." When the man exhibited a "bitch attitude" by not responding, Brian punched him and knocked him down. "One punch," Brian recalled. "I was surprised. The guy couldn't take a punch."

The next two assaults occurred when Brian and the same friend returned to the area to commit robberies, ostensibly because the friend wanted to steal a calling card to make telephone calls to another state. Because Brian's friend was a "rough-looking Black dude" of whom potential victims might be afraid, Brian's role was to "do the gay talk" and "lure" the victims. He enticed one target into the bushes, where he and his friend beat the victim and robbed him of money and a calling card. But when they tried this scheme again, their next target was able to escape:

> I told my friend, "As soon as I ask the guy for a light, rush him." The guy swung at my friend, and my friend ducked. The guy tried to run, but tripped. It was so funny watching this guy flip over in the air and then try to run. I was chasing him but dying laughing. . . . I made a mistake. I should have given him an uppercut when he lit my cigarette. The guy was big, about 6-foot-4 and husky, and we had a misconception that just because he was gay we could take him.

Brian's fourth assault involved the same basic plan, but it was committed with a different friend. Again, the plan went awry when the victim saw the second assailant:

> I got this guy and said, "Why don't we go in the bushes and do something?" But when the guy saw my friend he got nervous and took off. I chased him. He looked back at me like a scared deer.

Eric

Eric is a shy, wiry 26-year-old whose childhood was filled with numerous traumas, from parental alcoholism and death to adoption and abandonment. By age 15 he had garnered 10 arrests and was serving time in youth prison for a shooting. Economically marginalized and alienated from the political system, he resents "sniveling minorities" who are always "pissing and moaning." He said American Indians such as himself "have more right than Blacks to piss and moan, yet they don't."

Despite his avowed racism, Eric differentiated himself from skinhead friends, whom he said "will walk by a Black person and spit at him." Eric had been present when skinhead friends assaulted African Americans but said he did not participate. "It's not my place to stop them or condone it. You can't stop them."

Eric admitted numerous assaults on a variety of people, including four assaults on gay men. The one group attack occurred while he and some friends were en route to a concert. Having just broken up with a girlfriend, Eric had "a total fuck-it attitude" and was heavily intoxicated. When a group of businessmen began staring at Eric and his friends—who were sporting Mohawks, nose rings, tattoos, and camouflage attire—Eric's hotheaded friend Mike yelled, "What are you looking at?" The men laughed, prompting Mike to retort, "Are you guys a bunch of faggots or something? Suck my dick!" One of the businessmen yelled back, "Fuck you," and the fight was on.

Mike jumped out of the pickup truck and struck the businessman twice. The man picked up a metal pole and swung it at Eric, hitting him in the boot. Eric and his friends piled out of the truck and chased the man. "Mike kicked the shit out of him; all I did was kick him in the stomach. I was calling him faggot, cocksucker, puke." Eric said the businessmen were "probably fags," but he does not know for sure.

Eric recounted three other assaults on men whom he believed were homosexual. In one, he chased and kicked a biracial transvestite, for no reason other than that the man looked "weird" and was staring at him. Another time, he beat up a "fag" for stealing his cousin's jacket. ("He was a fag and a thief, so that made it twice as bad.") Most recently, he beat up "a total fag" acquaintance while the man was playing a video game at the home of one of Eric's relatives:

> He'd talk about his boyfriends all the time. One night I just got tired of it. I said, "Don't talk about that shit in front of me." He kept on, so I beat the shit out of him. I gave him an uppercut, and split his cheek open. I put his head through the glass table, got him down on the floor, and kicked him a bunch of times. He kept saying he'd had enough, but I said, "I don't think so." . . . The next day I felt bad. I apologized to him.

Eric stressed that he assaulted this man not because he was homosexual, but because "he wasn't respecting me. I didn't care that he's gay, if he'd shut up about it, be quiet about his preference."

Enforcement of Gender Norms

Although their assaults fall within most legal definitions of hate crime, Brian, Andrew, and Eric—like the rest of the informants I interviewed— all insisted that their assaults were not motivated by hatred of homosexuals. To reconcile the apparent contradiction between the socially normative attitudes often held by assailants and the viciousness and brutality of their behavior toward gay men and lesbians, during the course of my research I came to conceptualize the violence not in terms of individual hatred but as an extreme expression of American cultural stereotypes and expectations regarding male and female behavior.

From this perspective, assaults on homosexuals and other individuals who deviate from sex role norms are viewed as a learned form of social control of deviance rather than a defensive response to personal threat (Millham & Weinberger, 1977). Thus, heterosexism is not just a personal value system, it is a tool in the maintenance of *gender dichotomy*. In other words, through heterosexism, any male who refuses to accept the dominant culture's assignment of appropriate masculine behavior is labeled early on as a "sissy" or "fag" and then subjected to bullying (Green,

1987). Similarly, any woman who opposes male dominance and control can be labeled a lesbian and attacked (Pharr, 1988). The potential of being ostracized as homosexual, regardless of actual sexual attractions and behaviors, puts pressure on all people to conform to a narrow standard of appropriate gender behavior, thereby maintaining and reinforcing our society's hierarchical gender structure.

Eric exemplifies how heterosexual males, once they have incorporated a heterosexist ideology, appoint themselves as agents for the control of sexual deviance. In describing the three assaults on gay men that he committed while alone, Eric used shorthand explanations that assumed a shared cultural belief that his victims had violated unwritten codes of appropriate behavior and thus deserved punishment. In the first instance, Eric inflicted punishment for the gender-inappropriate act of cross-dressing; the fact that he offered no justification for this assault other than to repeatedly describe his transvestite victim's physical appearance (makeup, female clothing, and long braided hair) suggests that he believed the gender-norm beliefs upon which he acted are universally shared.

In the case of the man who had stolen his cousin's jacket, Eric inflicted punishment primarily for thievery; the man's identity as a "fag" merely provided additional justification for a beating that would have ensued anyway. In Eric's mind, "thief" and "fag" were equivalent concepts, as both entail violations of social norms shared by his peer group and society at large. Finally, in assaulting his relative's gay friend, Eric distinguished his victim's sexual inclinations, which were not problematic, from his refusal to be invisible. Thus, Eric was punishing the man not for homosexual acts but for so-called flaunting, that is, refusal to be ashamed of deviance. In each case, Eric was enforcing gender norms that he understood to be mandatory in our culture.

The enforcement of gender norms also explains Brian's calculated assaults on men whom he labeled "weak," and explains why he exhibited only shallow and unconvincing remorse. Indeed, Brian seemed driven by a visceral contempt for men he perceived as lacking in physical strength. More than once during our discussion, he nodded toward certain men walking by—men with slim builds and studious demeanors—as "pathetic" examples of prime candidates for assault. Brian's scorn was ironic in that he considered himself socially progressive and claimed to despise the fraternity ethos of "tribal," chest-thumping masculinity. Because Brian has a small build and has experienced male rape attempts, one explanation for his revulsion is defensive displacement of weakness. However, contempt for "weak," or insufficiently masculine, men is a central characteristic not just of Brian but of our entire culture (David & Brannon, 1976). Thus, cultural norms of masculinity help explain Brian's self-righteousness and lack of remorse, despite his professed support for gay rights and social tolerance.

Eric's and Brian's commitment to the enforcement of masculine norms stems from the nature of masculinity as an *achieved*, rather than ascribed, status. Masculinity and its converse, femininity, are relatively recent constructs of Western culture. Connell (1995) has argued that there is not one but many masculinities within contemporary Western society, with the dominant ideal—or *hegemonic masculinity*—operating more as a cultural standard than as an achievable status for the majority of men. Although hegemonic masculinity is somewhat elastic—its features change depending upon the labor needs of the state in a particular era—it generally connotes dominance, competitiveness, occupational achievement, and heterosexuality. McCarthy (1994) has traced these role prescriptions to a medieval warrior ethos concerning physical courage, strength, and honor that was repopularized during the 19th century in the service of American and European colonial expansionism.

The internalization of masculine subjectivities begins as early as preschool, when parents and teachers react more negatively to sex role deviations among boys than among girls (Green, 1987), and continues throughout adulthood. The peer group initiations of adolescence are particularly central in boys' incorporation of misogyny and heterosexism as essential components of masculine identity. This peer group indoctrination takes place not just among middle-class White boys, but across American cultures and economic classes. For example, the peer group has been described as playing a particularly powerful role in the socialization of African American boys (Franklin, 1984), who adopt masculine ideals of aggressiveness and antifemininity not only to succeed in the dominant culture (Cazenave & Leon, 1987), but also to rebel against Black women "as the inhibiting instruments of an oppressive system" (Grier & Cobbs, 1968, p. 52).

Adolescent males' sexual banter is a primary mode for the incorporation of an *antifemininity norm* (Thompson, Grisanti, & Pleck, 1985) emphasizing male dominance and female submission. Boys label women "bitches" and "sluts" and describe sexual intercourse as "fucking," "screwing," or "banging," symbolically associating female victimization with male dominance despite the fact that many boys do not privately relate to girlfriends in the stereotyped manner implied by such speech (Stockard & Johnson, 1980).

Organized sport, institutionalized during the Industrial Revolution as a test of masculinity, displays both this antifemininity norm and a competitive, hierarchical structure of organization. It models these hegemonic ideals both for athletes and for the much larger body of boys and men on the sidelines who benefit from male gender privilege without participating in direct displays of masculine power (Connell, 1995). In athletics, men must prove their masculinity by conquering, or "feminizing," other men (Dundes, 1985, p. 119). The ritual glorification of the masculine and vilification of the feminine thus demonstrate and celebrate masculine social power and dominance.

The antifemininity norm is a classic feature of other hierarchical male institutions, such as the military and the ultramasculine culture of prison. In the latter, prisoners are stripped of all social power except their status as men, and this too can be stolen from a man perceived as weak or passive. Through rape, men are symbolically emasculated and redefined as female to assume the role of property to their conquerors (Rideau & Wikberg, 1992). Prison rapists' stated motivations—"We're going to take your manhood" or "We're going to make a girl out of you" (Roskey, 1988, pp. 52-53)—illustrate that cultural expectations concerning masculinity are at the root of this ritual.

The antifemininity norm of hegemonic male culture explains the distinction drawn by Andrew between his gay friend, who is a "man's man," and effeminate gays such as the man he assaulted and the co-worker he threatened. For Andrew, the violation of male gender norms that effeminacy represents was more problematic than same-sex sexual conduct. This also explains research findings that a significant portion of heterosexuals' unwillingness to interact with both male and female homosexuals is premised on the belief that homosexuals behave in ways inappropriate to their anatomical sex (Millham & Weinberger, 1977). These gender norms are so deeply rooted in our culture that even among gay men and lesbians, drag queens and butch lesbians are often stigmatized by other homosexuals (Blachford, 1981). The consistent correlation found between gender stereotyping and heterosexism further bolsters the proposition that heterosexism is but one component of a broader ideology of hegemonic masculinity. Ultimately, then, homosexuals are culturally threatening more because they are perceived as violating essential gender norms than because they violate sexual taboos.

Peer Dynamics

Notably, all three assailants committed assaults either with or in front of friends, pointing to another social dimension of antigay violence. Brian and Eric in particular characterized their actions as assisting their friends. Brian saw himself as helping a friend who needed money and a calling card; Eric saw himself as protecting his young and hotheaded friend Mike. The peer group is especially influential for young men like Eric, who are alienated from institutions of society such as the school, the family, the workplace, religion, and politics. Pinderhughes (1991) has explored how marginalized young males establish their identity and self-worth by proving through toughness and hatred of the appropriate enemies that they are "down with the program" (p. 116).

In youthful peer groups, socially prohibited acts serve several instrumental functions. One of these is the garnering of social status by individuals who are often cut off from other methods of achieving it. A second function is to reduce intragroup competition by displacing it onto an external object—a surrogate victim scapegoated as deserving the abuse. A third function is to increase group solidarity and cohesion; this in turn bolsters interpersonal support in networks typically characterized by low cohesion and stability. Interviewing men convicted of robbery, for example, Cordilia (1986) identified a pattern in which social factors overrode monetary gain as a motive. In this pattern, the robbery was not planned until after the men began drinking together, and the crime served to solidify a disconnected group by providing it with a cooperative enterprise.

The phenomenon of group escalation, in which people engage in more extreme behaviors as part of a crowd than they would if alone, has been extensively documented and has been shown to be particularly powerful among teenagers and young adults (Csikszentmihalyi & Larson, 1984). Research into juvenile delinquency has largely adopted this explanation of crime as the outcome of group processes. Individuals may participate in criminal acts without fully intending to do so and without necessarily possessing values that condone crime:

> During the course of conversation, or while exchanging banter, someone may jokingly propose doing something delinquent. As the discussion continues, a situation of "pluralistic ignorance" develops in which each person believes that the others are more committed to carrying out the act than they really are. Rationalizing their behavior in various ways, they perform the deed in a state of "shared misunderstanding." (Mawson, 1987, p. 52)

Eric's feeling that he was compelled to join in the altercation once it was underway is thus explained by the dynamics of collective action, in which the group—often under the leadership of its most impulsive member—takes on a life of its own (Polansky, Lippitt, & Redl, 1950). Even when motives are consciously formulated, in such situations there is often a large gap between the original plan and the extent of actual destruction, with participants later expressing that things went further than they intended. The role of rationalization thus becomes important both to enable collective criminality in the first place and to reduce subsequent guilt. Rationalizations identified by Sykes and Matza (1957) include denial of responsibility, denial of injury, denial of the victim (e.g., the victim "asked for it"), condemnation of the condemners, and appeal to higher loyalties. Eric used several of these rationalizations in reframing the incident as self-defense (the man struck him first), claiming he was provoked (by being stared at), condemning his condemners as homosexuals with "special rights," and invoking peer loyalty.

The peer influences described by Eric and Brian are consistent with my survey results, in which *peer group dynamics*—including the desire to feel closer to friends, to live up to friends' expectations, and to prove both toughness and heterosexuality to friends—were the primary motivation for a distinguishable group of assailants. Peer dynamics was the only motivational factor in my survey that was significantly more endorsed by male than by female assailants,[5] suggesting its particular relevance in *male* group contexts.

Because it offers *direct*—rather than secondhand—evidence, group violence against homosexuals is an ideal way for men to demonstrate their masculinity to their peers. Not only is there the stereotype, mentioned by Brian, that homosexual men are unlikely to fight back, but in addition they are fairly easy to locate in urban areas and are less likely than others to report assaults to police (Harry, 1990). Thus, in group assaults the homosexual victim can be seen as fundamentally a dramatic prop, a vehicle for a ritualized conquest through which assailants demonstrate their commitment to heterosexual masculinity and male gender norms while simultaneously engaging in homosocial bonding with each other.

This is akin to the scapegoat function of women in group rape, a phenomenon with remarkable similarities to antigay violence. Motivations proffered in the literature on group or "party" rape include the exhibition of masculinity, the purging of homoerotic feelings, and homosocial bonding (Ehrhart & Sandler, 1986; Martin & Hummer, 1989). A combination of these factors is suggested by the ritualistic manner in which rapists take turns, converse about taking turns, watch each other, or engage in simultaneous sex with victims. "The ideas of 'sharing the girl among us fellows,' congregating around a common sexual object, and being sexually stimulated together as a group certainly have their homosexual implications," noted one early researcher who studied adolescent group rapists (Blanchard, 1959, p. 259).

Group rape has been studied most extensively in the context of the college fraternity, a hypermasculine subculture in which lonely and insecure young men from privileged backgrounds bond together into phallocentric brotherhoods that provide them with strength, power, and love. Because acknowledging physical love for each other would mean giving up their place in the heterosexual male hierarchy, fraternity members separate their emotions of love and compassion from sexual feelings and ritually displace the latter onto women whom they use together as sex objects, while accusing men who do not participate of homosexuality. As the thinly disguised homoeroticism of the "gang bang" suggests, fraternity members regard homosexuality with a complex mixture of "fear, hatred, and fascination" (Sanday, 1990, p. 122). The fascination is manifested in homoerotic forms of group physical contact, including not only group sex with women but also orgiastic dances in which the brothers dance arm in arm, occasionally naked and sometimes miming homosexual intercourse, until they lose control and fall down atop each other. The parallel hatred is manifested in constant antigay banter and even slogans such as "Drink Beer, Kill Queers" and "Club Faggots, Not Seals" on T-shirts, rubber stamps, and buses (Nardi & Bolton, 1991, p. 355; National Gay and Lesbian Task Force, 1992, p. 20).

Another illustration of the extrusion of homoeroticism from hypermasculine venues is the professional bodybuilding subculture, which incorporates a "gender narcissism" that disdains both women and, by extension, men perceived as effeminate (Klein, 1989, p. 16). Because homosexuals are considered effeminate, bodybuilders—many of whom are sexually active with other men, according to Klein's ethnographic study—continually reaffirm their masculinity through public derision of gay men, up to and including physical violence.

As these examples suggest, although both group rape and antigay violence are obviously illegal and frowned upon in polite society, they can nevertheless be seen as exaggerated social demonstrations of the gender role norms described earlier that are both expected of men and reinforced by men's greater structural power in society.

Thrill Seeking

For Brian, a primary motive in committing assaults was to "have fun." He and his friends launched their adventures with excited anticipation and high energy. They prepared like athletes before a game, stretching their limbs, rehearsing their moves, avoiding alcohol and drugs. Brian explained:

> It wasn't because we had something against gays, but because we could get some money and have some fun. It was a *rush.* A serious rush. Massive rush. Danger, fight-or-flight syndrome, pumps up the adrenaline. And when we get over on someone, it really heightens the rush. . . . It was nothing at all against gays. They're just an easy target. Gays have a reputation that they can't fight. It's a stereotype, it's not always true. . . . Women are easy targets, too, but that's cowardly. That's lame. I've never hit a woman. But if someone's male, and an adult, and the sizes are reasonable, then he's fair game. At least that was my attitude at the time.

This sporting tenor is not unusual. Consider this account by a man who was invited on a gay-hunting expedition at a college party by some young men who did not realize that he himself was openly gay:

> Nothing could better illustrate the casualness with which antigay violence is perpetrated than their casual invitation, the absence of . . . hostility or rancor motivating it. It was more like they were bored and looking for something interesting to do, to liven up the evening. . . . They were inviting me to join them in what was essentially a social activity. Our great grandfathers who grew up in rural areas used to go out and hunt rabbits and squirrels for fun. Nowadays, in urban areas, they hunt gays and Latinos. (Varnell, 1991, p. 4)

Factor analysis of survey respondents' motivations identified this thrill-seeking motivation as primary for a distinguishable group of assailants. Thrill seekers included both men and women who assaulted out of boredom, the desire for excitement and fun, and the wish to feel strong. A comparison of the survey accounts of thrill seekers and peer-driven assailants revealed both commonalities and differences. Both types of assailants exhibited only minimal animosity toward homosexuals. However, peer-driven assailants tended to recognize the harm to victims while downplaying their own roles and freedom of choice, whereas thrill seekers typically minimized the impact on victims by depicting incidents as harmless and amusing. This was certainly true of Brian, who jokingly described how funny his victims looked as they desperately tried to avoid being beaten and robbed.

The discovery of a distinguishable thrill-seeking motivation for anti-gay assault concurs with other study findings that alleviation of boredom is the most frequent reason given by teenagers for criminal and rebellious behavior in general and that homosexuals are the most frequent targets of thrill-motivated assaults (Comstock, 1991; Levin & McDevitt, 1993). But what is at the root of the pervasive boredom and social alienation suggested by this motivation?

Social Powerlessness

In contemporary American society, young people—from the poor to the upper middle classes—are systematically neglected and devalued. Lacking access to meaningful, challenging experiences, and sensing a declining potential for success in today's increasingly service-oriented economy, they are often frustrated, discouraged, and socially alienated (Côté & Allahar, 1994; Hersch, 1990). Young White males in particular face the contradiction of being taught to expect hegemonic masculine power while being denied any real access to it. This contradiction fosters "power-seeking, adventurist recreational activities at the expense of others who also lack power within the social order," such as women, racial minorities, and homosexuals (Comstock, 1991, p. 108). Trapped in a temporal vortex between devalued adolescence and adult male privilege, teenage males are given tacit permission to engage in a certain degree of rowdiness and aggression, under the auspices of "boys will be boys." This is particularly true for young men from more privileged strata, such as the fraternity boys discussed earlier, for whom peer group dynamics and thrill seeking often lead to exaggerated displays of masculinity regarding which society largely looks the other way.

However, if violence becomes a pervasive way of life and endures into adulthood, the scale tilts from socially excused to maladaptive. Eric's aggression, which led to 3 years behind bars and cost him an education, is illustrative of a violent lifestyle that falls outside the ideals of hegemonic masculinity. Describing how he drank and fought his way through adolescence, Eric said, "I used to beat people up, just to beat them up. When I ran out of people I didn't like, I'd beat up people my brother didn't like." Of his assault on the businessman, he commented, "I got satisfaction out of kicking the guy."

Eric's masculinity has the exaggerated quality of *masculine protest* (Adler, 1927/1992), in which violence is employed as an overcompensation for perceived weakness. Connell (1995) views this protest masculinity as a social, rather than individual, practice. In what he labels *marginalized masculinity*, economically and socially disempowered men like Eric "claim the potency that European culture attaches to masculinity" through a facade of power when their actual circumstances provide "no real resources for power" (p. 111). In other words, males who incorporate the gender-norm expectations of hegemonic masculinity yet cannot realize these expectations due to their economic or racial status may act out in extreme manners, often with homosexuals as their targets.

This is by no means to imply that the majority of men from lower-class or racial minority backgrounds respond to poverty and oppression with hypermasculinity and violence, even in the most compelling of peer group situations. In most cases, a predisposition is engendered through childhood socialization involving not only poverty and social oppression but also violent victimization and exposure to violence (Bandura, 1973; Eron, 1987). Eric, for example, experienced not only childhood violence but also parental abandonment, alcoholism, and death. And when Andrew was a child, his sadistic father routinely beat him with weapons while verbally deriding him. Andrew said it had taken him many years to learn to control the violent impulses engendered by this paternal abuse.

One of the hallmarks of the marginalized masculinity that may develop out of childhood poverty and violence is a preoccupation with a masculine front, or the protection of reputation and pride. Recall

Eric's explanation that his relative's gay friend deserved punishment for disrespecting him. And although the businessmen whom Eric and his friends assaulted "didn't even know it was coming," among Eric's peers the assault was far from surprising. For them, the men's eye contact, laughing derision, and profanity were provocative challenges requiring physical response. Indeed, cognitive research has identified sets of norms, rules, and expectations that are shared within subcultures and lead to this type of predictable, even ritualized, social aggression (Forgas, 1986).

Studying a group of economically and socially disenfranchised White youths similar to Eric's peer group, Pinderhughes (1991) found perceived powerlessness and victimization to drive their ritualized social aggression against both homosexuals and African Americans, whom they perceived as "taking over" (p. 99). In these situations, power and violence are in a sense opposites, for "where the one rules absolutely, the other is absent. Violence appears when power is in jeopardy" (Arendt, 1969, p. 56). Thus, whereas violence is often seen as an expression of power, in Eric's case it can be alternatively conceptualized as a response to real or perceived powerlessness, wherein affluent, presumably gay men wearing expensive clothing symbolize undeserved "special rights" for minorities.

This confluence of sexuality and economic class has historical origins. In the late 19th century, effeminacy signified not homosexuality but upper-class identity or aspiration, with the effeminacy of the idle aristocracy juxtaposed against the vigorous and productive nature of the working class (Sedgwick, 1985). Healy (1996) has extended this analysis to contemporary society, arguing that lower-class skinhead culture embodies a bourgeois caricature of working-class masculinity as rough and violent that is judged against a feminized middle class: "With the skinhead image being the ultimate sign of hard, White, working-class masculinity, anyone who wasn't a skinhead wasn't hard enough, so potentially the category of 'queer' encompassed *all* non-skins" (p. 49). In this analysis, homosexuals are targeted not only as sexual deviants but also as archetypal symbols of ruling-class oppression.

The perception of homosexuals as a privileged minority with "special rights" was verbalized not just by Eric but by other assailants I interviewed as well as by respondents in the group discussions that followed survey administrations. Some respondents believed that companies are required by law to have a specified percentage of gay workers and that certain apartment buildings are legally designated as all gay. This type of mythology—calculatedly promulgated by right-wing ideologues—is widespread. In a recent nationally syndicated column for youth, a teenage boy said he had "been told . . . they granted some sort of 'special rights' status for gays" (Minton, 1995, p. 8). The resentment engendered by these beliefs was cogently expressed by a young Texan who terrorized and murdered a gay man:

> I work all my life tryin' to have something nice and make something of myself. About the best job I can get is working in a restaurant makin' minimum wage. . . . From the time I was a kid it seemed like there was a lot against me, and yet here they [homosexuals] are, they're doing something that God totally condemns in the Bible. But look at everything they've got. . . . They've got all these good jobs, sit back at a desk or sit back in an air-conditioned building not having to sweat, not having to bust their ass, and they've got money. They've got the cars, they've got the apartments. They've got all the nice stuff in 'em. So, yeah, I resented that. (quoted in Bissinger, 1995, p. 88)

The class resentment expressed toward gay men in particular suggests that homosexuals symbolize not just gender nonconformity but also the *social privilege* afforded to wealthy White businessmen and denied to the working class and underclass. Central to this symbolism is the exclusion of women and non-Whites from the category of homosexual. Thus, even when heterosexuals encounter gay men of color and lesbians, they may place these individuals in categories other than homosexual. Indeed, a large body of research suggests that when people meet an individual from a stereotyped social group who does not fit their preexisting conceptions, rather than changing their image of the group in question, they may simply define the individual as atypical (Hewstone & Brown, 1986).

How then can we understand violence against lesbians and non-White homosexuals, which, based on victimization data, appears to be at least as prevalent as assaults on White gay men (Comstock, 1991; Tallmer, 1984)? In the case of gay men of color, when homosexuality is perceived as incompatible with a particular racial identity, openly gay men from that race may be stigmatized as having abandoned their racial identity in favor of a White-centered one. Among African Americans, for example, homosexuality is sometimes described as a non-Afrocentric lifestyle originating in slavery and penal rape and contributing to a shortage of marriageable men (for a review, see Johnson, 1981). In this view, openly gay Black men are race traitors who can be symbolically absorbed into the social category of the privileged White homosexual, discussed earlier.

In regard to attacks on lesbians, both my own research and that of von Schulthess (1992) suggest that these are often committed as the ultimate harassment of *women* rather than as a form of gay bashing. Thus, assailants may make antilesbian statements as escalating tactics during attacks on women, particularly when women respond to verbal provocation by becoming defiant or nonsubmissive. Despite the possibility of interview bias, the fact that the assailants I interviewed unanimously expressed more favorable attitudes toward lesbians than toward gay men suggests that they did not regard the two identities as morally equivalent. Indeed, several interviewees appeared to hold a primarily pornographic understanding of lesbianism (see Kite & Whitley, Chapter 3, this volume). As Eric put it, "I think lesbians are pretty cool. All of my friends think it would be cool to see lesbians [glances down in embarrassment]. Guys are different."

The conflation of sexuality and class, therefore, when reinforced by peer group pressures and the endorsement of dichotomous gender norms discussed earlier, provides an added impetus for some marginalized individuals to take out their frustration and rage on homosexual men in particular.

Conclusion

Analyzing assailants' self-disclosed motivations illustrates how a combination of primarily social factors, rather than a simple and singular psychological element such as hatred or repressed homosexuality, explains antigay violence. The mutually reinforcing melding of hierarchical gender norms, peer dynamics, youthful thrill seeking, and economic and social disempowerment explains how individuals as divergent as Brian, Andrew, and Eric ended up on such parallel missions. In a nation that glorifies violence and abhors sexual diversity, a minority perceived to violate gender norms functions as an ideal dramatic prop for young men to use in demonstrating their masculinity, garnering social approval, and alleviating boredom. This becomes more true as heterosexuality increasingly becomes a primary measure of masculinity (Herek, 1986) and as gay men and lesbians become increasingly visible in the media and popular culture. Furthermore, for members of economically and socially marginalized groups, gay men in particular are ideal targets because of their symbolic identification with upper-class privilege.

The three cases presented in this chapter illustrate how antigay violence can be seen primarily as an extreme manifestation of pervasive cultural norms rather than as a manifestation of individual hatred. This distinction explains why assailants typically express little remorse despite the fact that their expressions of cultural hostility are experienced by gay men and lesbians as vicious terrorism. This distinction is also critical if we hope to reach assailants and potential assailants at the clinical and educational levels, because people who have assaulted homosexuals typically do not recognize themselves in the stereotyped image of the hate-filled extremist.

Notes

1. An extensive discussion is beyond the scope of this chapter, but this assailant profile excludes childhood sissy bashing; school and workplace harassment; assaults in institutional settings such as the military, prisons, and law enforcement; and much antilesbian violence, which is more difficult to separate from the ubiquitous harassment of women (von Schulthess, 1992). Victimization data also overrepresent affluent White gay men while neglecting less visible homosexuals as well as heterosexuals who are mistakenly attacked (Berrill, 1992).

2. Survey measures were as follows: (a) an 89-item Heterosexist Violence Inventory developed for this study, (b) the short form of the Attitudes Toward Gay Men scale (Herek, 1988) and a parallel form for lesbian targets, (c) the Attitude Functions Inventory (Herek, 1987), (d) a modified Male Role Attitudes Scale (Pleck, Sonenstein, & Ku, 1993), and (e) a measure of parental and peer group social norms developed for this study.

3. Interviewee names used here are pseudonyms.

4. All direct quotes, unless otherwise noted, are statements made by interviewees.

5. The other three motivations identified through factor analysis of a 19-item motivational index were antigay ideology, thrill seeking, and self-defense.

References

Adler, A. (1992). *Understanding human nature* (C. Brett, Trans.). Oxford: Oneworld. (Original work published 1927)

Arendt, H. (1969). *On violence.* New York: Harcourt, Brace & World.

Bandura, A. (1973). *Aggression: A social learning analysis.* Englewood Cliffs, NJ: Prentice Hall.

Berrill, K. T. (1992). Anti-gay violence and victimization in the United States: An overview. In G. M. Herek & K. T. Berrill (Eds.), *Hate crimes: Confronting violence against lesbians and gay men* (pp. 19-45). Newbury Park, CA: Sage.

Bissinger, H. G. (1995, February). The killing trail. *Vanity Fair,* pp. 80-88, 142-145.

Blachford, G. (1981). Male dominance and the gay world. In K. Plummer (Ed.), *The making of the modern homosexual* (pp. 184-210). London: Hutchinson.

Blanchard, W. H. (1959). The group process in gang rape. *Journal of Social Psychology, 49,* 259-266.

Cazenave, N. A., & Leon, G. H. (1987). Men's work and family roles and characteristics: Race, gender, and class perceptions of college students. In M. S. Kimmel (Ed.), *Changing men: New directions in research on men and masculinity* (pp. 244-262). Newbury Park, CA: Sage.

Comstock, G. D. (1991). *Violence against lesbians and gay men.* New York: Columbia University Press.

Connell, R. W. (1995). *Masculinities.* Berkeley: University of California Press.

Cordilia, A. T. (1986). Robbery arising out of a group drinking context. In A. Campbell & J. J. Gibbs (Eds.), *Violent transactions: The limits of personality* (pp. 167-180). Oxford: Basil Blackwell.

Côté, J. E., & Allahar, A. L. (1994). *Generation on hold: Coming of age in the late twentieth century.* New York: New York University Press.

Csikszentmihalyi, M., & Larson, R. (1984). *Being adolescent.* New York: Basic Books.

David, D. S., & Brannon, R. (Eds.). (1976). *The forty-nine percent majority: The male sex role.* Reading, MA: Addison-Wesley.

Dundes, A. (1985). The American game of "smear the queer" and the homosexual component of male competitive sport and warfare. *Journal of Psychoanalytic Anthropology, 8,* 115-129.

Ehrhart, J. K., & Sandler, B. R. (1986). Party rape. *Response to the Victimization of Women and Children, 9*(1), 2-5.

Eron, L. D. (1987). The development of aggressive behavior from the perspective of a developing behaviorism. *American Psychologist, 42,* 435-442.

Ferenczi, S. (1952). The nosology of male homosexuality (homoeroticism). In E. Jones (Ed. and Trans.), *First contributions to psycho-analysis.* New York: Brunner/Mazel. (Original work published 1914)

Forgas, J. P. (1986). Cognitive representations of aggressive situations. In A. Campbell & J. J. Gibbs (Eds.), *Violent transactions: The limits of personality* (pp. 41-58). Oxford: Basil Blackwell.

Franklin, C. W. (1984). *The changing definition of masculinity.* New York: Plenum.

Franklin, K. (1996). *Hate crime or rite of passage? Assailant motivations in antigay violence.* Unpublished doctoral dissertation, California School of Professional Psychology, Alameda.

Goff, J. L. (1990). Sexual confusion among certain college males. *Adolescence, 25,* 599-614.

Green, R. (1987). *The "sissy-boy syndrome" and the development of homosexuality.* New Haven, CT: Yale University Press.

Grier, W. H., & Cobbs, P. M. (1968). *Black rage.* New York: Bantam.

Harry, J. (1990). Conceptualizing anti-gay violence. *Journal of Interpersonal Violence, 5,* 350-358.

Healy, M. (1996). *Gay skins: Class, masculinity and queer appropriation.* London: Cassell.

Herek, G. M. (1986). On heterosexual masculinity: Some psychical consequences of the social construction of gender and sexuality. *American Behavioral Scientist, 29,* 563-577.

Herek, G. M. (1987). Can functions be measured? A new perspective on the functional approach to attitudes. *Social Psychology Quarterly, 50,* 285-303.

Herek, G. M. (1988). Homosexuals' attitudes toward lesbians and gay men: Correlates and gender differences. *Journal of Sex Research, 25,* 451-477.

Hersch, P. (1990, July/August). The resounding silence. *Family Therapy Networker*, pp. 19-29.

Hewstone, M., & Brown, R. (1986). Contact is not enough: An intergroup perspective on the "contact hypothesis." In M. Hewstone & R. Brown (Eds.), *Contact and conflict in intergroup encounters* (pp. 1-44). Oxford: Basil Blackwell.

Johnson, J. M. (1981). *Influence of assimilation on the psychosocial adjustment of Black homosexual men.* Unpublished doctoral dissertation, California School of Professional Psychology, Berkeley.

Klein, A. M. (1989). Managing deviance: Hustling, homophobia, and the bodybuilding subculture. *Deviant Behavior, 10,* 11-27.

Levin, J., & McDevitt, J. (1993). *Hate crimes: The rising tide of bigotry and bloodshed.* New York: Plenum.

Martin, P. Y., & Hummer, R. A. (1989). Fraternities and rape on campus. *Gender & Society, 3,* 457-473.

Mawson, A. R. (1987). *Transient criminality: A model of stress-induced crime.* New York: Praeger.

McCarthy, B. (1994). Warrior values: A socio-historical survey. In J. Archer (Ed.), *Male violence* (pp. 105-120). London: Routledge.

Millham, J., & Weinberger, L. E. (1977). Sexual preference, sex role appropriateness, and restriction of social access. *Journal of Homosexuality, 2,* 343-357.

Minton, L. (1995, December 10). Fresh voices: "Special rights" and affirmative action. *Parade Magazine,* p. 8.

Nardi, P. M., & Bolton, R. (1991). Gay-bashing: Violence and aggression against gay men and lesbians. In R. Baenninger (Ed.), *Targets of violence and aggression* (pp. 349-400). Amsterdam: Elsevier Science.

National Gay and Lesbian Task Force. (1992). *Anti-gay/lesbian violence, victimization and defamation in 1991.* Washington, DC: Author.

National Gay and Lesbian Task Force. (1993). *Anti-gay/lesbian violence, victimization and defamation in 1992.* Washington, DC: Author.

Pervin, L. (1986). Persons, situations, interactions: Perspectives on a recurrent issue. In A. Campbell & J. J. Gibbs (Eds.), *Violent transactions: The limits of personality* (pp. 15-26). Oxford: Basil Blackwell.

Pharr, S. (1988). *Homophobia: A weapon of sexism.* Inverness, CA: Chardon.

Pinderhughes, H. L. (1991). *Ethnic and racial attitudes among youth and the rise in racial conflict in New York City.* Unpublished doctoral dissertation, University of California, Berkeley.

Pleck, J. H., Sonenstein, F. L., & Ku, L. C. (1993). Masculinity ideology: Its impact on adolescent males' heterosexual relationships. *Journal of Social Issues, 49*(3), 11-29.

Polansky, N., Lippitt, R., & Redl, F. (1950). An investigation of behavioral contagion in groups. *Human Relations, 3,* 319-348.

Rideau, W., & Wikberg, R. (1992). *Life sentences: Rage and survival behind bars.* New York: Times Books.

Roskey, M. L. (1988). *Ideology in instances of anti-gay violence.* Unpublished doctoral dissertation, University of California, Irvine.

Sanday, P. (1990). *Fraternity gang rape: Sex, brotherhood, and privilege on campus.* New York: New York University Press.

Sedgwick, E. K. (1985). *Between men: English literature and male homosocial desire.* New York: Columbia University Press.

Stockard, J., & Johnson, M. M. (1980). *Sex roles: Sex inequality and sex role development.* Englewood Cliffs, NJ: Prentice Hall.

Sykes, G., & Matza, D. (1957). Techniques of neutralization. *American Sociological Review, 22,* 664-670.

Tallmer, A. (1984). Anti-lesbian violence. In National Gay Task Force, *Task force report*. Washington, DC: National Gay Task Force.

Thompson, E. H., Grisanti, C., & Pleck, J. H. (1985). Attitudes toward the male role and their correlates. *Sex Roles, 13*, 413-427.

Varnell, P. (1991, November 21). Observer's notebook: Homophobia—notes and anecdotes. *Windy City Times*, p. 4.

von Schulthess, B. (1992). Violence in the streets: Anti-lesbian assault and harassment in San Francisco. In G. M. Herek & K. T. Berrill (Eds.), *Hate crimes: Confronting violence against lesbians and gay men* (pp. 65-75). Newbury Park, CA: Sage.

2

Homophobia in the Courtroom

An Assessment of Biases Against
Gay Men and Lesbians in a Multiethnic
Sample of Potential Jurors

DRURY SHERROD

PETER M. NARDI

In a recent California trial, a patient who had not revealed his HIV-positive status prior to surgery was sued by a nurse who failed to wear protective gloves while assisting in the operation. Although repeated tests over 2 years found no symptoms of HIV in the nurse, she nevertheless sued the patient for compensation for mental stress and anxiety that she might someday contract HIV.

Fearing that homophobia might bias jurors' verdicts in the upcoming trial, the defendant's attorneys and consultants recruited a group of people who closely matched the local jury pool. They then staged a mock trial in order to assess how similar jurors in a real trial would evaluate the disputed issues and to determine whether jurors' prejudices toward homosexuals might influence their verdicts. Indeed, so deep-seated were

AUTHORS' NOTE: We wish to express our appreciation to Mattson & Sherrod, Inc. (Los Angeles), for funding the project, and to Larry Mattson for his assistance and support. An earlier version of this chapter was presented at the conference "Sexual Orientation and the Law," Los Angeles, 1994.

the mock jurors' biases that, during the deliberations, one individual continually branded the defendant as "an out-and-out murderer," and others readily agreed with the charge. Lost in these mock jurors' minds were any notions of intent, injury, the right of the defendant to keep his HIV status private, and the obligation of the clinic to require its personnel to follow universal health care procedures. The mock jury found against the defendant, as eventually did the actual trial jury.

This incident demonstrates the potential influence of jurors' biases and fears on verdicts in trials involving gay and lesbian defendants or victims. It also suggests the desirability of developing profiles of potentially homophobic jurors and of identifying attitudes and values that frequently accompany homophobia, so that attorneys can attempt to screen such potentially biased jurors from jury panels.

In this chapter we discuss an ongoing research project that is designed to identify potentially homophobic jurors. Over the past two decades, many researchers have developed a variety of ways of measuring and assessing individuals' homophobic attitudes. Unfortunately, the majority of homophobia studies have been conducted with nonrandom convenience samples of predominantly White college students, and it is unclear how these findings relate to the more heterogeneous real-world population from which jurors are typically selected. The answer to this question is particularly important today, when citizen groups frequently make decisions that affect the rights and interests of gay men and lesbians—for example, when juries in state and federal courts decide civil or criminal lawsuits involving lesbians and gay men regarding custody rights, employment termination, insurance and spousal benefits, access to health care, patients' rights (as in the above example), and hate crimes committed because of the victim's sexual orientation. Equally important is an assessment of the role of homophobia in decision making among voters who cast ballots on propositions that aim to restrict the rights of lesbians and gay men and in elections involving gay and lesbian candidates.

Attitudes Toward Gay Men and Lesbians

Identifying the influence of homophobia in all of these settings requires research based on large, national, multiethnic, contemporary adult samples. However, with the exception of recent research by Herek and Capitanio (1996) involving a national probability sample of more than 500 multiethnic heterosexual adults, most studies of homophobia have either relied on relatively small, nonrandom, White student samples or have used only one or two rather general items to assess homophobia. For example, Whitley and Kite (1995) found in their review of 66 studies on attitudes toward homosexuals that very few employed national probability samples of adults and that the studies typically measured homophobia with one or two items. Similarly, of the 46 studies of homophobic attitudes reviewed by Schwanberg (1993), only 6 involved nonstudent samples; and of these 6, only 2 used large national probability random samples (Levitt & Klassen, 1974; Nyberg & Alston, 1976-1977), although both of these studies are nearly 20 years old, and the latter was based on a single interview item.

Results from these studies indicate that people scoring high in homophobia tend to be more authoritarian, less well educated, and more religious; they endorse more traditional sex roles; and they are more likely to be male, although a few studies have found no such gender differences, especially those that used general adult samples (Herek, 1991; Whitley & Kite, 1995). These studies further indicate that negative attitudes toward gay men and lesbians occur among those who are less likely to know or to come into contact with gay men or lesbians, who are more likely to live in the Midwest or the South, and who are more politically conservative (Herek, 1984, 1988; Herek & Capitanio, 1996). In addition, African Americans who hold negative attitudes toward gay men and lesbians are more likely to regard homosexuality as a choice and are less likely to believe that the social category "gay man" includes any Blacks (Herek & Capitanio, 1995).

Overall, these findings suggest that public reactions to gay men and lesbians at both the ballot box and the jury box may indeed be influenced by homophobia. However, because many of these studies are based on limited, disparate, and often problematic samples and methodologies, the findings need to be confirmed in a large, multiethnic, representative sample with more direct applicability to real-world settings, particularly to jurors (see Herek & Capitanio, 1995).

Jury Research

The presence of homophobic biases among potential jurors is especially troubling because research on jury decision making suggests that most jurors construct relatively simple narratives or "stories" in order to make sense of the evidence presented in a trial; most jurors construct these stories very early in the attorneys' opening statements; these stories then guide jurors' evaluation of the evidence during the cases in chief; and—most important for the present purposes—these stories generally arise from jurors' personal experiences regarding issues similar to those in the trial (Pennington & Hastie, 1992). In other words, jurors' biases and personal experiences influence their perceptions of the evidence presented at trial.

For example, in one study in which adult subjects were asked to view videotapes of an actual murder trial and to provide running protocols of their reactions to the trial, subjects who lived in high-crime areas viewed the defendant's carrying a large knife simply as a reasonable means of protection and self-defense. In contrast, subjects who lived in less crime-ridden areas viewed the same incident as evidence of the defendant's intent to commit a murder (Pennington & Hastie, 1986). In the same way, jurors who are biased against male homosexuals might view a patient's failure to disclose his HIV-positive status prior to surgery as evidence of the patient's intent to harm an unknowing health care worker.

Identifying Homophobic Jurors
During Jury Selection

In addition to constructing profiles of homophobic jurors, another goal of the present study was to determine how to identify potentially homophobic jurors during voir dire, the jury selection period that precedes a trial. This is the time when attorneys on each side have an opportunity to question potential jurors about their beliefs and attitudes on issues pertinent to the trial in order to determine whether the jurors can hear the evidence with an open mind. If a juror's answers convince the judge that the juror cannot be impartial, the judge can strike the juror from the panel. In addition, attorneys on each side also have a certain number of "peremptory challenges" (typically three to six) that they may use to excuse jurors whom they believe to be biased, for whatever reason.

Because some judges might not allow attorneys to question jurors directly about their attitudes toward homosexuality, as it could be awkward to ask such questions, and because some jurors might seek to hide their true biases in order to save face in the courtroom, in the present study we sought to identify proxy or surrogate questions that correlate highly with homophobic attitudes but that can be asked more easily during jury selection. In addition, we sought to determine which types of attitude questions are most predictive of homophobia within various ethnic and gender categories. Knowing the answers to these questions could save valuable time during the often brief jury selection period, because attorneys would not need to waste time asking jurors about attitudes that may not be highly predictive of homophobia in specific ethnic and gender categories.

How the Study Was Conducted

The Survey and Sample

The current study was conducted under the auspices of a jury research firm in which the first author is a partner. Because the firm, Mattson & Sherrod, Inc., is retained to conduct jury research on upcoming cases throughout the United States, its various research projects provided an ideal opportunity to gather data from a geographically diverse sample of White, Black, and Latino adults who were specifically recruited to match the demographic composition of federal and state jury panels across the country and who met the legal requirements for jury duty (such as being a registered voter and/or having a driver's license).

During a 3-year period, representative samples totaling 3,542 men and women from 15 states participated in mock juries and completed a questionnaire that assessed a wide range of opinions and self-reported behaviors.[1] Using specific criteria based on U.S. Census data and interviews with local attorneys, professional market research organizations recruited respondents by telephone until sample quotas were met. Depending on the region and the length of the mock trials, respondents received between $75 and $300 for participating in the project, which was a sufficient amount to encourage employed respondents to take a "sick" day or "personal" day off from work and to guarantee the representativeness of the sample (see Table 2.1 for a profile of respondents).

Although each research exercise involved a different case, jurors in every situation filled out an extensive questionnaire that included a standard set of about 150 demographic, lifestyle, and attitudinal questions. Among these questions was a 12-item Homophobia Scale designed to assess potential jurors' attitudes toward lesbians and gay men. These questions were designed to assess a range of personal prejudices (e.g.,

Table 2.1 Sample Demographics ($N = 3,542$)

Age	
Mean	42.2
Range	18-85
Gender	
Male	48.3%
Female	51.7%
Ethnicity	
African American	26.4%
Latino	18.6%
White	54.2%
Marital status	
Single	29.6%
Divorced/separated	15.7%
Married	50.2%
Widowed	4.5%
Education	
High school or technical school	40.3%
Some college	35.5%
College degree or more	24.1%
Household income (annual)	
Less than $20,000	40.7%
$21,000-40,000	39.0%
More than $40,000	20.3%
Political ideology	
Liberal	22.7%
Middle	51.0%
Conservative	26.3%
Region of residence	
Northeast	17.2%
Southeast	11.0%
Upper Midwest	8.3%
South	43.2%
West/Southwest	20.3%

attitudes toward gay and lesbian neighbors, gay and lesbian coworkers, gay and lesbian teachers, and the gay and lesbian "lifestyle") and a range of political beliefs (e.g., beliefs about the rights of gays and lesbians to have officially recognized marriages, to adopt children, to be free from discrimination in employment, and to have their civil rights protected). In addition, respondents were asked to indicate their links to any gay and lesbian acquaintances, friends, and relatives.

Factor analyses with varimax rotation and item-to-total score correlations were performed on the 12 Homophobia Scale items, resulting in the selection of the 9 strongest for the final scale (see Table 2.2). The 9 items of the final Homophobia Scale produced a reliability coefficient (Cronbach's alpha) of .908. Each item was scored on a 4-point scale, with higher scores representing more antigay sentiment. Total scores could range from 9 to 36, with higher scores indicating more homophobic attitudes. The mean score of the entire sample was 21.55, with a standard deviation of 8.

By treating the Homophobia Scale as a dependent variable, we were able to analyze jurors' homophobia scores as a function of their answers to a number of demographic, lifestyle, and attitudinal items (described in the next section). In this way, jury research that was ostensibly conducted for proprietary purposes (i.e., helping attorneys develop a jury strategy for a particular case) was able to yield a large, carefully recruited, geographically diverse, multiethnic sample for the purposes of constructing profiles of potentially homophobic jurors and of identifying voir dire questions that can be used to clarify jurors' biases.

Demographic Items and Attitude Questions

The remaining items in the questionnaire focused on several types of information, including (a) the respondent's demographics, such as sex, age, ethnicity, marital status, parenthood, employment, education, income, region of residence, political affiliation, religious affiliation, and military service; (b) behaviors indicative of the respondent's lifestyle, such as newspaper and magazine readership, frequency of church attendance, health and diet maintenance, financial practices, recreational activities, and use of consumer products; and (c) the respondent's attitudes, values, and fears pertaining to a number of topics, such as risk and harm, control and uncertainty, injury and disease, suffering and empathy, law and order, environmental pollution, government regulations, and personal responsibility.

Table 2.2 The Homophobia Scale

1. Do you think gay men and lesbians should be allowed to adopt children, just like heterosexuals?*
2. Do you think gay men and lesbians should be able to have officially recognized marriages, just like heterosexuals?*
3. Would it bother you if a gay male couple or a lesbian couple moved into the house or apartment next door to you?
4. Would you mind if your child's teacher was a gay man?
5. Would you mind if your child's teacher was a lesbian?
6. Do you think employers should be free to refuse to hire a person because of that person's sexual orientation?
7. Do you think being gay or lesbian is an acceptable lifestyle, just like other lifestyles people lead?*
8. Would you feel bothered in any way if you had to work closely with an individual who was gay or lesbian?
9. Do you think a person's sexual orientation should be a civil right that is protected by the government just like a person's ethnicity, religion, or sex?*

NOTE: The following response scale was used: 1 = no; 2 = probably not; 3 = probably; 4 = yes.
*Scoring was reversed for this item. α = .91.

Because the items that constituted the independent variables were constructed as stand-alone questions of the type used in jury selection during voir dire, rather than as additive components of traditional indexes or validated scales, it was necessary to reduce the total number of items to a more manageable size for the purposes of this study. Three criteria guided this process. First, in order to determine which items reflected sufficient variation in response, we calculated preliminary frequency percentage distributions and measurements of central tendency. Second, we gave priority to items that could be easily observed in the courtroom (e.g., ethnicity, sex, and age) and plausibly asked on a court-administered questionnaire or during oral voir dire. Finally, we selected items for their relevance to different gender and ethnic groupings. As a result of this process, 62 items were initially selected for further data analysis.

Analysis of variance (ANOVA) was used to assess the differences in mean Homophobia Scale scores among the response categories on each of the 62 items. The 23 items with an F value significant at $p < .0008$ (based on a Bonferroni correction) and not intercorrelated with other items in the set were entered into stepwise multiple regression equations in order to determine which items accounted for the most variance in respondents' Homophobia Scale scores.

Ethnic and Gender Differences in Homophobia

Because gender and ethnicity are routinely employed by attorneys as significant descriptor categories during jury selection, we performed ANOVA on respondents' mean Homophobia Scale scores by gender and ethnicity; this analysis revealed statistically significant differences. In order to understand the nature of these differences, we calculated comparisons among the six means using the Tukey-B test. As shown in Table 2.3, White males and Latino males scored significantly higher on the Homophobia Scale than did African American males and females, Latina females, and White females.

Beyond the overall finding that White and Latino males were more homophobic, on average, than other respondents, it is both theoretically important and pragmatically useful to identify the more homophobic members within all six gender and ethnic categories represented in the present study. Therefore, we calculated multiple regression equations in order to determine which of the 23 items accounted for the most variance in respondents' Homophobia Scale scores within each gender and ethnic category. Stepwise multiple regressions revealed that the most significant determinants of homophobia in each category were political conservatism and having few close gay and lesbian friends (see Table 2.4). Furthermore, among White and Latino males and females, the importance of religious beliefs was significantly linked with higher Homophobia Scale scores, and among Black and White males and Latina and White females, agreeing that "the world would be a better place if more people followed 'old-fashioned values' " was also a significant predictor of homophobia.

In addition, other characteristics were significantly associated with homophobia within specific ethnic and gender categories. For example, among Whites, the more homophobic respondents lived in the southern or central United States and attended church frequently. Among Black and White females, the more homophobic respondents were not regular readers of newspapers and agreed that the government was "doing enough to make sure industry does not pollute the environment." These

Table 2.3 Homophobia Scale Scores by Ethnicity and Gender

White males	22.93_a
Latino males	22.60_a
African American females	21.00_b
African American males	20.96_b
Latina females	20.91_b
White females	20.65_b

NOTE: For ANOVA of Homophobia Scale scores by gender and ethnicity, $F (5, 3493) = 10.63$, $p < .0001$. Means not sharing the same subscript differ significantly, using the Tukey-B test with a significance level of $p < .05$.

findings suggest the necessity of adapting voir dire questions to the ethnicity and gender of potential jurors.

Profiles of Homophobic Jurors

In light of the findings discussed above, we developed the following profiles of the most homophobic potential jurors within each ethnic/gender category:

White men. Among the White men, the most homophobic were those who did not have any close friends who are gay or lesbian, agreed that "the world would be a better place if more people followed 'old-fashioned values,' " were more conservative politically, agreed that religious beliefs are always important in guiding their daily decisions, were Protestant, attended religious services weekly, and lived in the South.

Latino men. For the Latino men, the most homophobic were those who did not have any close friends who are gay or lesbian, were more conservative, agreed that religious beliefs are always important in guiding their daily decisions, and had served in the U.S. armed forces.

Black women. Among the sample of African American female potential jurors, those with the highest homophobia scores attended religious services weekly, were more conservative politically, had few or no close gay/lesbian friends, agreed that "federal and state governments are doing enough to make sure industry does not pollute the environment," and did not read a local newspaper on a daily basis.

Table 2.4 Results of Stepwise Multiple Regressions for Ethnic and Gender Groups

Predictor Variable	Black Women	Black Men	Latina Women	Latino Men	White Women	White Men
Gay/lesbian friend	−.171	−.215	−.301	−.297	−.216	−.310
	[−.913]	[−1.165]	[−1.708]	[−1.859]	[−1.384]	[−2.368]
Political ideology	.174	.165	.147	.211	.220	.184
	[1.692]	[1.606]	[1.505]	[2.469]	[2.988]	[2.228]
Religion important	ns	ns	.147	.186	.164	.098
	ns	ns	[1.626]	[1.472]	[1.495]	[1.088]
Old values	ns	.145	.136	ns	.139	.205
	ns	[.891]	[1.158]	ns	[1.391]	[1.783]
Church attendance	.313	ns	ns	ns	.118	.122
	[4.831]	ns	ns	ns	[2.005]	[2.021]
Pollute environment	.146	ns	ns	ns	.093	ns
	[1.888]	ns	ns	ns	[1.366]	ns
Read paper	−.107	ns	ns	ns	−.079	ns
	[−.929]	ns	ns	ns	[−.754]	ns
South/other	ns	ns	ns	ns	.177	.077
	ns	ns	ns	ns	[2.234]	[1.991]
Married/other	ns	ns	.164	ns	ns	ns
	ns	ns	[2.055]	ns	ns	ns
Protestant/other	ns	ns	ns	ns	ns	−.128
	ns	ns	ns	ns	ns	[−2.534]
Veteran	ns	ns	ns	.142	ns	ns
	ns	ns	ns	[2.561]	ns	ns
Fate/planning	ns	ns	ns	ns	−.071	ns
	ns	ns	ns	ns	[−.714]	ns
Read magazines	ns	−.123	ns	ns	ns	ns
	ns	[−1.264]	ns	ns	ns	ns
Education	ns	ns	ns	ns	−.082	ns
	ns	ns	ns	ns	[−.545]	ns
R^2	.235	.127	.270	.262	.373	.398
R	.485	.357	.519	.512	.610	.631
N	498	432	331	325	979	929

NOTE: All regression coefficients shown in this table were significant at $p < .05$. For each variable, the standardized regression coefficient (β) is shown first (for comparisons within columns), with the unstandardized regression coefficient (b) in brackets (for comparisons across columns). The group mean was substituted for missing values of independent variables.

Black men. The most homophobic African American male potential jurors were those who had few or no close gay or lesbian friends, were more conservative, agreed that "the world would be a better place if more people followed 'old-fashioned values,' " and did not read any magazines on a regular basis.

Latina women. Among the Latina women in the sample, the most homophobic were those who had few or no close gay or lesbian friends, agreed that religious beliefs are always important in guiding their daily decisions, were currently married, were more conservative, and agreed that "the world would be a better place if more people followed 'old-fashioned values.' "

White women. The most homophobic White female potential jurors were those who were more conservative politically, agreed that religious beliefs are always important in guiding their daily decisions, had few or no close gay or lesbian friends, lived in the South, agreed that "the world would be a better place if more people followed 'old-fashioned values,' " attended religious services on a weekly basis, agreed that "federal and state governments are doing enough to make sure industry does not pollute the environment," did not read a local newspaper on a daily basis, had less education (high school or less), and believed that their "life is more controlled by fate than by planning."

Conclusions

The results of this study confirmed many of the determinants of homophobia noted by previous researchers (Herek, 1991; Whitley & Kite, 1995) but extended these findings to a large, geographically diverse, multiethnic adult sample. In addition, whereas most studies have focused on the effects of *either* ethnicity *or* gender on homophobia, this study evaluated the interactive effects of ethnicity *and* gender on homophobia. For example, whereas previous studies have determined that males are typically more homophobic than females, and that African Americans are no more homophobic than Whites (Herek & Capitanio, 1995), the current research found that White males and Latino males tended to be the most homophobic.

Furthermore, because this study included a number of questionnaire items that tapped a wide range of attitudes, values, fears, and lifestyle characteristics, it identifies the types of questions that could be posed by attorneys during voir dire jury selection in order to eliminate potential jurors who may be biased against lesbians and gay men. To the extent that jurors' biases influence their perceptions, organization, and reconstruction of the evidence presented by attorneys, these biases can affect jurors' verdicts and lead them to find unfairly against gay and lesbian defendants.

The findings in this study also suggest larger social and political implications. Because one of the most important correlates of positive attitudes toward lesbians and gay men is whether a respondent has a gay or lesbian friend, "coming out" and being "out" are necessary steps for gays and lesbians to take in the complex process of reducing homophobia and heterosexism in society. More important still is the role of political and social institutions in fostering a climate in which gay men and lesbians can openly express their sexual orientation without fear of prejudice or discrimination in the workplace, the voting booth, or the courtroom.

Appendix: Questionnaire Items

Gay/lesbian friend:
"Do you have any close friends who are gay or lesbian?" (no; probably not; probably; yes)

Political ideology:
"Politically you are:" (liberal; middle-of-the-road; conservative)

Religion important:
"How important are your religious beliefs in guiding your daily decisions?" (not important; sometimes important; often important; always important)

Old values:
"Do you think the world would be a better place if more people followed 'old-fashioned values'?" (no; probably not; probably; yes)

Church attendance:
"Do you try to attend religious services at your church or temple every week?" (no; yes)

Pollute environment:
"Are federal and state governments doing enough to make sure industry does not pollute the environment we live in?" (no; probably not; probably; yes)

Read paper:
"How thoroughly do you read your local newspaper every day?" (don't read it; scan it; somewhat thoroughly; thoroughly)

South/other:
"The postal ZIP code where you live" (responses coded as "South" included Florida, Tennessee, Missouri, Arkansas, and Texas; "Other" included New York, New Jersey, Pennsylvania, Maryland, Michigan, Minnesota, North Dakota, Colorado, Arizona, and California)

Married/other:
"Your present marital status:" (single; separated or divorced; married; widowed)

Protestant/other:
"Your religion:" (Protestant; Catholic; Jewish; other; none)

Veteran:
"Have you ever served in the U.S. Armed Forces?" (no; yes)

Fate/planning:
"My life is more controlled by fate than by planning." (disagree; somewhat disagree; somewhat agree; agree)

Read magazines:
"Do you read any magazines on a regular basis?" (no; 1 or 2; 3 or more)

Education:
"Your highest level of education:" (grade school; high school; technical school; junior college degree or some college; college degree; graduate degree)

Note

1. The 15 states were Arizona, Arkansas, California, Colorado, Florida, Maryland, Michigan, Minnesota, Missouri, New Jersey, New York, North Dakota, Pennsylvania, Tennessee, and Texas.

References

Herek, G. M. (1984). Beyond "homophobia": A social psychological perspective on attitudes toward lesbians and gay men. *Journal of Homosexuality, 10*(1-2), 1-21.

Herek, G. M. (1988). Heterosexuals' attitudes toward lesbians and gay men: Correlates and gender differences. *Journal of Sex Research, 25,* 451-477.

Herek, G. M. (1991). Stigma, prejudice, and violence against lesbians and gay men. In J. C. Gonsiorek & J. D. Weinrich (Eds.), *Homosexuality: Research implications for public policy* (pp. 60-80). Newbury Park, CA: Sage.

Herek, G. M., & Capitanio, J. P. (1995). Black heterosexuals' attitudes toward lesbians and gay men in the United States. *Journal of Sex Research, 32,* 95-105.

Herek, G. M., & Capitanio, J. P. (1996). "Some of my best friends": Intergroup contact, concealable stigma, and heterosexuals' attitudes toward gay men and lesbians. *Personality and Social Psychology Bulletin, 22*, 412-424.

Levitt, E., & Klassen, A. (1974). Public attitudes toward homosexuality: Part of the 1970 national survey by the Institute of Sex Research. *Journal of Homosexuality, 1*(1), 29-43.

Nyberg, K. L., & Alston, J. P. (1976-1977). Analysis of public attitudes toward homosexual behavior. *Journal of Homosexuality, 2*(2), 99-107.

Pennington, N., & Hastie, R. (1986). Evidence evaluation in complex decision making. *Journal of Personality and Social Psychology, 51*, 242-258.

Pennington, N., & Hastie, R. (1992). Explaining the evidence: Tests of the story model for juror decision making. *Journal of Personality and Social Psychology, 62*, 189-206.

Schwanberg, S. L. (1993). Attitudes towards gay men and lesbian women: Instrumentation issues. *Journal of Homosexuality, 26*(1), 99-136.

Whitley, B. E., Jr., & Kite, M. E. (1995). Sex differences in attitudes toward homosexuality: A comment on Oliver and Hyde (1993). *Psychological Bulletin, 117*, 146-154.

3

Do Heterosexual Women and Men Differ in Their Attitudes Toward Homosexuality?
A Conceptual and Methodological Analysis

MARY E. KITE

BERNARD E. WHITLEY, Jr.

Heterosexual men generally hold more negative attitudes toward homosexuality than do heterosexual women (for reviews, see Herek, 1984; Kite & Whitley, 1996). The sources of this difference, however, have yet to be fully understood. Two problems contribute to this lack of understanding. One is inattention to theoretical explanations for the sex difference (for exceptions, see Herek, 1986, 1988; Kite & Whitley, 1996). The other is a narrow empirical base that relies primarily on paper-and-pencil measures of college students' attitudes toward homosexuals in general, with little attention given to the attitudes of other populations, attitudes toward gay men and lesbians more specifically, assessments of other types of beliefs (e.g., concerning gay people's civil rights), or actual behavior toward gay people. In this chapter, we discuss these issues, beginning with an overview of theoretical explanations for sex differences in attitudes toward homosexuality.[1]

Gender Role Analysis of Sex Differences
in Attitudes Toward Homosexuality

A gender role analysis of sex differences in attitudes toward homosexuality is based on the assumption that heterosexuals' evaluations of gay men and lesbians are rooted in a broader belief system about women, men, and their appropriate roles (Deaux & Kite, 1987; Kite, 1994). This belief system has two consequences relevant to attitudes toward homosexuality. First, gender-associated beliefs appear to be inextricably linked; that is, people expect others' gender-associated characteristics to form a coherent package. They believe, for example, that people who possess stereotypically masculine traits also adopt stereotypically masculine roles and possess stereotypically masculine physical characteristics and, similarly, that those who possess feminine characteristics on one dimension are likely to be feminine on other dimensions (e.g., Deaux & Lewis, 1984; Rajecki, De Graaf-Kaser, & Rasmussen, 1992). Evidence that this belief system is tied to heterosexuals' perceptions of gay people comes from demonstrations that men who are described as having feminine characteristics are judged likely to be homosexual whereas women described as having masculine characteristics are judged likely to be lesbian (e.g., Deaux & Lewis, 1984; Martin, 1990; McCreary, 1994). People likewise infer that gay men have the gender-associated characteristics of heterosexual women and that lesbians have the gender-associated characteristics of heterosexual men (e.g., Kite & Deaux, 1987; Taylor, 1983). It is noteworthy, however, that the association between lesbianism and attributed masculinity appears to be much weaker than the association between gay male homosexuality and attributed femininity (e.g., Deaux & Lewis, 1984; Kite & Deaux, 1987; Martin, 1990; McCreary, 1994).

The second consequence of the gender belief system as relevant to antigay prejudice stems from people's evaluations of those who contradict traditional gender roles. In general, people who engage in role behaviors associated with the other sex (e.g., Costrich, Feinstein, Kidder, Marecek, & Pascale, 1975; Jackson & Cash, 1985) or who possess characteristics associated with the other sex (e.g., Laner & Laner, 1979, 1980) are not viewed positively. This may be particularly true for gay people, who, as discussed above, are stereotypically perceived as having cross-sex traits, roles, and physical characteristics and who are apparently disliked as a result (e.g., Laner & Laner, 1979, 1980), particularly by those with traditional gender role attitudes (e.g., Krulewitz & Nash, 1980). Men, for example, report that the worst possible insult that can be hurled at a man is "homosexual"; women list this label as the second worst insult for a man (Preston & Stanley, 1987).

These two aspects of the gender belief system may work to produce men's greater intolerance of homosexuality compared with women's. First, even though people expect consistency in others' gender-associated characteristics, these expectations appear to be more firmly held for men than for women. Research suggests that male gender roles are particularly nonpliant compared with female roles (see Stockard & Johnson, 1979). For example, gender-associated traits and gender-associated physical characteristics are more narrowly defined for men than for women (Hort, Fagot, & Leinbach, 1990). Second, violation of the traditional male gender role is seen as more egregious than violation of the traditional female gender role (see Herek, 1986; Kite & Whitley, 1996). People react more negatively to boys who possess female-typed traits than to girls who possess male-typed traits (Feinman, 1981).

If male gender roles are so clearly delineated, it follows that tolerance for those who are perceived as violating those roles (e.g., gay men) would be actively discouraged. This is particularly true for heterosexual men, for whom gender role conformity is acutely defined by American society (Bem, 1993). Men, more than women, are pushed to suppress any aspect of the self that might be associated with femininity (Herek, 1986). As a result, heterosexual men are especially likely to be pressured toward displaying antigay prejudice. That society responds differently to men's and women's gender role nonconformity can be explained by the generally higher status associated with the American male gender role compared with the American female gender role (Bem, 1993; Hogg & Turner, 1987; Lewin & Tragos, 1987; but see McCreary, 1994, for another viewpoint). Men, then, may simply have more to lose by overstepping their gender role boundaries and engaging in or endorsing homosexual behavior. In contrast, the cultural gender script allows greater flexibility for the female gender role; hence, women are allowed to hold more tolerant attitudes toward gender role violators. Similarly, it follows that heterosexuals of both sexes should be less likely to perceive lesbianism as a clear gender role violation; if women's roles are generally viewed as lower status, prejudice toward lesbians or engaging in lesbian behavior should not be as strongly culturally sanctioned. That lesbianism is largely invisible in American society, except as part of male-oriented eroticism (discussed below), highlights this perspective (see also Bem, 1993).

Psychodynamic Processes

Psychodynamic theories propose that prejudice stems from ego-defensiveness and the need to deny certain aspects of one's personality (Duckitt, 1992). From this viewpoint, heterosexuals' negative attitudes toward lesbians and gay men stem from a denial of sexual impulses in general or denial of attraction to same-sex others more specifically. The failure to recognize latent homosexual impulses purportedly produces irrational, negative responses toward gay people. The often-used (and often-misused) term *homophobia*, defined as an irrational, persistent fear or dread of homosexuals (MacDonald, 1976), has its roots in this perspective.

Relatively little research has directly explored the relationship between repressed homosexual impulses and attitudes toward gay men or lesbians. However, the finding that male heterosexuals have aversive reactions to depictions of the male body (e.g., Morin & Garfinkle, 1978) is typically explained by a psychodynamic perspective. Recently, Adams, Wright, and Lohr (1996) found that homophobic men in their sample showed greater physical arousal to consensual male homosexual activity than did nonhomophobic men, although the self-reported arousal of these individuals did not vary, suggesting that these homophobic men were repressing same-sex attraction. Moreover, homophobic and nonhomophobic men showed similar arousal levels to other types of erotica, including consensual female homosexual activity. Franklin (Chapter 1, this volume) has also provided evidence that, for at least a few men, antigay violence stems from a defensive reaction to their discomfort with their own sexual attraction to men.

Within the antigay prejudice literature, most research taking a psychodynamic perspective has focused on the relationship between psychodynamic personality characteristics such as dogmatism, gender role rigidity, religious conservatism, and, most commonly, authoritarianism and negative attitudes toward homosexuality (see Herek, 1984, for a review). In general, individuals who score high on these dimensions manifest the highest levels of antigay prejudice. Whether sex of respondent accounts for additional variance remains unresolved. Outside the literature on attitudes toward homosexuality, there has been little discussion of sex differences in authoritarianism (see Christie, 1991, for a review) or of sex differences in prejudice toward other social groups (see Ashmore & Del Boca, 1981; Duckitt, 1992). Pratto, Sidanius, Stallworth, and Malle (1994) found sex differences in authoritarianism, but Altemeyer (1988) did not. If there are no generalized sex differences in psychodynamic personality traits, it appears that to account adequately for sex differences in heterosexuals' attitudes toward homosexuality, theorists with a psychodynamic outlook must assume that such attitudes are a special case, with sex differences emerging because homosexuality raises a particular kind of threat that is specific to heterosexual men (e.g., Morin & Garfinkle, 1978). One possible source of this threat is that heterosexual men, who are unaccustomed to rejecting sexual advances (e.g., McCormick, 1979), feel more anxiety than do heterosexual women over the possibility of an invitation for same-sex relations. Heterosexual women, in contrast, have more readily available strategies for rejecting offers of sex (McCormick, 1979) and so may be relatively less threatened by the possibility of a same-sex approach. Supporting this idea, LaMar and Kite (in press) found that heterosexual women and men reported similar levels of discomfort at the idea of a sexual advance from a member of their sex, but that men were significantly less likely than women to agree that they would know how to respond to such a proposition. As Franklin (Chapter 1, this volume) has suggested, the anxiety produced by the threat of rejecting unwanted sexual advances may result in the defense mechanism of reaction formation; that is, heterosexual men may substitute feelings of anger and resentment toward gay men for the anxiety associated with unwanted sexual advances. Women's lower anxiety in similar situations would not necessitate such a defensive reaction.

The Sexualization of Lesbianism by Heterosexual Men

A third theoretical explanation for sex differences in attitudes toward homosexuality addresses the more specific finding that heterosexual men hold less negative attitudes toward lesbians than toward gay men, whereas heterosexual women hold approximately the same attitudes toward both groups (see Kite & Whitley, 1996). This explanation derives from heterosexual men's sexualization of women in American society (e.g., DeLamater, 1987; Sprecher & McKinney, 1993). As DeLamater (1987) has noted, "Generally, men seem more likely than women to perceive persons of the opposite sex in sexual terms" (p. 134). For example, a number of studies (reviewed by Sprecher & McKinney, 1993) have found that men are much more likely than women to attribute sexual intent to friendly behavior by members of the other sex. In addition, surveys have consistently found that men are more likely to be consumers of erotica in all its forms than are women (Fisher, 1983). Heterosexual men's tendency to view women in sexual terms may lead them to eroticize the idea of a woman making love to another woman. The positive erotic value thus assigned to lesbianism by heterosexual men may counteract the general stigma associated with homosexuality, resulting in attitudes toward lesbians that are less negative than those toward gay men. Because heterosexual women tend not to sexualize men in the same way, however, they may not sexualize male homosexuality and may therefore hold similar attitudes toward lesbians and gay men.

Although a number of writers have alluded to the idea that lesbianism has erotic value for heterosexual men (e.g., Reiss, 1986), researchers have conducted only a few studies to address this question. These researchers have used two methodological approaches to investigate this issue. Some have had participants rate slides or films that depict heterosexual and homosexual sexual activity (e.g., Gaughan & Gaynor, 1973; Greendlinger, 1985; Hatfield, Sprecher, & Traupmann, 1978; Levitt & Brady, 1965; Turnbull & Brown, 1977). Turnbull and Brown's (1977) results are typical: Although both male and female respondents rated homosexual acts more negatively than heterosexual acts, men rated lesbian sexual activity more positively than did women; there was no sex difference for ratings of gay male sexual activity. Using the other methodological approach, Nyberg and Alston (1977) asked their respondents to rate the ideas of men making love to men and of women making love to women as being either erotic or nonerotic. Their results show that only 7% of both male and female respondents found the idea of a man making love to another man erotic. However, 33% of their male respondents found the idea of a woman making love to another woman erotic, compared with only 10% of their female respondents.

These studies demonstrate that lesbianism does hold erotic value for at least some heterosexual men. But is this erotic value related to attitudes toward lesbians? Louderback and Whitley (1997) assessed male and female heterosexual respondents' ratings of the erotic value of male and female homosexuality and their attitudes toward lesbians and gay men.

Consistent with the results of previous research, female respondents reported attitudes toward lesbians that were similar to their attitudes toward gay men, whereas male respondents reported less negative attitudes toward lesbians than toward gay men. Furthermore, male respondents' ratings of the erotic value of lesbianism were much higher than their ratings of the erotic value of male homosexuality and much higher than female respondents' ratings of the erotic value of either male or female homosexuality. With perceived erotic value of homosexuality controlled, men's attitudes toward lesbians were more negative than before controlling for perceived erotic value and were similar to their attitudes toward gay men; women's attitudes toward both lesbians and gay men were essentially unaffected by controlling for the perceived erotic value of homosexuality. These results are consistent with the hypothesis that heterosexual men's less negative attitudes toward lesbians stem at least in part from the erotic value that they attribute to lesbianism.

We have described three theoretical perspectives on sex differences in attitudes toward homosexuality, each of which offers a plausible explanation for heterosexual men's greater negativity toward gay people. Connections across these perspectives, however, should not be overlooked. Herek's (1984, 1986) work on attitude functions, for example, points to a link between defensiveness toward homosexuality and gender role issues. Specifically, Herek argues that heterosexual male insecurity about homosexuality may stem from an inability to meet gender role expectations. Similarly, the sexualization of lesbianism may stem from the belief that women's deviation from prescribed gender roles is less serious than men's, or from more generalized beliefs about gender roles. Duckitt (1992) has argued that although the capacity for prejudice may exist in all humans, cultural conditions may determine both an individual's propensity to be prejudiced and the targets of those prejudicial reactions. Humans, then, may be predisposed to hold defensive attitudes toward threatening groups, but societal shaping of cultural roles may heavily influence the choice of the derogated out-group, as well as the direction and strength of prejudice toward that group.

Meta-Analysis of Sex Differences in Attitudes Toward Homosexuality

We conducted a meta-analysis of the available literature on sex differences in attitudes toward homosexuality through September 1993

(Kite & Whitley, 1996). Our analysis was based on 112 studies and included a total of 46,966 male and 53,858 female respondents. From these studies, we obtained 167 effect sizes. We further classified these effect sizes as representing attitudes toward homosexual persons, attitudes toward homosexual behavior, and attitudes toward gay people's civil rights. We based our predictions on the gender role analysis of sex differences in attitudes toward homosexuality described earlier and on the proposition that, because different types of judgments about an attitude object can be based on different sources of information (e.g., Esses, Haddock, & Zanna, 1993), these judgments need not be consistent. Finally, within each category, to the extent possible, we considered moderators of the effect sizes.

Attitudes Toward
Homosexual Persons

We predicted a sex difference in heterosexuals' attitudes toward homosexual persons, arguing that men's more rigid adherence to gender roles would lead to their more negative attitude. This prediction was borne out. The average correlation between sex and attitude was $r = .19$.[2] (Positive correlations indicate that men hold more negative attitudes.) We further expected, however, that men's negativity would be particularly acute when the attitude object was a gay man or a person of unspecified sex rather than a lesbian. This prediction, too, held. Sex differences were largest when the person being rated was a gay man ($r = .25$) or of unspecified sex ($r = .27$). For the latter category, it is likely that the perceivers assumed the questions referred to gay men (see Black & Stevenson, 1984; Haddock, Zanna, & Esses, 1993). In contrast, the sexes did not differ when the attitude object was a lesbian ($r = .00$). We explained these findings by noting that gay men may be viewed as violators of the male gender role, leading heterosexual men to evaluate them particularly negatively. In contrast, heterosexual men may be less likely to view lesbianism as a gender role violation, and hence are less derogatory toward those individuals. If female gender roles are less constrained, however, heterosexual women might be free to express greater acceptance of both gay men and lesbians. The sexualization of lesbianism, described earlier, provides a more detailed explanation for how gender roles might account for this finding.

Attitudes Toward
Homosexual Behavior

Our prediction of sex differences in attitudes toward homosexual behavior also relied on a gender role analysis. Specifically, we reasoned
that if sexuality more generally is an important aspect of the gender
belief system (Deaux & Kite, 1987), heterosexual men might be more
likely to view homosexual behavior as inappropriate and would therefore hold more negative attitudes toward that behavior than would
women. We were more tentative about this prediction, however, because
men generally hold more permissive attitudes toward sexual behavior than do women (e.g., Oliver & Hyde, 1993). The average effect size
($r = .13$) indicated that men were more negative than women toward
homosexual behavior, although the size of this difference was significantly smaller than that for attitudes toward homosexual persons. Apparently, heterosexual men's permissive sexual attitudes do not extend
to homosexuality.

Attitudes Toward Gay
People's Civil Rights

Although the results described above provide clear evidence for heterosexual men's greater negativity toward homosexuality, we did not
expect these results to generalize to all types of attitudes toward homosexuality, because attitudes toward a particular group need not be consistent (e.g., Esses et al., 1993). Herek's (1991) review of national opinion
poll data showed greater acceptance of gay civil rights than of either
homosexual behavior or homosexual people (see also Strand, Chapter 6,
this volume). Moreover, national surveys rarely have found sex differences in this area (but see Herek & Capitanio, 1995; Herek & Glunt, 1993).
We therefore reasoned that heterosexual women and men might differ
in their attitudes toward homosexuality and still hold similar views
about gay people's civil rights.

Our meta-analysis found essentially no overall sex difference in heterosexuals' attitudes toward the civil rights of lesbians and gay men
($r = .02$). However, 4 of the 16 studies found that men held more negative
attitudes than women, with an average difference of about one third of
a standard deviation. The 12 studies that found no sex difference were

all conducted as part of the General Social Survey (Wood, 1990) and dealt with free speech rights, asking respondents, for example, whether or not they would allow a "homosexual" to give a speech in their community. In contrast, the 4 studies that found sex differences included questions about rights that could be construed as related to gender role: military service, homosexual marriage, and adoption. The results of a Gallup Poll published after completion of our meta-analysis fit the same pattern: Men expressed more negative attitudes than did women on the issue of gays serving in the military (Moore, 1993). These results are consistent across national probability samples and convenience samples of college students (e.g., Harris & Vanderhoof, 1995). Thus, as with heterosexuals' attitudes toward homosexual persons and behavior, gender role issues may be a key to understanding sex differences in attitudes toward gay civil rights. Men are more negative than women on gender role-related issues, whereas there is no difference on gender role-neutral issues.

Additional new data suggest that the pattern changes slightly when gay male and lesbian targets are considered separately (LaMar & Kite, in press; but see Harris & Vanderhoof, 1995). Heterosexual college students' ratings of gender role-related civil rights differed by both sex of rater and sex of the person being rated. Heterosexual men reported less acceptance for gay men's than for lesbians' civil rights, but heterosexual women's acceptance did not differ by sex of person being rated. This pattern mirrors the comparisons of attitudes toward gay men and lesbians found in our meta-analysis. Finally, heterosexual men were more willing to accept discrimination (e.g., housing, job) against gay men than against lesbians, but heterosexual women's acceptance of this type of discrimination was similar for gay men and lesbians. Attitudes toward free speech were not assessed. Because no other studies we know of have examined heterosexuals' attitudes toward the civil rights of gay men and lesbians separately, it is difficult to know whether the results emerged because of the specific use of target labels (i.e., heterosexual men will derogate gay men almost regardless of the question asked), because of methodological issues such as study population (discussed below), or because a gender role analysis cannot account for all aspects of heterosexuals' attitudes toward gay people's civil rights. Given the current political landscape and recent legislative attempts to restrict the rights of gay men and lesbians, this issue is crucial and deserves considered investigation.

Study Population as a Moderator of Effect Size

In the case of both attitudes toward homosexual persons and attitudes toward homosexual behavior, we were able to consider whether study population (e.g., college students versus other adults) moderated the sex difference in attitudes toward homosexuality. In both cases, sex differences were smallest for nonprofessional adults and largest for college students. Our analysis of attitudes toward homosexual persons also included graduate students and professionals; the effect size for this group fell between college students and other adults. Analysis of attitudes toward homosexual behaviors also included high school students, for whom the sex difference was largest.

Interpretation of these population differences is difficult because many factors co-occur with study population (e.g., age, education; see Whitley & Kite, 1995, for a discussion). Other confounds also obscure interpretation of these results. For example, the majority of studies on sex differences in attitudes toward homosexual persons and behavior used convenience samples of college students. In contrast, most studies using national or regional probability samples of adults have assessed only attitudes toward the civil rights of gay men; when other dependent variables were used, they were usually measured with single items of unknown validity. To determine how well the research using college students generalizes to the population at large, survey researchers must use well-validated measures of attitudes toward homosexual persons and behavior. Studies that have done so have obtained inconsistent results. Herek and Glunt (1993) found sex differences of about the same magnitude as the average effect size for studies using college student samples, and Herek and Capitanio (1995) found a similar sex difference with an African American sample. However, additional data collected by Herek and Capitanio (1996) were consistent with the majority of prior survey studies finding no sex difference in attitudes toward either lesbians or gay men. The question of the generalizability of the research conducted with college students is therefore still unresolved.

Gender Roles and Attitudes Toward Homosexuality

The gender role approach to understanding sex differences in attitudes toward homosexuality implies that gender role attitudes should mediate those sex differences. That is, when sex differences in gender role attitudes are controlled, sex differences in attitudes toward homosexuality should disappear. Statistically, the hypothesis predicts that there should be correlations between respondent sex and gender role attitudes, between respondent sex and attitudes toward homosexuality, and between gender role attitudes and attitudes toward homosexuality, and that the partial correlation between respondent sex and attitudes toward homosexuality should be near zero when gender role attitudes are controlled (Baron & Kenny, 1986).

Before examining the data on this question, it is important to note that the concept of gender role is an example of what Carver (1989) has called a multifaceted construct. It is composed of several related components, each of which can have different relationships to another variable, such as attitudes toward homosexuality. Three components of gender role have been studied in relation to heterosexuals' attitudes toward homosexuality (Whitley, 1987). Gender role self-concept is assessed through self-reports of gender role-related personality traits, such as those included in Spence, Helmreich, and Stapp's (1975) Personal Attributes Questionnaire (PAQ). These scales typically provide two scores: one for traits stereotypically associated with men (variously labeled as masculine, instrumental, or agentic) and another for traits stereotypically associated with women (variously labeled as feminine, expressive, or communal). Gender role behavior is assessed through self-reports of the frequency of behaviors that men and women engage in at different rates, such as those included in Orlofsky, Ramsden, and Cohen's (1982) Sex Role Behavior Scale. Finally, gender role attitudes are assessed by the degree to which respondents endorse statements that reflect traditional or nontraditional gender roles, such as those included in Spence and Helmreich's (1972) Attitudes Toward Women Scale (AWS).

In order for any of these gender role constructs to mediate sex differences in attitudes toward homosexuality, scores on measures of the constructs must correlate with scores on measures of attitudes toward homosexuality. In a meta-analysis of 10 studies of the relationship between gender role self-concept and attitudes toward homosexuality, Whitley (1995) found a mean correlation of $r = .00$ for male-associated traits and a mean correlation of $r = -.09$ for female-associated traits, indicating that these constructs could have no mediating effect. Similarly, in the only study that included gender role behaviors, Whitley (1987) found a correlation of only $r = .10$ between self-reports of male-associated behaviors and attitudes toward homosexuality and a correlation of only $r = -.06$

between self-reports of female-associated behaviors and such attitudes. In contrast, our meta-analysis found that scores on measures of gender role attitudes had a mean correlation of $r = .44$ with scores on measures of attitudes toward homosexuality. We also found that when sex differences in gender role attitudes were controlled (men holding more traditional attitudes), the average partial correlation between gender role attitudes and attitudes toward homosexuality was only $r = .02$. These results indicate that sex differences in attitudes toward homosexuality are related to differences in gender role attitudes, but not to sex differences in gender role self-concept or gender role behaviors.

We must place a qualification on the conclusions just stated. Recent research suggests that men who score higher on extreme gender role involvement, a trait that Mosher (1991) has called *hypermasculinity*, also express more negative attitudes toward homosexuality (e.g., Mosher, 1991; Patel, Long, McCammon, & Wuensch, 1995), even though hypermasculinity scores are relatively independent of gender role attitudes as assessed by the AWS (Mosher, 1991). Thus, hyper-gender-role involvement may be related to heterosexuals' attitudes toward homosexuality independent of respondents' gender role attitudes. Although a parallel hyperfemininity scale has been developed for women (Murnen & Byrne, 1991), no research has reported its relation to attitudes toward homosexuality.

Conservative Gender Role Attitudes or General Conservatism?

Although the gender role interpretation of sex differences in attitudes toward homosexuality is appealing, one might ask whether it is the gender role relatedness of those attitudes or their reflection of generally conservative versus liberal social and political viewpoints that leads them to be correlated with attitudes toward homosexuality. For example, scores on measures of sexism (endorsement of traditional gender role beliefs), racism, and antigay attitudes are all intercorrelated (Bierly, 1985; Qualls, Cox, & Schehr, 1992). Scores on measures of authoritarian and conservative attitudes correlate with scores on measures of both racism and sexism (e.g., Altemeyer, 1988; Pratto et al., 1994) and have an average correlation of $r = .41$ with scores on measures of antigay attitudes (Whitley, 1997).

It is therefore possible that sexism, racism, and antigay attitudes are all facets or manifestations of the higher-order construct of authoritarian conservatism, at least for the predominantly White, heterosexual respondent samples used in the research. This possibility raises the question of whether the specific construct of sexism has a relationship to antigay attitudes beyond that generated by the relationship between the general construct of authoritarian conservative attitudes. We were able to locate only two studies that addressed this issue by examining the correlation of traditional sex role attitudes with attitudes toward homosexuality, controlling for conservative beliefs (Agnew, Thompson, Smith, Gramzow, & Currey, 1993; Whitley, 1987). Although these studies found significant partial correlations, indicating that both conservatism and sexism had an independent relationship to attitudes toward homosexuality, their attitude measures did not distinguish among attitudes toward homosexual persons, behavior, and civil rights. Given the complexity of attitudes toward homosexuality, replication and extension of this research is needed to provide a complete answer to the question posed in the above section heading. Moreover, preliminary data analysis in our laboratory (LaMar & Kite, 1996) suggests that when attitudes toward women's roles (as assessed by the FEM scale; Smith, Ferree, & Miller, 1975) are controlled for, attitude toward the male gender role (as assessed by the Attitudes about Masculinity Scale; Brannon & Juni, 1984) makes an independent contribution to heterosexuals' attitudes toward gay people, suggesting another avenue for further study.

Other Gaps in the Research Literature

Despite the large number of studies on sex differences in heterosexuals' attitudes toward homosexuality, significant gaps exist in the research literature. In addition to those already suggested, some possible directions for future research include making greater use of behavior as a dependent variable and studying responses to lesbians and gay men as individuals rather than as social groups.

Behavior Toward Lesbians and Gay Men

Although there has been a great deal of research on sex differences in expressed attitudes toward lesbians and gay men, few studies have used behavior toward lesbians and gay men as a dependent variable. In making this statement, we define behavioral dependent variables rather narrowly as direct observation of positive or negative actions, self-reports of positive or negative actions, and what Aronson, Ellsworth, Carlsmith, and Gonzales (1990) have called *behavioroid* measures—having research participants make a commitment to perform an action, even if that action is not carried out. These variables include such behaviors as self-reports of antigay aggression, observation of interpersonal distance in laboratory interactions with persons described as being gay, and agreeing to meet with a person described as being gay. We take this narrow approach because it seems to us that other types of behavioral measures—such as self-reports of desired levels of intimacy with lesbians or gay men, nonverbal behaviors, and the content of conversations—bear less resemblance to the types of negative behaviors that lesbians and gay men experience in their everyday lives (e.g., Berrill, 1990; Herek, 1993).

Behavioral studies are important because the attitude-behavior relationship can be very weak and can vary as a function of other variables in the research situation (e.g., Eagly & Chaiken, 1993). In fact, of the five studies that used a dependent variable that met our definition of behavioral (Karr, 1978; Kite, 1992; Lord, Lepper, & Mackie, 1984; Patel et al., 1995; San Miguel & Millham, 1976), only Karr's found a simple attitude-behavior relationship. However, two of the studies did identify variables that moderated the attitude-behavior relationship. Lord et al. (1984) found a moderate relationship when the target person's reported traits fully matched the respondents' personal stereotypes of gay men, but no relationship when the target person's traits only partly fit the stereotype. San Miguel and Millham (1976) found a relationship when the target person was similar to the respondent but not when he was dissimilar and when the outcome of an interaction was negative but not when it was positive. The other studies found no relationship between antigay attitudes and behavior. Thus, like other attitude-behavior relationships, that between heterosexuals' attitudes toward homosexuality and their behavior toward lesbians and gay men can vary as a function of situational factors (e.g., Kite, 1994). For example, Franklin (Chapter 1, this volume) has suggested that negative attitudes toward lesbians and gay men can lead people to perceive negative actions directed at lesbians and gay men to be permissible. However, she further notes that additional, situational, factors—such as youthful thrill seeking, peer group norms, and the felt need to exercise masculine power—must be present before the negative attitudes are expressed as negative behaviors. Consequently, one should not generalize from sex differences in antigay attitudes to sex differences in antigay behavior.

Unfortunately, all five studies assessed only men's behavior, four using only gay male targets, so there is almost no information in the research literature on sex differences in behavior toward lesbians and gay men, although research on antigay violence shows that it is most commonly perpetrated by men (e.g., Berrill, 1990). Research is therefore clearly needed to answer a number of questions. Are there sex differences in heterosexuals' behavior directed toward lesbians and gay men? If so, what variables, especially sex of target person, moderate that relationship? Are there sex differences in the attitude-behavior relationship? If so, what psychological processes cause that difference? The answers to questions such as these can give direction to interventions aimed at reducing antigay behavior in society.

Attitudes Toward Individuals Versus
Attitudes Toward Social Groups

Most studies of sex differences in attitudes toward lesbians and gay men assess respondents' attitudes toward lesbians and gay men as social groups rather than as individuals. However, when interacting with lesbians and gay men, heterosexuals are responding to concrete individuals in all their complexity, rather than to abstract and perhaps simplistically construed social groups. People's responses may differ in these two situations because presenting respondents with a social group as an attitude object calls their stereotypes of the group to mind, which are usually negative with respect to lesbians and gay men (e.g., Lord et al., 1984). Not surprisingly, then, several studies have shown that people respond more negatively to lesbians and gay men presented in a stereotyped manner than when they are presented as "average" people (Laner & Laner, 1979, 1980; Lord et al., 1984).

Therefore, the question arises of whether the sex differences that are found when heterosexuals rate lesbians and gay men as social groups are also found when they rate individual lesbians and gay men who behave in a nonstereotypic manner. The results of this type of research are mixed. Only one study found the typical outcome in which male respondents rate gay men more negatively than lesbians and rate gay men more negatively than do female respondents (Cuenot & Fugita, 1982). Three studies found no sex of respondent or sex of target effects (Kite, 1992, 1994; Shaffer & Wallace, 1990). One pair of related studies found that men rated lesbians and gay men similarly but rated gay men more negatively than did women (Laner & Laner, 1979, 1980). Another study found that men rated both heterosexual and homosexual men more negatively than did women (Gross, Green, Storck, & Vanyur, 1980). Finally, San Miguel and Millham (1976) found that men's reactions to a gay man varied as a function of their attitudes toward homosexuality (see also Kite, 1992), the extent to which they perceived the gay man to be similar to themselves, and whether their interaction with the gay man was positive or negative.

Clearly, more research is needed on how heterosexual men and women respond to individual lesbians and gay men and on what factors affect those responses. The answers to questions such as these are especially important given that classroom presentations by lesbians and gay men, either live or on videotape, are commonly used as attitude-change interventions in colleges and universities (Stevenson, 1988). Such research must, however, be carefully designed to maximize its generalizability to real-life interactions. For example, only two of the studies described above (Cuenot & Fugita, 1982; San Miguel & Millham, 1976) had research participants interact with another person; participants in the other studies either read summaries of information about the people they evaluated or viewed a videotape of a simulated interview. Research of the latter variety lacks much of the richness of the face-to-face interactions of everyday life.

The ways in which interacting with "average" lesbians and gay men affect respondents' stereotypes also need to be assessed, given that people often see members of social groups who do not fit their stereotypes as "exceptions to the rule" and so maintain the stereotype for the social group as a whole (Brewer, 1988), resulting in little real attitude change. For example, Herek and Capitanio (1996) found that heterosexuals who had contact with only one lesbian or gay man held attitudes similar to those who had never had contact with someone they knew to be gay; however, heterosexuals who knew two or more gay people had more favorable attitudes. As Rothbart and John (1985) have suggested, a per-

son who knows more than one member of a group may find it difficult
to dismiss their behavior as atypical.

Distinguishing Between Attitudes
Toward Lesbians and Attitudes
Toward Gay Men

In closing, we want to reiterate a point that others have made before
us (e.g., Herek, 1994): It is essential to distinguish between attitudes
toward lesbians and attitudes toward gay men. Our meta-analysis found
that only 7% of the studies reviewed specifically examined attitudes
toward lesbians, and that all of these studies were limited in that they
assessed only the "persons" component of the attitude and used only
college student respondent samples. In contrast, 59% of the studies simply described the attitude object using the term *homosexual,* which, as
noted earlier, many interpret as meaning *gay man.* Another 18% of the
studies specified gay men as the attitude objects, and 16% of the studies
assessed attitude toward both lesbians and gay men but combined these
responses into a single attitude score. Consequently, little is known about
the ways in which attitudes toward lesbians are similar to and different
from attitudes toward gay men.

Making a distinction between the two sets of attitudes is important
both empirically and theoretically. Empirically, our meta-analysis found
a clear interaction between sex of respondent and sex of attitude object:
Men and women held similar attitudes toward lesbians, but men were
more negative toward gay men. Consequently, researchers must control
both sex of respondent and sex of attitude object to get an accurate picture of the meaning of their results. Research conducted with only male
or only female respondents rating only lesbians or only gay men may
not generalize to other combinations of respondents and attitude objects.
Theoretically, the processes underlying men's and women's attitudes
toward lesbians and gay men may differ. For example, we earlier noted
the possibility that men's less negative attitudes toward lesbians may
result from men's sexualization of lesbianism.

Both theoretical and empirical requirements therefore indicate the necessity of distinguishing between attitudes toward lesbians and attitudes
toward gay men. Such well-focused research and theory can only better
our understanding of attitudes toward both lesbians and gay men and

point to better interventions aimed at alleviating the negative aspects of those attitudes.

Notes

1. Our theoretical analysis concerns *heterosexuals'* attitudes toward gay men and lesbians. In describing our own research and that of others, however, we describe the findings more generally. Although the majority of the respondents in these studies are likely heterosexual, few researchers specifically exclude gay men, lesbian, and bisexual participants. Although the impact of this inclusion is likely minimal, it is not completely correct to assume that these data reflect only heterosexuals' viewpoints. Certainly, a literature based on respondents who report exclusive heterosexuality would provide clearer tests of our hypotheses.

2. Kite and Whitley (1996) reported effect sizes as *d*. However, to make results more accessible, we have converted those effects sizes to *r* in this presentation. This conversion has no effect on interpretation of the results.

References

Adams, H. E., Wright, L. W., & Lohr, B. A. (1996). Is homophobia associated with homosexual arousal? *Journal of Abnormal Psychology, 105,* 440-445.

Agnew, C. R., Thompson, V. D., Smith, V. A., Gramzow, R. H., & Currey, D. P. (1993). Proximal and distal predictors of homophobia: Framing the multivariate roots of out-group rejection. *Journal of Applied Social Psychology, 23,* 2013-2042.

Altemeyer, B. (1988). *Enemies of freedom: Understanding right-wing authoritarianism.* San Francisco: Jossey-Bass.

Aronson, E., Ellsworth, P. C., Carlsmith, J. M., & Gonzales, M. H. (1990). *Methods of research in social psychology* (2nd ed.). New York: McGraw-Hill.

Ashmore, R. D., & Del Boca, F. K. (1981). Conceptual approaches to stereotypes and stereotyping. In D. L. Hamilton (Ed.), *Cognitive processes in stereotyping and intergroup behavior* (pp. 1-35). Hillsdale, NJ: Lawrence Erlbaum.

Baron, R. M., & Kenny, D. A. (1986). The mediator-moderator variable distinction in social psychological research: Conceptual, strategic, and statistical considerations. *Journal of Personality and Social Psychology, 51,* 1173-1182.

Bem, S. L. (1993). *The lenses of gender: Transforming the debate on sexual inequality.* New Haven, CT: Yale University Press.

Berrill, K. T. (1990). Anti-gay violence and victimization in the United States. *Journal of Interpersonal Violence, 5,* 274-294.

Bierly, M. M. (1985). Prejudice toward contemporary outgroups as a generalized attitude. *Journal of Applied Social Psychology, 15,* 189-199.

Black, K. N., & Stevenson, M. R. (1984). The relationship of self-reported sex-role characteristics and attitudes toward homosexuality. *Journal of Homosexuality, 10*(1-2), 83-93.

Brannon, R., & Juni, S. (1984). A scale for measuring attitudes about masculinity. *Psychological Documents, 14,* 6-7.

Brewer, M. B. (1988). A dual process model of impression formation. In T. K. Srull & R. S. Wyer (Eds.), *Advances in social cognition* (Vol. 1, pp. 1-36). Hillsdale, NJ: Lawrence Erlbaum.

Carver, C. S. (1989). How should multifaceted personality constructs be tested? Issues illustrated by self-monitoring, attributional style, and hardiness. *Journal of Personality and Social Psychology, 56,* 577-585.

Christie, R. (1991). Authoritarianism and related constructs. In J. P. Robinson, P. R. Shaver, & L. S. Wrightsman (Eds.), *Measures of personality and social psychological attitudes* (Vol. 1, pp. 501-571). New York: Academic Press.

Costrich, N., Feinstein, L., Kidder, L., Marecek, J., & Pascale, L. (1975). When stereotypes hurt: Three studies of penalties for sex-role reversals. *Journal of Experimental Social Psychology, 11,* 520-530.

Cuenot, R. G., & Fugita, S. S. (1982). Perceived homosexuality: Measuring heterosexual attitudinal and nonverbal reactions. *Personality and Social Psychology Bulletin, 8,* 100-106.

Deaux, K., & Kite, M. E. (1987). Thinking about gender. In B. B. Hess & M. M. Ferree (Eds.), *Analyzing gender: A handbook of social science research* (pp. 92-117). Newbury Park, CA: Sage.

Deaux, K., & Lewis, L. L. (1984). Structure of gender stereotypes: Interrelationships among components and gender label. *Journal of Personality and Social Psychology, 46,* 991-1004.

DeLamater, J. (1987). Gender differences in sexual scenarios. In K. Kelley (Ed.), *Females, males and sexuality: Theories and research* (pp. 127-139). Albany: State University of New York Press.

Duckitt, J. (1992). Psychology and prejudice. *American Psychologist, 47,* 1182-1193.

Eagly, A. H., & Chaiken, S. (1993). *The psychology of attitudes.* Fort Worth, TX: Harcourt Brace Jovanovich.

Esses, V. M., Haddock, G., & Zanna, M. P. (1993). Values, stereotypes, and emotions as determinants of intergroup attitudes. In D. M. Mackie & D. L. Hamilton (Eds.), *Affect, cognition, and stereotyping: Interactive processes in group perception* (pp. 137-166). New York: Academic Press.

Feinman, S. (1981). Why is cross-sex-role behavior more approved for girls than for boys? A status characteristics approach. *Sex Roles, 7,* 289-300.

Fisher, W. A. (1983). Gender, gender-role identification, and response to erotica. In E. R. Allgeier & N. B. McCormick (Eds.), *Changing boundaries: Gender roles and sexual behavior* (pp. 261-284). Mountain View, CA: Mayfield.

Gaughan, E. J., & Gaynor, M. W. (1973). College student ratings of arousal value of pornographic photographs. *Proceedings of the Annual Convention of the American Psychological Association, 8,* 409-410.

Greendlinger, V. (1985). Authoritarianism as a predictor of response to heterosexual and homosexual erotica. *High School Journal, 68,* 183-186.

Gross, A. E., Green, S. K., Storck, J. T., & Vanyur, J. M. (1980). Disclosure of sexual orientation and impressions of male and female homosexuals. *Personality and Social Psychology Bulletin, 6,* 307-314.

Haddock, G., Zanna, M. P., & Esses, V. M. (1993). Assessing the structure of prejudicial attitudes: The case of attitudes toward homosexuals. *Journal of Personality and Social Psychology, 65,* 1105-1118.

Harris, M. B., & Vanderhoof, J. (1995). Attitudes towards gays and lesbians serving in the military. *Journal of Gay and Lesbian Social Services, 3*(4), 23-51.

Hatfield, E., Sprecher, S., & Traupmann, J. (1978). Men's and women's reactions to sexually explicit films: A serendipitous finding. *Archives of Sexual Behavior, 7,* 583-592.

Herek, G. M. (1984). Beyond "homophobia": A social psychological perspective on attitudes toward lesbians and gay men. *Journal of Homosexuality, 10*(1-2), 1-21.

Herek, G. M. (1986). On heterosexual masculinity: Some psychical consequences of the social construction of gender and sexuality. *American Behavioral Scientist, 29*, 563-577.

Herek, G. M. (1988). Heterosexuals' attitudes toward lesbians and gay men: Correlates and gender differences. *Journal of Sex Research, 25*, 451-477.

Herek, G. M. (1991). Stigma, prejudice, and violence against lesbians and gay men. In J. C. Gonsiorek & J. D. Weinrich (Eds.), *Homosexuality: Research implications for public policy* (pp. 60-80). Newbury Park, CA: Sage.

Herek, G. M. (1993). Documenting prejudice against lesbians and gay men on campus: The Yale Sexual Orientation Survey. *Journal of Homosexuality, 25*(4), 15-29.

Herek, G. M. (1994). Assessing heterosexuals' attitudes toward lesbians and gay men: A review of empirical research with the ATLG scale. In B. Greene & G. M. Herek (Eds.), *Lesbian and gay psychology: Theory, research, and clinical applications*. Thousand Oaks, CA: Sage.

Herek, G. M., & Capitanio, J. P. (1995). Black heterosexuals' attitudes toward lesbians and gay men in the United States. *Journal of Sex Research, 32*, 95-105.

Herek, G. M., & Capitanio, J. P. (1996). "Some of my best friends": Intergroup contact, concealable stigma, and heterosexuals' attitudes toward gay men and lesbians. *Personality and Social Psychology Bulletin, 22*, 412-424.

Herek, G. M., & Glunt, E. K. (1993). Interpersonal contact and heterosexuals' attitudes toward gay men: Results from a national survey. *Journal of Sex Research, 30*, 239-244.

Hogg, M. A., & Turner, J. C. (1987). Intergroup behaviour, self-stereotyping and the salience of social categories. *British Journal of Social Psychology, 26*, 325-340.

Hort, B. E., Fagot, B. I., & Leinbach, M. D. (1990). Are people's notions of maleness more stereotypically framed than their notions of femaleness? *Sex Roles, 23*, 197-212.

Jackson, L. A., & Cash, T. F. (1985). Components of gender stereotypes: Their implications for inferences on stereotypic and nonstereotypic dimensions. *Personality and Social Psychology Bulletin, 11*, 326-344.

Karr, R. G. (1978). Homosexual labeling and the male role. *Journal of Social Issues, 34*(3), 73-83.

Kite, M. E. (1992). Individual differences in males' reactions to gay males and lesbians. *Journal of Applied Social Psychology, 22*, 1222-1239.

Kite, M. E. (1994). When perceptions meet reality: Individual differences in reactions to lesbians and gay men. In B. Greene & G. M. Herek (Eds.), *Lesbian and gay psychology: Theory, research, and clinical applications*. Thousand Oaks, CA: Sage.

Kite, M. E., & Deaux, K. (1987). Gender belief systems: Homosexuality and the implicit inversion theory. *Psychology of Women Quarterly, 11*, 83-96.

Kite, M. E., & Whitley, B. E., Jr. (1996). Sex differences in attitudes toward homosexual persons, behavior, and civil rights: A meta-analysis. *Personality and Social Psychology Bulletin, 22*, 336-353.

Krulewitz, J. E., & Nash, J. E. (1980). Effects of sex role attitudes and similarity on men's rejection of male homosexual. *Journal of Personality and Social Psychology, 38*, 67-74.

LaMar, L. M., & Kite, M. E. (1996). [Male and female gender role attitude and sex differences in attitudes toward homosexuality]. Unpublished raw data.

LaMar, L. M., & Kite, M. E. (in press). Sex differences in attitudes toward homosexuality: A multi-dimensional perspective. *The Journal of Sex Research*.

Laner, M. R., & Laner, R. H. (1979). Personal style or sexual preference: Why gay men are disliked. *International Review of Modern Sociology, 9*, 215-228.

Laner, M. R., & Laner, R. H. (1980). Sexual preference or personal style? Why lesbians are disliked. *Journal of Homosexuality, 5*(4), 339-356.

Levitt, E. E., & Brady, J. P. (1965). Sexual preferences in young adults and some correlates. *Journal of Clinical Psychology, 21,* 347-354.

Lewin, M., & Tragos, L. M. (1987). Has the feminist movement influenced adolescent sex role attitudes? A reassessment after a quarter century. *Sex Roles, 16,* 125-135.

Lord, C. G., Lepper, M. R., & Mackie, D. (1984). Attitude prototypes as determinants of attitude-behavior consistency. *Journal of Personality and Social Psychology, 46,* 1254-1266.

Louderback, L. A., & Whitley, B. E., Jr. (1997). Perceived erotic value of homosexuality and sex-role attitudes as mediators of sex differences in heterosexual college students' attitudes toward lesbians and gay men. *Journal of Sex Research, 34,* 175-182.

MacDonald, A. P., Jr. (1976). Homophobia: Its roots and meanings. *Homosexual Counseling Journal, 3*(1), 23-33.

Martin, C. L. (1990). Attitudes and expectations about children with nontraditional and traditional gender roles. *Sex Roles, 22,* 151-165.

McCormick, N. B. (1979). Come-ons and put-offs: Unmarried students' strategies for having and avoiding sexual intercourse. *Psychology of Women Quarterly, 4,* 194-211.

McCreary, D. R. (1994). The male role and avoiding femininity. *Sex Roles, 31,* 517-531.

Morin, S. F., & Garfinkle, E. M. (1978). Male homophobia. *Journal of Social Issues, 34*(1), 29-47.

Moore, D. W. (1993, April). Public polarized on gay issue. *Gallup Poll Monthly,* pp. 30-34.

Mosher, D. L. (1991). Macho men, machismo, and sexuality. *Annual Review of Sex Research, 2,* 199-247.

Murnen, S. K., & Byrne, D. (1991). Hyperfemininity: Measurement and initial validation of the construct. *Journal of Sex Research, 26,* 479-489.

Nyberg, K. L., & Alston, J. P. (1977). Homosexual labeling by university youths. *Adolescence, 12,* 541-546.

Oliver, M. B., & Hyde, J. S. (1993). Gender differences in sexuality: A meta-analysis. *Psychological Bulletin, 114,* 29-51.

Orlofsky, J. L., Ramsden, M. W., & Cohen, R. S. (1982). Development of the revised Sex Role Behavior Scale. *Journal of Personality Assessment, 46,* 632-638.

Patel, S., Long, T. E., McCammon, S. L., & Wuensch, K. L. (1995). Personality and emotional correlates of self-reported antigay behaviors. *Journal of Interpersonal Violence, 10,* 354-366.

Pratto, F., Sidanius, J., Stallworth, L. M., & Malle, B. F. (1994). Social dominance orientation: A personality variable predicting social and political attitudes. *Journal of Personality and Social Psychology, 67,* 741-763.

Preston, K., & Stanley, K. (1987). "What's the worst thing . . . ?" Gender-directed insults. *Sex Roles, 17,* 209-219.

Qualls, R. C., Cox, M. B., & Schehr, T. J. (1992). Racial attitudes on campus: Are there gender differences? *Journal of College Student Development, 33,* 524-529.

Rajecki, D. W., De Graaf-Kaser, R., & Rasmussen, J. L. (1992). New impressions and more discrimination: Effects of individuation on gender-label stereotypes. *Sex Roles, 27,* 171-185.

Reiss, I. L. (1986). *Journey into sexuality: An exploratory voyage.* Englewood Cliffs, NJ: Prentice Hall.

Rothbart, M., & John, O. P. (1985). Social categorization and behavioral episodes: A cognitive analysis of the effects of intergroup contact. *Journal of Social Issues, 41*(3), 81-104.

San Miguel, C. L., & Millham, J. (1976). The role of cognitive and situational variables in aggression toward homosexuals. *Journal of Homosexuality, 2*(1), 11-27.

Shaffer, D. R., & Wallace, A. (1990). Belief congruence and evaluator homophobia as determinants of the attractiveness of competent homosexual and heterosexual males. *Journal of Psychology and Human Sexuality, 3*(1), 67-87.

Smith, E. R., Ferree, M. M., & Miller, F. D. (1975). A short scale of attitudes toward feminism. *Representative Research in Social Psychology, 6,* 51-58.

Spence, J. T., & Helmreich, R. L. (1972). The Attitudes Toward Women Scale: An objective instrument to measure attitudes toward the rights and roles of women in contemporary society. *JSAS Catalog of Selected Documents in Psychology, 2,* 66. (Ms. No. 153)

Spence, J. T., Helmreich, R. L., & Stapp, J. (1975). Ratings of self and peers on sex role attributes and their relations to self-esteem and conceptions of masculinity and femininity. *Journal of Personality and Social Psychology, 32,* 29-39.

Sprecher, S., & McKinney, K. (1993). *Sexuality.* Newbury Park, CA: Sage.

Stevenson, M. R. (1988). Promoting tolerance for homosexuality: An evaluation of intervention strategies. *Journal of Sex Research, 25,* 500-511.

Stockard, J., & Johnson, M. M. (1979). The social origins of male dominance. *Sex Roles, 5,* 199-218.

Taylor, A. (1983). Conceptions of masculinity and femininity as a basis for stereotypes of male and female homosexuals. *Journal of Homosexuality, 9*(1), 37-53.

Turnbull, D., & Brown, M. (1977). Attitudes toward homosexuality and male and female reactions to homosexual and heterosexual slides. *Canadian Journal of Behavioral Science, 9,* 68-80.

Whitley, B. E., Jr. (1987). The relationship of sex-role orientation to heterosexuals' attitudes toward homosexuals. *Sex Roles, 17,* 103-113.

Whitley, B. E., Jr. (1995). *Sex-role orientation and attitudes toward homosexuality: A meta-analysis.* Unpublished manuscript, Ball State University, Department of Psychological Science.

Whitley, B. E., Jr. (1997, April). *Authoritarian/conservative attitudes and attitudes toward homosexuality.* Paper presented at the annual meeting of the Eastern Psychological Association, Washington, DC.

Whitley, B. E., Jr., & Kite, M. E. (1995). Sex differences in attitudes toward homosexuality: A comment on Oliver and Hyde (1993). *Psychological Bulletin, 117,* 146-154.

Wood, F. W. (Ed.). (1990). *An American profile: Opinions and behavior, 1972-1989.* Detroit, MI: Gale Research.

4

The Relationship Between Stereotypes of and Attitudes Toward Lesbians and Gays

ANGELA SIMON

Research over the past several years has provided us with much information on the correlates of individuals' attitudes toward lesbians and gay men. Investigations have shown that negative attitudes toward lesbians and gays are associated with traditional views regarding the roles and behavior of women (e.g., Agnew, Thompson, Smith, Gramzow, & Currey, 1993; Harry, 1995; Herek, 1988, 1994; Simon, 1995b, 1996; see also Kite & Whitley, Chapter 3, this volume); conservative, nonpermissive attitudes toward sex (e.g., Ficarrotto, 1990; Simon, 1995b, 1996); the belief that homosexuality is "caused" by social or environmental factors (Herek & Capitanio, 1995; Simon, 1996; Whitley, 1990); negative interpersonal experiences with lesbians and gays, or a lack of homosexual acquaintances or friends (e.g., Agnew et al., 1993; D'Augelli & Rose, 1990; Herek, 1988, 1994; Herek & Capitanio, 1996; Herek & Glunt, 1993; Simon, 1995b, 1996; Whitley, 1990); religiosity factors such as membership in traditionally conservative religions and frequent attendance at religious services (Agnew et al., 1993; Fisher, Derison, Polley, Cadman, & Johnston, 1994; Herek, 1994; Herek & Capitanio, 1995; Seltzer, 1992; Simon, 1996); and being older and having relatively little education (Herek, 1984; Herek & Capitanio, 1996; Herek & Glunt, 1993).

Although many possible correlates of attitudes toward homosexuals have been examined, the relationship between such attitudes and stereotypes of homosexuals has not received widespread attention. Stereotypes abound in popular culture, with homosexuals widely perceived as promiscuous recruiters and corrupters of children, who cannot have committed relationships, have not yet met the right man (for lesbians) or right woman (for gay males), and want to be men (for lesbians) or want to be women (for gay males; see ELAN/PFLAG, 1992; *Fairy Tales,* 1995). Is it inevitable that heterosexuals who hold such beliefs will also have overall negative attitudes toward homosexuals? Do individuals with generally positive attitudes toward homosexuals reject these negative beliefs? What are the implications of the relationship between stereotypes and attitudes for stereotype change and prejudice reduction?

In the world outside the social psychological laboratory, these questions can be framed in the following ways. Can a politico wholeheartedly reject the ideas that lesbians and gays cannot have committed relationships, cannot be good parents, and are antifamily but still strongly support antigay legislation such as the Defense of Marriage Act (1996)? Can a religious leader firmly believe that homosexuals recruit and corrupt children and are child molesters but still support pro-gay legislation, for example, a law that would protect a homosexual elementary school teacher from job discrimination? Is it possible for military personnel to steadfastly reject the notions that lesbians and gays are promiscuous and are sexual predators (especially in communal shower settings like those favored in the military) but still adamantly oppose the idea of openly homosexual women and men serving in the armed forces? Can judicial figures make rulings in favor of lesbians and gays, such as the 1996 Hawaii same-sex marriage ruling (*Baehr v. Miike,* 1996) and the 1996 Colorado Amendment 2 decision (*Romer et al. v. Evans et al.,* 1996), while at heart believing that lesbians and gays are immoral, want special civil rights, and are psychologically abnormal? Should a gay man who is in a social situation where negative attitudes toward gays prevail work on dismantling others' negative stereotypes of gays in order to reduce prejudice? Likewise, should a lesbian who is in a homophobic work environment focus on eradicating negative beliefs about lesbians in order to make her situation more tolerable?

Social scientists have not yet thoroughly explored how heterosexuals' negative and positive stereotypes of lesbians and gay men are related to their attitudes and prejudice toward lesbians and gays. My major purpose in this chapter is to review some of the work that has been conducted in this area from both a general social psychological perspective and a more specific lesbian and gay studies orientation. The chapter concludes with a discussion of how this work may be utilized for the purposes of stereotype change and prejudice reduction.

Social Psychological Research on Stereotypes and Attitudes

Stereotypes and Other Constructs

Although different definitions of stereotypes appear in the social psychological literature, most theorists agree that stereotypes are beliefs (e.g., Hamilton & Trolier, 1986; Judd & Park, 1993; Smith, 1993). Ashmore and Del Boca (1981) have defined stereotypes as "a set of beliefs about the personal attributes of a group of people" (p. 16). This conceptualization of stereotypes, which has been adopted by many social psychological researchers (e.g., Eagly & Mladinic, 1989; Haddock, Zanna, & Esses, 1993; Jussim, Nelson, Mannis, & Soffin, 1995; Stroebe & Insko, 1989), guides the discussion in this chapter.

Many early social psychologists equated stereotypes with prejudice, but most contemporary psychologists draw a distinction between the two constructs (Ashmore & Del Boca, 1981). Prejudice is generally considered to be an attitude. For example, Esses, Haddock, and Zanna (1993) have maintained that an attitude toward a social group can be viewed as a "favorable or unfavorable overall evaluation of a social group, with an unfavorable evaluation being labeled prejudice" (p. 138). Similarly, Stephan and Stephan (1993) have held that "prejudice consists of negative evaluations of social groups" (p. 125). These latter views of prejudice are compatible with those of other theorists (e.g., Smith, 1993; Stroebe & Insko, 1989) and with my own.

Social psychologists agree that stereotypes and prejudice should be related to each other. According to Fishbein and Ajzen (1975), prejudice, like any other attitude, is a function of beliefs about the attitude object as well as the evaluations of those beliefs. In their model, beliefs and stereotypes are synonymous, with attitudes considered evaluative and beliefs considered cognitive (Ajzen, 1989; Fishbein & Ajzen, 1975). In Zanna and Rempel's (1988) model, an attitude (including prejudice) is an evaluation of an object that is based on three separable sources of information: cognitive information or beliefs, affective information (i.e., feelings or emotions), and information concerning past behavior toward the object. Cognitive information or beliefs include consensually and individually held stereotypes about the social group (Esses et al., 1993). Once formed, the attitude (prejudice) can be independent of the stereotypic beliefs upon which it was based.

Both models predict that stereotypes of a social group should positively correlate with attitudes toward that group—for example, that negative stereotypes should be related to prejudice. Indeed, most social psychologists adhere to the view that negative stereotypes and prejudice are strongly interrelated, but surprisingly little research has been conducted on this relationship (Stangor, Sullivan, & Ford, 1991). What follows is a review of some of the more recent work in social psychology that has focused on these linkages.

Research on the Relationship Between Stereotypes and Attitudes

Some social psychological researchers have found that stereotypes of social groups are positively correlated with attitudes toward those groups. However, these researchers have also found that other constructs may be stronger predictors of attitudes.

In a 1993 book chapter, Esses, Haddock, and Zanna reviewed some of their own work in this area. In one study, individual stereotypes (i.e., all characteristics that an individual attributes to members of a social group) and attitudes toward six ethnic groups were assessed. Results revealed significant and moderate correlations for the two constructs across groups, with positive stereotypes associated with positive attitudes. In another study described by Esses et al. (1993), relationships among attitudes, individual stereotypes, symbolic beliefs (i.e., beliefs that social groups violate or uphold cherished values and norms), and emotions for several social groups (including homosexuals) and social issues were examined. Relationships between stereotypes and attitudes were generally significant, with correlations ranging from small to moderate; emotions or feelings about the social group were most consistently related to attitudes.

In research that is especially relevant to this chapter, Haddock et al. (1993) examined these same relationships for the target social group "homosexuals." In two studies, they found that, overall, stereotypic beliefs or individual stereotypes were significantly positively correlated with attitudes toward homosexuals and accounted for a significant proportion of explained variance. Higher correlations were observed for symbolic beliefs and affect (see also Haddock & Zanna, Chapter 5, this volume). Likewise, Stangor et al. (1991) assessed individuals' attitudes toward, emotional responses toward, and stereotypes of different social groups, including homosexuals. The results of two studies showed that individually held stereotypes were weakly to moderately predictive of attitudes; emotional responses were stronger, more consistent predictors of attitudes.

Eagly and her colleagues' research has shown that affect does not necessarily play a larger and stronger role than cognition in the prediction of attitudes. Eagly and Mladinic (1989) found that both personal/individual stereotypes and social/consensual stereotypes (i.e., shared beliefs about the characteristics possessed by members of a social group) correlated positively and significantly with attitudes for the groups women, men, Democrats, and Republicans; correlations ranged in size from small to moderate. In a later study, Eagly, Mladinic, and Otto (1994) found that beliefs (i.e., personal stereotypes) about women, men, Democrats, Republicans, abortion on demand, affirmative action, and welfare assistance for the poor were moderately and significantly correlated with attitudes toward these social groups and issues. Personal stereotypes were also moderately good predictors of these attitudes. The relationships between beliefs and attitudes were stronger than the relationships between affects and attitudes.

Other researchers whose primary interest was not in evaluating the cognitive and affective components of attitudes have also examined the stereotype-attitude relationship. For example, Stephan and Stephan (1993) have reported on a study they conducted in which correlations between stereotypes of and attitudes toward six national groups (Moroccans, Russians, Japanese, Chinese, Americans, Indians) were obtained for two different samples. Correlations were positive, but not always significant, with the highest values being of moderate magnitude (see also Stephan, Ageyev, Coates-Shrider, Stephan, & Abalakina, 1994). Although it was not the main focus of their work, Jussim et al. (1995) have presented correlations between measures of stereotypes and attitudes for various types of targets, including a homosexual target. Correlations were generally positive, significant, and moderate to strong, although some correlations, including those for the homosexual target, were of low magnitude.

This brief review reveals a fact on which many social scientists have remarked: Research results offer mixed support for a *strong* association between stereotypes and attitudes (Ashmore & Del Boca, 1981; Esses et al., 1993; Stangor et al., 1991; Stephan & Stephan, 1993; Stroebe & Insko, 1989). Stereotypes may not be as strong as some other factors in predicting attitudes, but that issue is not the focal point of this chapter. The focus here is on the relationship between stereotypes and attitudes, and the evidence suggests that negative stereotypes are moderate predictors of prejudice. This means that for some individuals, negative stereotypes are strongly associated with prejudice, but the two are not necessarily linked. The presence of a moderate relationship between stereotypes and attitudes suggests that it is possible for individuals who adhere to negative stereotypes of a social group to simultaneously possess positive attitudes toward that group as a whole. This is a counterintuitive yet interesting proposition, one that is further explored in the following section.

Research on the Relationship Between Stereotypes of and Attitudes Toward Lesbians and Gay Men

For the most part, the stereotypes of homosexuals evident in popular culture are like those revealed by empirical research. Some empirically derived stereotypes of lesbians include the beliefs that lesbians tend to be independent, to not be easily influenced, to not give up easily, to have a need for security, to be significantly different from the "normal, healthy adult," to be positive toward females, to be masculine, to have short hair, to be negative toward males, to be too blatant, and to be a bad influence on children (Eliason, Donelan, & Randall, 1993; Kite & Deaux, 1987; Page & Yee, 1985; Taylor, 1983). Gay men are stereotyped to be interested in sex, to be emotional, to have a need for security, to be neat, to enjoy art and music, to be significantly different from the "normal, healthy adult," to be positive toward males, to be feminine, to have high-pitched voices, to wear jewelry, to be creative, and to be complicated (Kite & Deaux, 1987; Page & Yee, 1985; Simon, Glassner-Bayerl, & Stratenwerth, 1991; Taylor,

1983). Clearly, there are many beliefs regarding homosexuals. What are the interrelationships between these types of beliefs or stereotypes and attitudes and prejudice?

Research on the Generic Term *Homosexuals*

One way to begin exploring stereotypes of lesbians and gays and their possible relationships to prejudice is by reviewing research on the use of the term *homosexuals* as a generic. There has not been a great deal of work on this issue, but it appears that the term *homosexual* is often interpreted to mean "male homosexual" specifically; this tendency seems to be greater among men than among women (Black & Stevenson, 1984; Haddock et al., 1993; see also Haddock & Zanna, Chapter 5, and Kite & Whitley, Chapter 3, this volume).

Black and Stevenson (1984) have noted that stereotyping of the generic term *homosexual* may have implications for attitudes, in that some individuals who interpret *homosexual* as meaning male homosexual may have more negative attitudes than those who do not interpret the term this narrowly. Haddock et al. (1993) did not find this trend.

My own work partially supports the above findings (Simon, 1995a). Self-identified heterosexual college undergraduates from a southeastern university completed attitude and stereotype measures. Data from 208 participants (160 women and 48 men) were included in the analyses reported here. Participants were randomly assigned to one of three conditions. In the *homosexual* (HO) condition, subjects were asked to complete a sex-unspecified version of the 20-item Attitudes Toward Lesbians and Gay Men (ATLG) scale (Herek, 1988). ATLG scores can range from 20 to 180, with higher scores indicating more negative attitudes. After completion of the attitude scale, subjects were asked to rate how descriptive each of a series of 65 phrases was of the individual whom they were thinking of while completing the scale. Participants in the *female homosexual* (FH) and the *male homosexual* (MH) conditions were submitted to this same procedure but were asked to think of "female [male] homosexuals and female [male] homosexuality specifically" in the respective conditions. All participants were asked whom they were generally or specifically thinking of while completing the attitude scale.

Of interest here are the responses of the 68 subjects in the HO condition: 14 (21%) indicated that they were thinking of homosexual men only; 27 (40%) said that they were thinking of both homosexual women and men; and 26 (38%) said that sometimes they thought of homosexual women, sometimes homosexual men, and sometimes both. One female subject indicated that she thought of homosexual women only. There were no notable differences by subject sex. A series of t tests were conducted on the ATLG scores of participants in the HO condition. All possible pairwise comparisons were made between the scores of participants who thought of male homosexuals only, who thought of both homosexual women and men, and who sometimes thought of either or both. The mean ATLG score of the group who thought of male homosexuals only was higher ($M = 106.14$, $SD = 44.89$) than either of the other two groups ($M = 94.11$, $SD = 43.60$ for the group who thought of both sexes; $M = 95.89$, $SD = 38.59$ for the group who thought of sometimes one sex and sometimes both); however, these differences were not significant (at $p < .05$).

In sum, there appears to be some tendency for individuals to stereotype the group "homosexuals" to mean male homosexuals. Heterosexuals who exhibit this tendency may possess more prejudice than others, but this relationship appears to be weak to moderate at best. Consistent with my earlier review of general social psychological research, stereotyping of homosexuals is not inevitably linked to prejudice toward them.

Research on the Relationship Between Stereotypes and Attitudes

Not surprisingly, research focusing specifically on the relationship between stereotypes of and attitudes toward lesbians and gay men is quite limited. Unlike the previously reviewed social psychological work, the bulk of research in this area does not appear to have been specifically designed to assess the stereotype-attitude relationship. Yet useful information regarding this association can be extracted. For example, Laner and Laner (1980) found that a stereotypic lesbian target (i.e., hypofeminine; undecided major; enjoys motorcycle riding; wears jeans, leather jacket, and no makeup) was liked less than other types of lesbian and nonlesbian targets. These authors reported on results from one of their earlier studies that showed that stereotypic gay males (i.e., hypomasculine) were somewhat disliked. If liking is considered an assessment of attitude—not uncommon in this area of research—then it can be concluded that Laner and Laner found evidence for a positive relationship between stereotyping and prejudice, with greater negative stereotyping associated with stronger negative attitudes.

Dew (1985) found that female participants who expressed conservative sex role attitudes (toward homosexuality and women's rights) associated homosexuality with unattractive female targets, whereas females with more liberal sex role attitudes did not consistently make this association. Male participants made the homosexuality-unattractiveness association regardless of their attitudes. This research suggests that prejudice toward homosexuals is associated with the tendency to stereotype lesbians negatively, that is, to view them as unattractive.

Some additional evidence for a positive relationship between negative stereotypes and prejudice comes from the work of Jackson and Sullivan (1990), who found that cognition and affect predicted male subjects' evaluations of male homosexuals. For example, negative affect (e.g., how angry or disgusted subjects felt) predicted whether a homosexual applicant would be recommended for acceptance into graduate school, and negative affect and stereotypic beliefs concerning creativity and morality predicted whether subjects believed a homosexual applicant would be successful in graduate school. These were not the same patterns as for the heterosexual target.

More straightforward evidence also exists. For example, Gentry (1987) found significant, positive correlations of low to moderate magnitude between intolerance (measured by a social distance scale toward female homosexuals and toward male homosexuals) and agreement with several negative stereotypic statements about female and male homosexuals. For instance, the more intolerant female and male subjects were, the more likely they were to agree with statements such as "Female (male) homosexuals should not be allowed around children," "Female (male) homosexuals belong in jail," and "Female (male) homosexuals need psychiatric care" (p. 201).

An association between negative stereotypes and prejudice has also been revealed in the work of Sigelman, Howell, Cornell, Cutright, and Dewey (1990). Male participants who expressed a highly intolerant attitude toward gays perceived a gay male stimulus person as having more gay-stereotyped traits (e.g., unaggressive, gentle, weak, unmasculine) than did more tolerant male participants. Highly intolerant subjects also perceived the gay male stimulus person as having significantly more gay-stereotyped traits than other stimulus persons (e.g., a male heterosexual), whereas no significant differences emerged for the less intolerant subjects.

Preliminary results from my previously mentioned study demonstrate the existence of a positive relationship between negative stereotypes and prejudice, but the strength of this relationship is not yet clear (Simon, Cassity, Giovannini, & Baker, 1995). As described above, participants were randomly assigned to the homosexual, the female homosexual, or the male homosexual condition. Participants completed the ATLG scale and then rated how descriptive each of a series of 65 phrases was of the individual whom they were thinking of while completing the attitude scale. Ratings of the phrases were made on a scale ranging from 1 (*very nondescriptive*) to 9 (*very descriptive*). A total of 38 of the 65 descriptors were preexperimentally judged by independent raters to be applicable to both female and male homosexuals. Of these 38, 17 were judged to be positive stereotypes of homosexuals and 21 were judged to be negative stereotypes. These descriptors were utilized in the present analyses and are listed in Table 4.1.

Positive and negative stereotype scores were calculated for each subject through summing of the ratings across the two different sets of items. Approximate quartile ATLG values were used to create four attitudinal groups: extremely positive, positive, negative, and extremely negative. Again, data from 160 women and 48 men are included in the analyses presented here. Preliminary analyses revealed no significant differences by group label or subject sex, so data were collapsed across these variables.

Positive stereotype scores were submitted to a one-way ANOVA, with attitudinal group serving as the independent variable. A significant effect for attitudinal group emerged, $F(3, 195) = 14.11$, $p < .001$. As shown in Table 4.2, positive stereotypes were seen as less descriptive of the lesbian, gay, or homosexual target as attitudes toward the group became more negative. Negative stereotype scores were submitted to the same one-way ANOVA by attitudinal group. Again, a significant effect for attitudinal group emerged, $F(3, 194) = 37.28$, $p < .001$. As shown in Table 4.3, negative stereotypes were seen as more descriptive of the lesbian, gay, or homosexual target as attitudes toward the group became more negative. These results show a definite positive relationship between stereotypes of homosexuals and attitudes toward homosexuals. However, they also make it clear that prejudiced individuals do not have entirely nega-

Table 4.1 Positive and Negative Descriptors Used for Stereotype Scores

Positive Descriptors	Negative Descriptors
Has a good sense of humor	Feels ashamed of self
Is a loving romantic partner	Thinks of self as better than heterosexuals
Is self-confident	Is extremely politically liberal
Is sensitive	Is lonely
Is nice	Takes on the roles of the opposite sex in romantic relationships
Is creative	
Is willing to stand up for self	Is confused
Is caring	Is bitter
Is gentle	Is rebellious
Is compassionate	Is psychologically sick
Is intelligent	Publicly displays affection for romantic partner
Is loving toward all people	
Is understanding	Lacks self-control
Is independent	Attempts to come on to heterosexuals
Is open-minded	Is a scary/threatening individual
Is friendly	Is self-centered
Is happy	Wants special political rights
	Attempts to convert children to homosexuality
	Is not a Christian
	Spreads AIDS
	Is too open about his or her sexuality
	Has no morals
	Had a bad experience with someone of the opposite sex

tive stereotypes of homosexuals and that nonprejudiced individuals do not completely reject such negative beliefs.

In sum, the research reviewed here offers support for the existence of a relationship between stereotypes of and attitudes toward lesbians and gays. However, compelling evidence for a strong association between the two constructs is still absent. Negative stereotypes are associated with prejudice toward lesbians and gays, but the two are not fundamentally linked. Here again, the research suggests that it is possible for individuals who adhere to negative stereotypes of homosexuals to simultaneously possess positive attitudes toward the group as a whole.

Table 4.2 Mean Positive Stereotype Scores by Attitudinal Group

	Stereotype Scores	
Attitudinal Group	*M*	*SD*
Extremely positive	126.02	17.44
Positive	120.61	20.06
Negative	108.62	17.97
Extremely negative	103.64	22.08

NOTE: Scores can range from 17 to 153, with higher scores indicating positive terms are descriptive of the target.

Table 4.3 Mean Negative Stereotype Scores by Attitudinal Group

	Stereotype Scores	
Attitudinal Group	*M*	*SD*
Extremely positive	71.77	19.25
Positive	80.48	18.86
Negative	91.30	23.34
Extremely negative	113.02	21.02

NOTE: Scores can range from 21 to 189, with higher scores indicating negative terms are descriptive of the target.

Conclusions and Future Directions

Although there may not yet be a confirmed, extremely powerful relationship between negative stereotypes of and prejudice toward homosexuals, the bulk of empirical research suggests that a moderate relationship exists between these constructs. What are the implications of this relationship for stereotype change and prejudice reduction?

At the outset, it is necessary to note that limitations of laboratory research may hamper successful use of these data for stereotype reduction and attitude change in the real world. For example, the bulk of the research reviewed here utilized college undergraduates as participants. The typical college student is quite unlike the average homophobic, middle-aged adult with a low educational level. It is clear that ideas for prejudice reduction gleaned entirely from empirical research with students may not be workable with the general population. Furthermore, the stereotypes that are utilized in laboratory research often do not mirror the real-world stereotypes that heterosexuals actually possess. Again, strategies for stereotype and attitude change outside the laboratory may be affected.

The research results also make it clear that strategies for prejudice reduction that focus on changing negative stereotypes will not work for many heterosexuals with antigay attitudes. Changing the negative beliefs of individuals for whom there is a strong positive association between stereotypes and attitudes may result in decreased prejudice. However, what of those individuals for whom this association is not strong? What about the politician or military leader who supports antigay policies yet does not hold negative stereotypes of lesbians and gays? Clearly, the strategies used to decrease the prejudice of such individuals must focus on aspects other than stereotype change. And what of the religious leader or judge who strongly adheres to negative stereotypes of lesbians and gay men, yet possesses remarkably little prejudice toward homosexuals? Should we attempt to change the negative stereotypes of such individuals, or, because their prejudice is already low, should we disregard the negative stereotypes?

These limitations and difficulties notwithstanding, information on the relationship between stereotypes and attitudes can still be useful to social scientists who are designing studies specifically aimed at changing heterosexuals' negative stereotypes of and prejudice toward homosexuals. I review below a few of the many possible uses of this knowledge in initiating stereotype and attitude change. In addition, information on the linkages between negative stereotypes and prejudice can have practical use for lesbians and gays themselves. I discuss some of these applications below also.

Stereotypes, Prejudice, and Attitude Change

The *contact hypothesis* holds that under certain conditions, contact between members of a majority and a minority social group can result in decreased bias of the former, the in-group, toward the latter, the out-group (Amir, 1976; Brewer & Kramer, 1985; Rajecki, 1982). Several favorable contact conditions must be present and several unfavorable conditions absent for contact to work in decreasing bias (e.g., Amir, 1969, 1976), but the powerful potential of contact for reducing homonegativism among heterosexuals has been demonstrated. For example, research on attitude correlates, reviewed at the beginning of this chapter, demonstrates that two contact variables—having positive interpersonal experiences with homosexuals and having homosexual acquaintances or friends—are strongly correlated with positive attitudes toward lesbians and gays (Agnew et al., 1993; D'Augelli & Rose, 1990; Herek, 1988, 1994; Herek & Capitanio, 1996; Herek & Glunt, 1993; Simon, 1995b, 1996; Whitley, 1990).

Social psychologists have noted many weaknesses of the contact hypothesis, and empirical support for it has been mixed. One pressing problem is that positive attitude change created in the contact situation often does not generalize from the target out-group member(s) to the out-group as a whole (Hewstone & Brown, 1986; Wilder & Thompson, 1980). Several possible solutions to this problem of nongeneralizability are available, and all of them can benefit from information on the positive links between stereotypes of and attitudes toward social groups, specifically homosexuals.

Wilder's (1984) work suggests that contact with a typical, likable out-group member will result in a favorable evaluation of that individual on the part of in-group members and will facilitate positive attitude change that generalizes to the larger out-group. In designing a contact study, a social scientist could make use of the information available on stereotypes and on the stereotype-prejudice relationship to create a target out-group member who is the optimal blend of typicality and likableness. For instance, work on the content of stereotypes reveals that the typical lesbian is perceived as being masculine and as having short hair. The research on the association between stereotypes and attitudes suggests that positive attitude or likableness is often associated with the beliefs that lesbians are not unattractive, are not confused, and are intelligent. This information suggests that a social scientist interested in creating a potentially successful contact condition would benefit from using a lesbian target out-group member who is physically somewhat attractive but who also has some distinguishing masculine characteristics (e.g., short hair, an athletic build, a strong jaw) and who is successful in a field that traditionally requires intellectual competence (e.g., college professor, medical doctor, clinical psychologist). Of course, this is just one of many possible types of potentially "successful" target out-group members. This idea is like that employed by Rothbart and John (1985), who held that generalizable stereotype change (i.e., attitude change) may occur when in-group members encounter an out-group member who disconfirms the stereotype (e.g., a lesbian being a successful college professor) but who is typical enough to activate the larger group label (e.g., a lesbian who has short hair and an athletic build and who may even periodically "remind" the in-group members that she is a lesbian).

Research on stereotype change suggests that another way to create generalizability is through the use of subgrouping. Subgrouping involves an experimental procedure in which members of a group are presented in smaller clusters, or subgroups. Although all subgroups are similar in some way, some subgroup members confirm the larger group stereotype and other subgroups disconfirm it. Subgrouping has been found to lead to a less stereotypic, more variable view of the members of the group as a whole (Maurer, Park, & Rothbart, 1995; Park, Ryan, & Judd, 1992). In terms of the discussion here, this research suggests that if a contact situation could be created using several different subgroups of lesbians or gays—all of which are linked by the label "homosexual" but each of which confirms or disconfirms the prevailing stereotypes— stereotype and attitude change will occur and will generalize to other members of the out-group. Once again, research on the links between stereotypes of and prejudice toward lesbians and gays could be used to create optimal clusters, utilizing confirming and disconfirming attributes that have been demonstrated to be at least moderately associated with nonprejudicial views of homosexuals.

Maurer et al. (1995) did make use of the gay male stereotype in one of their studies. For example, one of their *confirming* subgroups included gay males who were described as fashion conscious and sexually promiscuous, whereas another confirming group was described as having their feelings easily hurt and unable to get enough intimacy in their relationships. The *disconfirming* subgroup consisted of gay males described as masculine and involved in long-term relationships. The research reviewed earlier suggests that these stereotypic beliefs are the same ones often associated with the presence or absence of prejudice.

In designing studies in which prejudice reduction depends, to some degree, on the manipulation of stereotypes, it is important to keep in mind that both low- and high-prejudice individuals have negative stereotypes. The existence of this tendency has been powerfully demonstrated by Devine (1989) in a now widely cited investigation. Based on the results of three studies, Devine concluded that high- and low-prejudice subjects are equally knowledgeable of the content of certain cultural stereotypes; stereotypes are automatically activated for both high- and low-prejudice subjects; and, when conditions for controlled processing are present, low-prejudice (but not high-prejudice) subjects consciously inhibit the automatic activation of stereotypes and consciously replace them with their personal beliefs, which predominantly reflect equality and negations of stereotypes. Discussion of the process by which these tendencies emerge for low-prejudice individuals is beyond the scope of this chapter, but explications of this model are available (e.g., Devine & Monteith, 1993; Devine, Monteith, Zuwerink, & Elliot, 1991; Monteith, Devine, & Zuwerink, 1993). What is important for the discussion here is that when researchers design studies within the contact paradigm, it is not necessarily crucial that they manipulate the makeup of target out-group members so that they have a complete absence of negative attributes, because low levels of prejudice can coexist with negative stereotypes. Studies on the contact hypothesis may sometimes be hindered by researchers being overly concerned with manipulating out-group members to be wholly positive representatives of their larger groups. Other matters should take precedence in studies of this type.

The techniques for prejudice reduction outlined here obviously would be most easily employed in laboratory settings. Again, the limitations of such an approach should be recognized. At the least, psychologists should recruit older, nonstudent, heterosexual participants for such studies, because younger college students do not seem generally to be virulently homophobic. Recent work by Herek and Capitanio (1996) also suggests that contact with homosexuals may work best in reducing prejudice when heterosexuals interact with multiple lesbians and gay men, when heterosexuals interact with homosexuals with whom they have close relationships, and when heterosexuals learn of homosexual persons' sexual orientation directly from the homosexual individuals. The use of multiple contacts can be or already is being utilized in the prejudice reduction strategies mentioned above. Creating an experimental situation in which direct disclosure of sexual orientation occurs between heterosexual study participants and homosexual targets in the context of an intimate relationship would be difficult but possible if a prejudice reduction study like one described above is conducted longitudinally rather than in a single session. Prejudice reduction may be more substantial in studies conducted over many sessions; however, this type of laboratory study would still not reflect what occurs in real life, where disclosure usually occurs in the midst of an ongoing, intimate relationship. Other types of prejudice reduction strategies would have to be created to mimic this.

Practical Applications

In their interactions with heterosexuals, lesbian and gay individuals themselves can use information on negative stereotyping and prejudice to highlight attributes they already possess, thereby possibly initiating positive evaluations of themselves by social perceivers (Wilder, 1984). For example, suppose a gay man who has been in a 10-year monogamous relationship is in a predominantly heterosexual social situation where the prevailing attitude toward gays is negative. If he knows that prejudice is associated with the belief that "all gay men lack sexual self-control," he may choose to make a point of emphasizing that he, a gay male, has been involved in a long-term, committed relationship. This may result in some perceivers having more favorable and less hostile evaluations of him. (Unfortunately, research on subtyping [e.g., Maurer et al., 1995; Rothbart & John, 1985] indicates that this more favorable attitude will probably not generalize to the larger out-group.)

Likewise, imagine that a lesbian who has had a history of positive experiences and close friendships with men is in a rather homonegative work situation. She knows that negative attitudes toward lesbians are associated with the belief that all lesbians have had bad experiences with others of the opposite sex. When opportunities arise, she may make it a point to talk about the many male friends that she, a lesbian, has had in her lifetime. Again, this strategy may promote more favorable or less hostile evaluations of the lesbian individual by some of her coworkers.

Social psychological research is quite valuable when everyday people can use the knowledge obtained from such research for practical purposes. The above are just two examples of how lesbians and gay men can personally apply the knowledge gained from social science research to create a less hostile environment for themselves.

References

Agnew, C. R., Thompson, V. D., Smith, V. A., Gramzow, R. H., & Currey, D. P. (1993). Proximal and distal predictors of homophobia: Framing the multivariate roots of out-group rejection. *Journal of Applied Social Psychology, 23,* 2013-2042.

Ajzen, I. (1989). Attitude structure and behavior. In A. R. Pratkanis, S. J. Breckler, & A. G. Greenwald (Eds.), *Attitude structure and function* (pp. 241-274). Hillsdale, NJ: Lawrence Erlbaum.

Amir, Y. (1969). Contact hypothesis in ethnic relations. *Psychological Bulletin, 71,* 319-342.

Amir, Y. (1976). The role of intergroup contact in change of prejudice and ethnic relations. In P. A. Katz (Ed.), *Towards the elimination of racism* (pp. 245-308). New York: Pergamon.

Ashmore, R. D., & Del Boca, F. K. (1981). Conceptual approaches to stereotypes and stereotyping. In D. L. Hamilton (Ed.), *Cognitive processes in stereotyping and intergroup behavior* (pp. 1-35). Hillsdale, NJ: Lawrence Erlbaum.

Baehr v. Miike, 1996 WL 694235 (Haw. Cir. Ct., 1st Cir. Dec. 3, 1996).

Black, K. N., & Stevenson, M. R. (1984). The relationship of self-reported sex-role characteristics and attitudes toward homosexuality. *Journal of Homosexuality, 10*(1-2), 83-93.

Brewer, M. B., & Kramer, R. M. (1985). The psychology of intergroup attitudes and behavior. *Annual Review of Psychology, 36*, 219-243.

D'Augelli, A. R., & Rose, M. L. (1990). Homophobia in a university community: Attitudes and experiences of heterosexual freshmen. *Journal of College Student Development, 31*, 484-491.

Defense of Marriage Act, Pub. L. No. 104-199 (1996).

Devine, P. G. (1989). Stereotypes and prejudice: Their automatic and controlled components. *Journal of Personality and Social Psychology, 56*, 5-18.

Devine, P. G., & Monteith, M. J. (1993). The role of discrepancy-associated affect in prejudice reduction. In D. M. Mackie & D. L. Hamilton (Eds.), *Affect, cognition, and stereotyping: Interactive processes in group perception* (pp. 317-344). New York: Academic Press.

Devine, P. G., Monteith, M. J., Zuwerink, J. R., & Elliot, A. J. (1991). Prejudice with and without compunction. *Journal of Personality and Social Psychology, 60*, 817-830.

Dew, M. A. (1985). The effect of attitudes on inferences of homosexuality and perceived physical attractiveness in women. *Sex Roles, 12*, 143-155.

Eagly, A. H., & Mladinic, A. (1989). Gender stereotypes and attitudes toward women and men. *Personality and Social Psychology Bulletin, 15*, 543-558.

Eagly, A. H., Mladinic, A., & Otto, S. (1994). Cognitive and affective bases of attitudes toward social groups and social policies. *Journal of Experimental Social Psychology, 30*, 113-137.

ELAN (Eugene Lesbians Against Nine)/PFLAG (Parents and Friends of Lesbians and Gays). (1992). *Dispelling 9 common myths about lesbians and gays.* Eugene, OR: Author.

Eliason, M., Donelan, C., & Randall, C. (1993). Lesbian stereotypes. In P. N. Stern (Ed.), *Lesbian health: What are the issues?* (pp. 41-54). Washington, DC: Taylor & Francis.

Esses, V., Haddock, G., & Zanna, M. (1993). Values, stereotypes, and emotions as determinants of intergroup attitudes. In D. M. Mackie & D. L. Hamilton (Eds.), *Affect, cognition, and stereotyping: Interactive processes in group perception* (pp. 137-166). New York: Academic Press.

Fairy Tales. (1995). (Available from Good Catch! P.O. Box 1756, Old Chelsea Station, New York, NY 10011)

Ficarrotto, T. J. (1990). Racism, sexism, and erotophobia: Attitudes of heterosexuals toward homosexuals. *Journal of Homosexuality, 19*(1), 111-116.

Fishbein, M., & Ajzen, I. (1975). *Belief, attitude, intention, and behavior: An introduction to theory and research.* Reading, MA: Addison-Wesley.

Fisher, R. D., Derison, D., Polley, C. F., III, Cadman, J., & Johnston, D. (1994). Religiousness, religious orientation, and attitudes towards gays and lesbians. *Journal of Applied Social Psychology, 24*, 614-630.

Gentry, C. S. (1987). Social distance regarding male and female homosexuals. *Journal of Social Psychology, 127*, 199-208.

Haddock, G., Zanna, M. P., & Esses, V. M. (1993). Assessing the structure of prejudicial attitudes: The case of attitudes toward homosexuals. *Journal of Personality and Social Psychology, 65*, 1105-1118.

Hamilton, D. L., & Trolier, T. K. (1986). Stereotypes and stereotyping: An overview of the cognitive approach. In J. F. Dovidio & S. L. Gaertner (Eds.), *Prejudice, discrimination, and racism* (pp. 127-164). Orlando, FL: Academic Press.

Harry, J. (1995). Sports ideology, attitudes toward women, and anti-homosexual attitudes. *Sex Roles, 32,* 109-116.

Herek, G. M. (1984). Beyond "homophobia": A social psychological perspective on attitudes toward lesbians and gay men. *Journal of Homosexuality, 10*(1-2), 1-21.

Herek, G. M. (1988). Heterosexuals' attitudes toward lesbians and gay men: Correlates and gender differences. *Journal of Sex Research, 25,* 451-477.

Herek, G. M. (1994). Assessing heterosexuals' attitudes toward lesbians and gay men: A review of empirical research with the ATLG scale. In B. Greene & G. M. Herek (Eds.), *Lesbian and gay psychology: Theory, research, and clinical applications* (pp. 206-228). Thousand Oaks, CA: Sage.

Herek, G. M., & Capitanio, J. P. (1995). Black heterosexuals' attitudes toward lesbians and gay men in the United States. *Journal of Sex Research, 32,* 95-105.

Herek, G. M., & Capitanio, J. P. (1996). "Some of my best friends": Intergroup contact, concealable stigma, and heterosexuals' attitudes toward gay men and lesbians. *Personality and Social Psychology Bulletin, 22,* 412-424.

Herek, G. M., & Glunt, E. K. (1993). Interpersonal contact and heterosexuals' attitudes toward gay men: Results from a national survey. *Journal of Sex Research, 30,* 239-244.

Hewstone, M., & Brown, R. (1986). Contact is not enough: An intergroup perspective on the "contact hypothesis." In M. Hewstone & R. Brown (Eds.), *Contact and conflict in intergroup encounters* (pp. 1-44). Oxford: Basil Blackwell.

Jackson, L. A., & Sullivan, L. A. (1990). Cognition and affect in evaluations of stereotyped group members. *Journal of Social Psychology, 129,* 659-672.

Judd, C. M., & Park, B. (1993). Definition and assessment of accuracy in social stereotypes. *Psychological Review, 100,* 109-128.

Jussim, L., Nelson, T. E., Mannis, M., & Soffin, S. (1995). Prejudice, stereotypes, and labeling effects: Sources of bias in person perception. *Journal of Personality and Social Psychology, 68,* 228-246.

Kite, M. E., & Deaux, K. (1987). Gender belief systems: Homosexuality and the implicit inversion theory. *Psychology of Women Quarterly, 11,* 83-96.

Laner, M. R., & Laner, R. H. (1980). Sexual preference or personal style? Why lesbians are disliked. *Journal of Homosexuality, 5*(4), 339-356.

Maurer, K. L., Park, B., & Rothbart, M. (1995). Subtyping versus subgrouping processes in stereotype representation. *Journal of Personality and Social Psychology, 69,* 812-824.

Monteith, M. J., Devine, P. G., & Zuwerink, J. R. (1993). Self-directed versus other-directed affect as a consequence of prejudice-related discrepancies. *Journal of Personality and Social Psychology, 64,* 198-210.

Page, S., & Yee, M. (1985). Conception of male and female homosexual stereotypes among university undergraduates. *Journal of Homosexuality, 12*(1), 109-118.

Park, B., Ryan, C. S., & Judd, C. M. (1992). The role of meaningful subgroups in explaining differences in perceived variability for in-groups and out-groups. *Journal of Personality and Social Psychology, 63,* 553-567.

Rajecki, D. W. (1982). *Attitudes: Themes and advances.* Sunderland, MA: Sinauer Associates.

Romer et al. v. Evans et al., 116 S.Ct. 1620 (1996).

Rothbart, M., & John, O. P. (1985). Social categorization and behavioral episodes: A cognitive analysis of the effects of intergroup contact. *Journal of Social Issues, 41*(3), 81-104.

Seltzer, R. (1992). The social location of those holding antihomosexual attitudes. *Sex Roles, 26,* 391-398.

Sigelman, C. K., Howell, J. L., Cornell, D. P., Cutright, J. D., & Dewey, J. C. (1990). Courtesy stigma: The social implications of associating with a gay person. *Journal of Social Psychology, 13,* 45-56.

Simon, A. (1995a). [Attitudes toward and stereotypes of homosexuals]. Unpublished raw data.

Simon, A. (1995b). Some correlates of individuals' attitudes toward lesbians. *Journal of Homosexuality, 29*(1), 89-103.

Simon, A. (1996). *Southeastern college students' attitudes toward lesbians and gay men: Are folk beliefs true?* Manuscript submitted for publication.

Simon, A., Cassity, D., Giovannini, D. L., & Baker, C. B. (1995, November). *The influence of group label on stereotypes of and attitudes toward homosexuals.* Paper presented at the meeting of the Kentucky Academy of Science, Bowling Green.

Simon, B., Glassner-Bayerl, G., & Stratenwerth, I. (1991). Stereotyping and self-stereotyping in a natural intergroup context: The case of heterosexual and homosexual men. *Social Psychology Quarterly, 54,* 252-266.

Smith, E. R. (1993). Social identity and social emotions: Toward new conceptualizations of prejudice. In D. M. Mackie & D. L. Hamilton (Eds.), *Affect, cognition, and stereotyping: Interactive processes in group perception* (pp. 297-315). New York: Academic Press.

Stangor, C., Sullivan, L. A., & Ford, T. E. (1991). Affective and cognitive determinants of prejudice. *Social Cognition, 9,* 359-380.

Stephan, W. G., Ageyev, V., Coates-Shrider, L., Stephan, C. W., & Abalakina, M. (1994). On the relationship between stereotypes and prejudice: An international study. *Personality and Social Psychology Bulletin, 20,* 277-284.

Stephan, W. G., & Stephan, C. W. (1993). Cognition and affect in stereotyping: Parallel interactive networks. In D. M. Mackie & D. L. Hamilton (Eds.), *Affect, cognition, and stereotyping: Interactive processes in group perception* (pp. 111-136). New York: Academic Press.

Stroebe, W., & Insko, C. A. (1989). Stereotype, prejudice, and discrimination: Changing conceptions in theory and research. In D. Bar-Tal, C. F. Graumann, A. W. Kruglanski, & W. Stroebe (Eds.), *Stereotyping and prejudice: Changing conceptions* (pp. 3-34). New York: Springer-Verlag.

Taylor, A. (1983). Conceptions of masculinity and femininity as a basis for stereotypes of male and female homosexuals. *Journal of Homosexuality, 9*(1), 37-53.

Whitley, B. E., Jr. (1990). The relationship of heterosexuals' attributions for the causes of homosexuality to attitudes towards lesbians and gay men. *Personality and Social Psychology Bulletin, 16,* 369-377.

Wilder, D. A. (1984). Intergroup contact: The typical member and the exception to the rule. *Journal of Experimental Social Psychology, 20,* 177-194.

Wilder, D. A., & Thompson, J. E. (1980). Intergroup contact with independent manipulation of in-group and out-group interaction. *Journal of Personality and Social Psychology, 38,* 589-603.

Zanna, M. P., & Rempel, J. K. (1988). Attitudes: A new look at an old concept. In D. Bar-Tal & A. W. Kruglanski, *The social psychology of knowledge* (pp. 315-334). Cambridge: Cambridge University Press.

5

Authoritarianism, Values, and the Favorability and Structure of Antigay Attitudes

GEOFFREY HADDOCK

MARK P. ZANNA

A few years ago, while walking down one of the main streets of Toronto, Canada, the first author witnessed an event that made a lasting impression on him. Among the crowd enjoying the sunshine and warmth of a beautiful summer afternoon were a pair of men who were holding hands and walking quickly down the street. As they darted past, the author wondered why these men seemed in such a hurry. Soon after he asked himself that question, the reason for their behavior became evident. Following not more than 20 yards behind the pair was a group of young skinheads who were casting vulgar insults and threats at the two men. Thankfully, the large number of shoppers and tourists in the street allowed the pair to disappear into the crowd.

Around the time of this event, we had just analyzed the results of a study in which we assessed the structure of attitudes toward various social groups. One of the target groups included in this study of Cana-

AUTHORS' NOTE: Preparation of this chapter was facilitated by Social Sciences and Humanities Research Council of Canada (SSHRC) doctoral and postdoctoral fellowships to the first author, and by an SSHRC research grant to the second author. We would like to thank Frances Mallozzi for her collaboration and assistance with the prejudice reduction study.

dian university students was "homosexuals." The timing of this research and the witnessing of the treatment of the two men described above not only exemplified the importance of social psychology for our understanding of everyday human behavior, it also helped generate a research program that has sought to understand the underlying structure of antigay attitudes.

In this chapter, we review research we have conducted in order to study antigay prejudice. This work has covered four general topics: (a) the structure of antigay attitudes, (b) the relation between right-wing authoritarianism (RWA; Altemeyer, 1988) and antigay attitudes, (c) the role of perceived value dissimilarity and antigay attitudes, and (d) techniques that may be effective in changing antigay attitudes. We begin the chapter by describing the model of attitude that has guided our research and explaining how this model can be applied to the study of prejudicial attitudes. Second, we describe a study that examined the underlying structure of antigay attitudes and the role of RWA in relation to the favorability and structure of these attitudes (Haddock, Zanna, & Esses, 1993). Third, we discuss research that examined how negative attitudes translate into discriminatory behavior and the importance of values and perceived value dissimilarity in understanding and changing antigay attitudes. We conclude by reviewing some implications of our work and proposing some questions for future research.

Defining the Attitude Concept

The framework from which our research is derived comes from contemporary theorizing in the general area of attitudes. In the attitude literature, it has been suggested that evaluations, cognitions, and affective responses are separable yet related aspects of attitudes (e.g., Eagly & Chaiken, 1993; Zanna & Rempel, 1988). The distinctions among these components have led to the development of *multicomponent* models of attitude. These models share the basic tenet that attitudes are overall evaluations of objects that are derived from three general sources of information: (a) cognitive information, (b) affective information, and (c) behavioral information. *Cognitive information* refers to beliefs or thoughts about an attitude object. For instance, an individual may express the belief that a particular politician is intelligent and advocates economic policies that promote equality. *Affective information* refers to feelings or emotions associated with an attitude object. For instance, an individual may indicate that a particular politician makes him or her feel angry and disgusted. *Behavioral information* refers to past behaviors or behavioral intentions with respect to an attitude object. For instance, an individual might report the positive experience of meeting a political candidate during an election campaign.

How does this multicomponent model of attitude lend itself to the study of prejudice? We have suggested that an intergroup attitude be defined as a favorable or unfavorable overall evaluation of a social group (Esses, Haddock, & Zanna, 1993). In terms of the role of cognition in intergroup attitudes, we have postulated that two separate types of beliefs are relevant. One type of cognitive information is *stereotypic beliefs*, that is, characteristics attributed to typical members of a target group (e.g., the belief that typical members of a group are friendly or unintelligent). This is the most popular conception of the cognitive component of prejudice, and the evaluative implications of stereotypes have generally been taken as the cognitive component of intergroup attitudes (Ashmore & Del Boca, 1981; Eagly, Mladinic, & Otto, 1994). Cognitions about social groups, however, may not be derived entirely from stereotypic beliefs. For instance, Rokeach (1968) discovered that perceived similarity in values serves as an important determinant of interpersonal attraction. In addition, research on the importance of values in the expression of symbolic racism (e.g., McConahay, 1986; Sears, 1988) has led us to believe that other general, abstract beliefs are also relevant to the cognitive component of prejudicial attitudes. We refer to these beliefs as *symbolic beliefs.* Symbolic beliefs are beliefs that social groups violate or promote the attainment of cherished values, customs, and traditions (e.g., the perception that typical members of a group promote freedom of expression or violate the attainment of world peace).

In contrast, the affective component of intergroup attitudes focuses on the evaluative implications of the emotions that are elicited by members of different social groups (e.g., typical group members may evoke feelings of fear or admiration). Although not entirely independent of the cognitive component of prejudice, assessing the affective component of intergroup attitudes provides information that is not captured through simple assessment of individuals' beliefs. For example, research by Esses et al. (1993) and Stangor, Sullivan, and Ford (1991) has found that emotional responses toward social groups make a significant unique contribution to the prediction of prejudicial attitudes.[1]

Applying a General Model of Attitude to Studying the Structure of Antigay Prejudice

The primary purpose of our initial study was to determine the relative importance of stereotypes, symbolic beliefs, and affective associates in predicting attitudes toward the group *homosexuals*.[2] However, we were also interested in assessing the extent to which the individual difference variable of right-wing authoritarianism (RWA) (Altemeyer, 1988) might: (a) be related to both the favorability and structure of attitudes and (b) moderate the relative importance of stereotypes, symbolic beliefs, and affective responses in predicting attitudes. As described by Altemeyer (1988), high authoritarians are extremely self-righteous individuals who maintain a strong acceptance of traditional values and norms, possess a general willingness to submit to legitimate authority, and display a general tendency to aggress against others (especially those who threaten their conventional values and norms). High authoritarians are characterized as being most committed to maintaining the traditional family structure and feel threatened by liberalization and individuals who threaten their conventional values.

In addition to the simple maintenance of traditional values, research has discovered that values play an extremely important role in the lives of high authoritarians. For instance, using a procedure developed by Schwartz (1992), we have found that authoritarianism is positively correlated with value importance ratings in both college and adult samples (Haddock & Zanna, 1993; Rohan & Zanna, 1996). Thus, not only do high authoritarians maintain traditional values, they also rate their values as more important in guiding their everyday lives.

How might authoritarianism be related to the favorability and structure of antigay attitudes? First, consistent with past research (e.g., Altemeyer, 1988), we expected high RWAs to maintain particularly negative attitudes. Second, we expected that with their more traditional outlook and the greater emphasis placed on values in guiding their lives, high RWAs would be especially likely to perceive homosexuals as maintaining and promoting values that violate RWAs' highly conventional value system, perhaps leading to symbolic beliefs serving as the primary determinant of their relatively more intolerant attitudes. Consistent with this hypothesis, our previous research revealed that attitudes toward groups that are evaluated particularly negatively by high RWAs are usually based upon symbolic beliefs (Esses et al., 1993). In contrast, low

RWAs were thought to be more willing to perceive value differences as acceptable, thus leading symbolic beliefs to play a less important role in predicting the attitudes of these individuals. Consequently, stereotypes and affective responses were expected to be particularly important in predicting the relatively more tolerant attitudes of low authoritarians.

Study 1:
The Structure of Antigay Attitudes

Subjects

This study involved 145 students (73 females, 72 males) enrolled in introductory psychology classes at the University of Waterloo.[3]

Materials

To measure attitudes, subjects were asked to complete a 101-point evaluation thermometer, upon which each subject provided a number between 0° and 100° to indicate his or her overall evaluation of typical members of the target group. The thermometer measure has been used successfully in past research in the domain of intergroup attitudes (e.g., Esses et al., 1993; Sears, 1988; Stangor et al., 1991).

Stereotypic beliefs were assessed by having subjects list the characteristics they would use to describe typical group members. Having completed this task, they then rated each characteristic on a 5-point scale ranging from *very negative* (−2) to *very positive* (+2). Finally, subjects indicated the percentage of group members who possess each characteristic. A stereotype score was calculated by: (a) multiplying the valence of each response by the proportion of group members believed to possess that characteristic, (b) summing these products, and (c) dividing by the number of characteristics listed.

Symbolic beliefs were assessed by having subjects list the values, customs, and traditions that they believed are blocked or facilitated by typical group members. Upon completing this task, they then rated the extent to which each value, custom, or tradition is blocked or facilitated by typical group members on a 5-point scale ranging from *almost always blocked* (−2) to *almost always facilitated* (+2). Finally, subjects indicated the percentage of group members whom they believe block or facilitate each value. A symbolic belief score was calculated in the same manner as for the measure of stereotypes.

Affective responses were assessed by having subjects list the feelings or emotions they experience when they see, meet, or think about typical members of the group. They then rated the valence of each emotion on a 5-point scale ranging from *very negative* (–2) to *very positive* (+2). Finally, they indicated the percentage of group members who elicit each emotion. An affect score was calculated in the same manner as for the measure of stereotypes.

Right-wing authoritarianism was assessed through the use of the RWA scale (Altemeyer, 1988), a 30-item, 9-point scale on which higher scores represent higher levels of authoritarianism. Respondents are asked to indicate the extent of their agreement or disagreement with statements such as "In these troubled times laws have to be enforced without mercy, especially when dealing with the agitators and revolutionaries who are stirring things up" and "People should pay less attention to the Bible and the other traditional forms of religious guidance and instead develop their own personal standards of what is moral and immoral" (this item reverse scored). In the studies described in this chapter, an abbreviated 10-item version of the scale was used ($\alpha = .75$).

Procedure

Homosexuals was one of five target groups that subjects evaluated during the session (the others were *English Canadians, French Canadians, Native Canadians,* and *Pakistanis*). Whereas all subjects completed the attitude measure first, the order of the predictor variables and of the target groups was counterbalanced. Finally, subjects completed the abbreviated RWA scale, provided demographic information, and were fully debriefed.[4]

Results

Favorability of responses. How favorable or unfavorable were subjects in their perceptions of the group? Overall, subjects' attitudes toward homosexuals were negative ($M = 40.84$, $SD = 25.48$), and significantly more negative than their attitudes toward any of the other target groups studied. In comparison, the mean attitude scores for the other target groups ranged from 81.08 (for the target group English Canadians) to 58.01 (for the target group Pakistanis).

The means for all of the predictor variables (and the attitude measure) are presented in Table 5.1. In each case, the mean predictor score is negative. In addition, each of the predictors contained large amounts of variability, indicating that different subjects were willing to provide disparate beliefs and feelings.

Relations among predictor variables. To ensure that the predictor variables were not redundant, Pearson product-moment correlations were computed. These correlations are presented in Table 5.2. Not surprisingly, the correlations are all positive, meaning that positive stereotypes were typically associated with positive symbolic beliefs and positive affective associates. However, the correlations were not high enough to suggest that the variables were eliciting completely identical information.

The different types of information elicited by the different measures is also revealed through a content analysis of subjects' open-ended responses. Conducting this analysis also allowed us to determine the most frequently elicited (i.e., consensual) responses. With respect to stereotypes, our subjects most frequently reported that homosexuals are effeminate, emotional, friendly, and artistic. For the symbolic beliefs measure, the group was perceived as promoting freedom, blocking the attainment of the traditional family, and promoting peace. The emotions most frequently elicited were feelings of disgust, discomfort, and confusion.

The prediction of attitudes. To determine the relative importance of stereotypes, symbolic beliefs, and affective associates in predicting attitudes, a regression analysis was performed in which the stereotype, symbolic belief, and affect scores were entered simultaneously. This approach allowed us to both (a) determine the total proportion of variance in attitudes accounted for by the three predictor variables and (b) assess the unique contribution of each variable in predicting attitudes.

The results of this analysis are presented in the top panel of Table 5.3. Together, the three predictor variables accounted for 40.1% of the variance in attitudes. The standardized regression coefficients are also presented in Table 5.3. They reveal that both symbolic beliefs ($\beta = .379$, $p < .001$) and affective associates ($\beta = .303$, $p < .001$) uniquely contributed to

Table 5.1 Study 1: Mean Perceptions of Homosexuals

Variable	Mean (SD)
Attitude	40.84
	(25.48)
Stereotypic beliefs	−.17
	(.85)
Symbolic beliefs	−.27
	(1.04)
Affect	−.57
	(.82)

SOURCE: Adapted from Haddock, G., Zanna, M. P., & Esses, V. M. (1993). Assessing the structure of prejudicial attitudes: The case of attitudes toward homosexuals. *Journal of Personality and Social Psychology, 65*, 1105-1118. Copyright 1993 by the American Psychological Association.
NOTE: Standard deviations are in parentheses.

Table 5.2 Study 1: Correlations Among Predictor Variables

	Stereotype	Symbolic	Affect
Stereotypic beliefs	—	.44**	.61**
Symbolic beliefs		—	.36**
Affect			—

SOURCE: Adapted from Haddock, G., Zanna, M. P., & Esses, V. M. (1993). Assessing the structure of prejudicial attitudes: The case of attitudes toward homosexuals. *Journal of Personality and Social Psychology,, 65*, 1105-1118. Copyright 1993 by the American Psychological Association.
**$p < .001$.

the prediction of attitudes. Stereotypes, on the other hand, were not uniquely predictive of attitudes ($\beta = .102$, *ns*).

RWA and the favorability and structure of attitudes. Consistent with past research, there was a significant negative correlation between RWA scores and attitudes ($r = -.42$, $p < .001$). High authoritarians expressed less favorable attitudes than did low authoritarians. In addition, high authoritarians were also more likely to express negative stereotypes, symbolic beliefs, and affective associates than were low authoritarians (all $ps < .05$).

Table 5.3 Study 1: Regression Analyses

Variable	Final Beta Coefficient
All subjects ($N = 145$)	
Stereotypic beliefs	.102
Symbolic beliefs	.379***
Affect	.303***
High RWAs ($N = 48$)	
Stereotypic beliefs	−.214
Symbolic beliefs	.343*
Affect	.318
Low RWAs ($N = 48$)	
Stereotypic beliefs	.434***
Symbolic beliefs	.157
Affect	.348**

SOURCE: Adapted from Haddock, G., Zanna, M. P., & Esses, V. M. (1993). Assessing the structure of prejudicial attitudes: The case of attitudes toward homosexuals. *Journal of Personality and Social Psychology, 65,* 1105-1118. Copyright 1993 by the American Psychological Association.
*$p < .05$; **$p < .01$; ***$p < .001$.

To assess the relative importance of stereotypes, symbolic beliefs, and affective associates in predicting attitudes among high and low authoritarians, separate regression analyses were performed for each of these groups.[5] Conducting separate analyses for high and low RWAs not only allowed us to assess differences in the unique contribution of each predictor variable but also provided us the opportunity to determine whether the three predictor variables accounted for equivalent proportions of variance in attitudes for high and low RWAs. The results of these analyses are presented in Table 5.3. Among high RWAs, the three predictor variables accounted for 16.0% of the variance in their attitudes. The standardized regression coefficients are also presented in Table 5.3. The unique contribution of symbolic beliefs was significant ($\beta = .343, p < .05$), whereas the unique contribution of affect approached significance ($\beta = .318, p < .085$). Stereotypes did not uniquely contribute to the prediction of attitudes for high RWAs ($\beta = −.214, ns$).

Among low RWAs, the findings were strikingly different. For these individuals, the three predictor variables accounted for 60.2% of the variance in their attitudes. The standardized regression coefficients reveal that the unique contributions of both stereotypes ($\beta = .434, p < .001$) and affective associates ($\beta = .348$, $p < .01$) were significant. In contrast, symbolic beliefs were not uniquely predictive of attitudes ($\beta = .157$, *ns*) for low RWAs. Thus, not only did the predictor variables account for more variance among low RWAs, the attitudes of these less bigoted individuals were derived from different sources of information.

Discussion

The results of this study revealed that, among our sample, attitudes toward homosexuals were negative, particularly among high authoritarians. In addition, the stereotypes, symbolic beliefs, and affective information our respondents associated with the group were also negative (and especially negative among high authoritarians).

Overall, attitudes were best predicted by symbolic beliefs and affective responses. Interestingly, stereotypes, which are generally taken as the cognitive component of prejudice, did not uniquely predict attitudes. Thus, in order to understand attitudes toward gay men and lesbians more effectively, one must assess more than simply the evaluative implications of individuals' stereotypic beliefs.

We hypothesized that the relative importance of stereotypes, symbolic beliefs, and affective associates might differ as a function of individual differences in right-wing authoritarianism. The results strongly supported our expectations. Among high authoritarians, attitudes were best predicted by symbolic beliefs that gays hinder the attainment of subjects' cherished values. Conversely, stereotypic beliefs and affective associates were very useful in predicting the attitudes of low authoritarians. For these individuals, symbolic beliefs were not uniquely predictive of attitudes toward the group.

Recall that the initial aims of our research were to discover the structure of antigay attitudes and the role of RWA in relation to the favorability and structure of these attitudes. Although our initial study confirmed our expectations, we elected to conduct a second study (Haddock et al., 1993, Study 2) that served to replicate and extend the main findings of the study just described. In this second study, high RWAs once again expressed the most negative attitudes, and, as in the first study, their attitudes were best uniquely predicted by the evaluative implications of their symbolic beliefs. In contrast, the attitudes of low RWAs were once again best uniquely predicted by the evaluative implications of their stereotypic beliefs. This second study also included a measure of past behavioral experiences, to determine if this source of information would be uniquely predictive of attitudes only among high RWAs. The results supported the hypothesis (see Haddock et al., 1993, for an extended discussion of this study).

Thus, these two studies, taken together, served to answer the initial aims of our research. Having satisfied this goal, we turned our attention to three new issues. First, we wondered how negative attitudes would translate into discriminatory behavior. Specifically, we were interested in assessing how attitude favorability and attitude structure would predict one form of antigay discrimination. Second, given the important role of value-based symbolic beliefs in predicting the attitudes of high RWAs, we decided to examine in more detail the importance of values and perceived value dissimilarity in understanding antigay prejudice. Third, given that the attitudes of high and low RWAs are based on different types of beliefs (symbolic beliefs among high RWAs and stereotypic beliefs among low RWAs), we wondered whether strategies that experimentally manipulated the favorability of either consensual symbolic beliefs or stereotypes about gay men would have different effects on changing the attitudes of high and low authoritarians. The remaining portion of the chapter introduces research we have conducted to begin to answer these questions.

Study 2:
The Relation Between
Antigay Attitudes and Discriminatory Behavior

As exemplified by the event described at the beginning of this chapter, antigay prejudice is not simply the expression of a negative attitude; it is often accompanied by discriminatory behavior. In order to begin to explore the role of attitude favorability and attitude structure in predicting one form of antigay discrimination, we had 63 subjects participate in a two-session study on social attitudes. In the first session, subjects completed the attitude, affect, cognition, and RWA measures. Two weeks later, as part of the second session, they completed a short survey ostensibly given on behalf of the University of Waterloo Psych Society (i.e., the undergraduate psychology association). Subjects were (mis)informed that researchers within the psychology department had been approached by the Psych Society and asked to distribute to research participants a short survey concerning the funding of student organizations. In a letter introducing the survey, subjects were told that the student government was being forced to cut funding to student organizations by 20% and that the Psych Society was interested in soliciting psychology students' impressions of this issue. They were further informed that their responses on the survey might influence the student government's final budgetary decision. Subjects were then given a subset of 10 campus organizations and the funding that they ostensibly received for that academic year. They were then asked to indicate the amount of funding they believed each group should be allocated for the following year, with the restriction that, overall, the funds for the 10 groups had to be reduced by 20%. Embedded in the list of various academic, social, and recreational clubs used in the survey was the university's organization for lesbians and gay men, the Gay and Lesbian Liberation Organization of Waterloo (GLLOW).[6]

We hypothesized that negative attitudes based upon symbolic beliefs would produce the greatest level of discrimination on this nonreactive behavioral measure. To test this hypothesis, we conducted an analysis in which we derived an index that allowed us to quantify the source of cognitive information most consistent with an individual's attitude. If negative attitudes based upon symbolic beliefs (rather than stereotypic beliefs) led to particularly negative funding allocations, it would provide initial evidence that these value-based beliefs have important behavioral consequences.

Prior to conducting the analysis, we needed to compute an index that would allow us to quantify the consistency among individuals' attitudes, symbolic beliefs, and stereotypes. Following the work of Chaiken, Pomerantz, and Giner-Sorolla (1995), we computed scores that represented the extent to which individuals' symbolic belief and stereotype scores were consistent with their attitudes. We computed this index by first standardizing subjects' scores on the three measures. We then calculated the absolute difference between the attitude and symbolic belief scores (ATT/SYM scores) and the attitude and stereotype scores (ATT/STR scores). We then subtracted the ATT/SYM score from the ATT/STR score to create an index that represented the degree to which attitudes are based on symbolic beliefs versus stereotypic beliefs. A more positive score on this consistency index would represent a smaller discrepancy (and, therefore, greater consistency) between individuals' attitudes and symbolic beliefs. Employing a tertile split on attitude favorability and a

median split on the consistency index, we conducted a 3 (relatively fa-
vorable/neutral/unfavorable attitude) × 2 (attitude most consistent
with either symbolic beliefs or stereotypes) analysis of variance
(ANOVA), using subjects' funding allocations for GLLOW as the dependent variable.

The analysis revealed a main effect of attitude favorability. Subjects
with unfavorable attitudes proposed greater cuts to GLLOW's funding
(mean percentage funding reduction = 42%) than did subjects with relatively neutral (25%) or favorable attitudes (27%). More important, the
analysis revealed a marginally significant interaction between favorability and basis of attitudes ($p < .10$). Subjects whose negative attitudes were
based upon (i.e., were more consistent with) symbolic beliefs proposed
the largest funding cut for GLLOW (reducing funds by an average of
52%) and proposed significantly greater cuts than subjects with relatively neutral (22%) or favorable (25%) attitudes based upon symbolic
beliefs. In contrast, subjects whose negative attitudes were based upon
(i.e., were more consistent with) stereotypic beliefs proposed cuts (36%)
that were not different from those of subjects with relatively neutral
(28%) or favorable (29%) attitudes based upon stereotypes. Furthermore,
among those subjects with particularly negative attitudes, those based
upon symbolic beliefs tended to propose greater cuts than those based
upon stereotypes ($p < .10$). This difference existed even though these
individuals maintained equally negative attitudes. Thus, overall, these
results provide preliminary evidence that symbolic beliefs have important consequences, in that negative attitudes based upon these beliefs are
translated into negative behavior.

Study 3:
Perceptions of Value Dissimilarity,
RWA, and Antigay Attitudes

We have found that value-based symbolic beliefs serve as an important predictor of antigay attitudes, especially among high authoritarians. What is it about these symbolic beliefs that lead them to play an
important role in predicting the attitudes of these more closed-minded
individuals? Perhaps high authoritarians perceive homosexuals as
maintaining a value system markedly different from their own, and perhaps it is these perceived differences in values that serve as the primary

determinant of their (negative) attitudes. Given the important role of these beliefs, we have sought to understand more clearly the roles of values and perceptions of value dissimilarity in antigay prejudice.

Perceived value dissimilarity refers to the extent to which people view themselves and members of an out-group as differing in their perceived importance of basic human values (Struch & Schwartz, 1989). These differences are posited to have a range of negative consequences. As Struch and Schwartz (1989) have pointed out, "The greater the perceived value dissimilarity between an in-group and out-group in their hierarchies of basic values, the more inhumane the out-group is perceived to be" (pp. 365-366). In previous research, we had found that perceived value dissimilarity plays a substantial role in mediating the relation between RWA and males' attitudes toward feminists (Haddock & Zanna, 1994, Study 4). We became interested in understanding the relation between perceived value dissimilarity and our measures of symbolic beliefs, attitudes, and authoritarianism, to determine the extent to which accounting for values would have an impact on the relation between RWA and antigay attitudes.

To begin to address this question, we had 151 subjects complete a questionnaire package that, in addition to the attitude, affect, cognition, and RWA measures, included a set of questions that asked about the respondent's important values and the values he or she perceived as important among typical homosexuals. We created these questions by adapting a technique for measuring values proposed by Schwartz (1992) in which participants are asked to rate, on 9-point scales, the extent to which a series of 56 values serve as guiding principles in their lives. These 56 values correspond to 11 motivational types of values.[7] Due to time constraints, our subjects rated 22 of these values, 2 for each of the 11 types. Furthermore, they performed this task twice. First, they rated the extent to which the values serve as guiding principles in their own lives. This provided us with an assessment of each individual's personal value profile ("own profile"). Immediately after completing this task, participants rated the extent to which the same 22 values serve as guiding principles in the life of a typical homosexual. This provided us with an assessment of each participant's perception of homosexuals' values ("homosexual profile").

A perceived value dissimilarity score was computed in the following manner. First, for each of the 11 value types, we computed an index by taking the mean rating of the two items for that type. This was done separately for their own profile ratings and for their homosexual profile ratings. Second, we created a value discrepancy score for each value type by taking the absolute difference between their own profile mean and their homosexual profile mean. Finally, we computed a perceived value dissimilarity score by taking the mean of the value discrepancy scores across the 11 value types.

Results

The mean perceived value dissimilarity score was 1.17, indicating that subjects viewed themselves as somewhat different from homosexuals in the extent to which the 11 value types served as important principles in life. Scores on this measure were positively associated with RWA scores ($r = .40$, $p < .001$) and, not surprisingly, negatively correlated with attitudes ($r = -.49$, $p < .001$). Thus, high authoritarians perceived greater value dissimilarity, and those who perceived greater value dissimilarity held more negative attitudes.

Next, we examined the extent to which perceived value dissimilarity was associated with our measures of stereotypes, symbolic beliefs, and affective responses. We were most interested in the relation between perceived value dissimilarity and our measure of symbolic beliefs. Overall, perceived value dissimilarity was most highly correlated with symbolic beliefs ($r = -.42$, $p < .001$). This correlation, however, was moderated by authoritarianism. Among high RWAs, the perceived value dissimilarity-symbolic belief relation was strong, $r = -.44$, $p < .01$. In contrast, this correlation was nonsignificant among low RWAs ($r = .08$, ns). Furthermore, the difference between these correlations was significant ($Z = 2.71$, $p < .01$). Thus, among only high authoritarians, the greater the perceived value dissimilarity, the more negative the symbolic beliefs.

Most important, we considered the question of how much of the RWA-attitude relation could be accounted for by jointly considering symbolic beliefs and perceived value dissimilarity. To answer this question, we computed the semipartial correlation between RWA and attitudes, removing the effects of perceived value dissimilarity and symbolic beliefs. The RWA-attitude relation in this particular study was $r = -.40$ ($p < .001$). After perceived value dissimilarity and symbolic beliefs were partialed out, this correlation was no longer significant ($r = -.11$). In contrast, partialing out the stereotype and affect scores did not appreciably affect the RWA-attitude relation, $r = -.35$, $p < .001$. Thus, the RWA-attitude relation may be largely mediated by the effect of values (as assessed in two different ways).

Together, then, our research that has examined the roles played by values and perceived value dissimilarity in antigay attitudes has revealed that these roles are important, both in predicting one form of discriminatory behavior and in mediating the correlation between authoritarianism and antigay attitudes. These findings led us to consider the possibility that antigay attitudes, especially among high authoritarians, might be most effectively changed through (positive) modification of individuals' symbolic beliefs about the group. In our next study, we considered the possibility of changing the attitudes of male high and low RWAs by attempting to modify either their symbolic beliefs or stereotypes about gay men.

Study 4:
Changing Antigay Attitudes
by Modifying Stereotypes or Symbolic Beliefs

Not surprisingly, the question of how to reduce antigay prejudice has generated a considerable amount of research. For instance, Herek (1991) described two techniques thought to be successful in reducing the prevalence of prejudice against gay men: educational programs and personal contact. Unfortunately, neither approach seems particularly suited for modifying the attitudes of high RWAs. For instance, an explanation for the success of educational programs is that they serve to refute stereotypes. On the basis of our results, one might expect this technique to be most successful in changing the attitudes only of low authoritarians. To change the attitudes of high authoritarians, approaches intended to increase the favorability of symbolic beliefs are likely necessary. Regarding the impact of personal contact, Altemeyer (1988) noted that contact with gay males is uncommon among high RWAs, which suggests that this technique, on its own, may not be successful. Thus, we are left with the question of how to go about changing the attitudes of those individuals most inclined to express antigay prejudice. Given our findings regarding the importance of values in predicting the negative attitudes of high RWAs, we believe that a consideration of the structural basis of high and low RWAs' attitudes might help answer this question.

The general paradigm underlying our attitude change study follows from our previous research. Recall that the attitudes of high RWAs are derived primarily from symbolic beliefs, whereas the attitudes of low RWAs are derived primarily from stereotypic beliefs. This pattern generates the question of whether manipulating the favorability of either stereotypic or symbolic beliefs about gay individuals will lead to differential attitude change among high and low RWAs. Because the attitudes of high RWAs are derived primarily from the evaluative implications of their symbolic beliefs, strategies that focus on changing these persons' stereotypes about gay men are likely to be ineffective. Rather, changing the attitudes of these more intolerant individuals might require strategies that increase the favorability of their symbolic beliefs about the group. Among low RWAs, recall that these individuals are somewhat more favorable in their perceptions of gay men and that these attitudes are generally derived from their stereotypes about the group. Thus, strategies designed to change their stereotypes about gay men are likely to be as effective as, or more effective than, strategies designed to modify their symbolic beliefs about the group.

How might one attempt to increase the favorability of subjects' stereotypes or symbolic beliefs about gay men? We followed procedures used in research that has addressed how the concentration of confirming and disconfirming stereotypic information affects attitudes toward stigmatized groups (e.g., Hewstone, 1994). In this paradigm, participants learn about individual group members who both disconfirm negative consensual stereotypes and confirm positive consensual stereotypes. For instance, if a particular group is consensually perceived as unfriendly (a negative characteristic) and intelligent (a positive characteristic), subjects learn about individual group members who are both friendly and intelligent. After subjects read descriptions of numerous group members, their impressions of the target group become more favorable (Hewstone, 1994).

We decided to adopt this paradigm in our study. However, rather than limiting this procedure to the study of stereotypes, we extended it so that instead of receiving stereotypic information, subjects received information describing group members who disconfirmed negative consensual symbolic beliefs and confirmed positive consensual symbolic beliefs. Thus, if group members are consensually perceived as hindering the attainment of the traditional family and promoting the attainment of freedom, subjects learn about individual group members who place high value on both the nuclear family and individual freedom.

Briefly, the study took the following form. In the context of an impression formation task, high and low RWAs read descriptions of six individual group members. Two types of descriptions were used, each highlighting different information. Some subjects read descriptions intended to change negative stereotypes, whereas others read descriptions intended to change negative symbolic beliefs. After learning about these individuals, subjects rated their impressions of these individuals. It was expected that high RWAs would express more favorable perceptions if presented with disconfirming symbolic belief information, whereas low RWAs would express more favorable perceptions if presented with disconfirming stereotypic belief information.

What type of information was used in the description of the six target individuals? We used the consensual stereotypes and symbolic beliefs that were derived from the content analyses of our open-ended measures. The most commonly elicited stereotypes included the traits effeminate, emotional, and artistic, whereas the most commonly elicited symbolic beliefs included beliefs that group members hinder the attainment of the nuclear family and promote the attainment of equality, freedom, and peace. From this information, we constructed descriptions of six target individuals. Overall, subjects received six pieces of information for each target. In the stereotype condition, two of the statements served to disconfirm negative stereotypic beliefs about gay men. For instance, subjects read a profile of an individual described as masculine and unemotional. A third statement served to confirm a positive consensual stereotype (e.g., that the target is artistic). A fourth statement provided information suggesting that the target confirms a positive symbolic belief (e.g., that the target strongly believes in the value of freedom). Finally, the remaining two pieces of information contained statements irrelevant to the group. In the symbolic beliefs condition, the dispersion of information followed the same pattern; that is, two pieces of information served to disconfirm negative consensual symbolic beliefs, and a third confirmed a positive consensual symbolic belief. A fourth statement provided information suggesting that the target confirmed a positive stereotype, and the final two pieces of information contained statements irrelevant to the group.

The procedure of the study was as follows. Subjects were informed that the study was being conducted to assess the extent to which individuals form impressions of others based on limited information. They were then told that during the previous academic year, the psychology department had members of various campus organizations volunteer for detailed psychological interviews in order to help train clinical psychology graduate students. From these interviews, subjects were instructed that the department possessed detailed personality descriptions of members of numerous campus organizations and that these descriptions had been condensed to determine whether individuals could accurately form impressions on the basis of this limited information. They were then told that their task was to read these thumbnail sketches and complete a series of questions assessing their impressions of the target individuals. Subjects were then presented with different envelopes and informed that each envelope contained descriptions of six members of a particular campus organization. In reality, however, all envelopes contained information about gay men. Some envelopes contained the stereotype descriptions, whereas the others contained the symbolic belief descriptions. Each subject then selected an envelope, thus assigning himself to condition. The subjects then read the six personality sketches and subsequently completed a series of questions regarding their impressions (i.e., attitudes) of each target. These questions asked subjects the extent to which they liked, respected, and wished to be friends with each target. Finally, participants completed the GLLOW funding measure, which was independently introduced as a ballot being administered by the Psych Society.

In addition to the two information type conditions, we also included a control condition of high and low RWAs who only completed the GLLOW student funding measure. Thus, this study took the form of a 3 (stereotypic information/symbolic belief information/control group) × 2 (high/low RWA) between-subjects factorial design.[8] Forty male subjects participated in the study.[9] Overall, on the measure of attitude, we predicted that there would be a significant main effect of authoritarianism. High RWAs should express more negative impressions of the target than low RWAs. More interestingly, however, we expected the interaction between information type and authoritarianism to be significant. Specifically, among high RWAs, those presented with symbolic belief information should express significantly more favorable evaluations than those presented with stereotypic information. Among low RWAs, those presented with stereotypic belief information should express more favorable evaluations (though this effect might be less pronounced due to their relatively tolerant attitudes). On the GLLOW funding measure, we expected similar findings. Most important, among high RWAs, we expected those presented with symbolic belief information to propose less substantial cuts compared with those in the stereotype and control conditions. Among low RWAs, we expected those presented with stereotypic belief information to propose less substantial cuts compared with those in the symbolic belief and control conditions. As well, among control subjects, low authoritarians should propose less substantial reductions than high RWAs.

The results were generally consistent with the hypothesis. On the attitude measure, the analysis revealed a significant main effect of information type, $F(1, 24) = 5.78, p < .05$.[10] Overall, subjects who received the symbolic belief information were more favorable in their evaluations than were subjects in the stereotypic belief condition. In addition, the interaction between RWA and information type was marginally significant, $F(1, 24) = 3.82, p = .06$. As predicted (and displayed in Table 5.4), high RWAs evaluated the targets more favorably after reading the symbolic beliefs information ($M_{sym} = 5.71, M_{ster} = 3.62; F(1, 24) = 9.40, p < .01$), whereas among low RWAs, perceptions of the targets did not differ as a function of information type ($M_{sym} = 5.54, M_{ster} = 5.28; F < 1$). Thus, the evaluations of high RWAs were affected by the type of information, with more positive judgments being made when subjects learned that the six individuals disconfirmed negative consensual symbolic beliefs (and confirmed positive symbolic beliefs).

On the GLLOW funding measure, the results of two sets of analyses were generally supportive of the hypothesis. To test the hypothesis most directly, we conducted an analysis in which we constructed contrast weights that allowed us to determine the level of support for our predicted interaction.[11] This contrast proved to be marginally significant ($t = 1.69, p = .10$). Further support for the hypothesis comes from the funding allocations of subjects in the two experimental conditions. In a 2×2 analysis of variance (in which we excluded control group subjects), the interaction between authoritarianism and information type was marginally significant, $F(1, 24) = 3.02, p = .09$. High RWAs who read the symbolic belief information tended to advocate less substantial reductions ($M = 31\%$) compared with those who read the stereotypic belief disconfirming information ($M = 57\%$), $F(1, 24) = 2.51, p = .08$. The funding allocations of low RWAs did not differ as a function of information type ($F < 1$). Comparisons between high and low RWAs within each experimental condition are also informative. As expected, high RWAs did recommend a significantly greater budget reduction than did low RWAs in the stereotype condition (57% versus 22%, respectively; $t = 2.03, p < .05$). However, the typical relation between RWA and antigay hostility (Haddock et al., 1993) was entirely eliminated in the symbolic belief condition

Table 5.4 Study 4: Mean Attitudes as a Function of Condition and Authoritarianism

	Condition	
Authoritarianism	Symbolic Belief	Stereotypic Belief
High	5.71	3.62
Low	5.54	5.28

NOTE: Scores range from 1 to 9, with higher scores representing more favorable attitudes.

(31% versus 35% for high and low RWAs, respectively; $t < 1$). Thus, reading about gay individuals who disconfirmed negative consensual symbolic beliefs tended to make high RWAs perceive group members more favorably and led to less pronounced funding cuts to a gay and lesbian student organization.

Overall, these findings, although preliminary in nature, suggest that different types of information may be differentially successful in changing antigay attitudes among high RWAs. Most notably, they imply that campaigns designed to reduce antigay prejudice by focusing on altering stereotypes might benefit from also considering the roles of values and perceptions of value dissimilarity.

General Conclusions and Future Research Possibilities

Our program of research developed out of an initial desire to explore the structure of antigay attitudes. Although a large number of studies have examined the relation between antigay attitudes and various individual difference constructs, research examining the underlying structure of these attitudes has been much less prevalent. Thus, our initial work sought to examine the structure of these attitudes, as well as to assess the relation between right-wing authoritarianism and antigay prejudice. The results of this work present a picture that is both complex and interesting. With respect to the favorability of attitudes, our initial studies revealed that extremely negative antigay attitudes are very prevalent among our university samples, especially among individuals high in right-wing authoritarianism. Overall, authoritarianism was negatively associated with the favorability of attitudes, affective responses, and cognitive beliefs about the group.

With respect to the structure of antigay attitudes, our research has revealed a number of interesting effects. In our original studies (Haddock et al., 1993), stereotypic beliefs, overall, did not uniquely predict attitudes. Rather, it appears as though value-based symbolic beliefs serve as an important predictor of prejudice, particularly among high RWAs. The attitudes of these bigoted individuals derive primarily from their beliefs that homosexuals violate important values. Additional research has replicated this finding with numerous social and ethnic target groups (e.g., Esses et al., 1993; Haddock & Zanna, 1994). These findings have important implications for the general area of prejudicial attitudes. For instance, our findings suggest that attempts to understand and predict intergroup attitudes by focusing exclusively on the favorability of stereotypes are unlikely to provide a complete representation of the structure of individuals' attitudes. Thus, we would suggest that future research designed to assess the structure of prejudice needs to include other types of measures that are derived from general models of the attitude concept. Similarly, these results also suggest that strategies designed to change attitudes by attempting to modify individuals' stereotypes may produce limited benefits among those with particularly negative attitudes (as our subsequent research suggests).

The results of our initial studies led us to become interested in three additional issues that we have started to investigate: (a) how negative attitudes translate into discriminatory behavior, (b) the role that perceived value dissimilarity plays in the relation between right-wing authoritarianism and antigay prejudice, and (c) the effects of modifying either stereotypes or symbolic beliefs on changing individuals' attitudes. Initial research exploring these issues has produced promising results. For instance, using our student group funding allocation measure, we determined that negative attitudes derived from symbolic beliefs led to the greatest level of antigay discrimination. Second, we have found that the consideration of measures of perceived value dissimilarity and symbolic beliefs plays an important role in mediating the relation between authoritarianism and antigay attitudes. Finally, a study examining the differential effects of modifying consensual stereotypic versus symbolic beliefs about gay men revealed that among high RWA male subjects, information attempting to disconfirm negative symbolic beliefs (and confirm positive symbolic beliefs) produced more favorable attitudes.

While providing some preliminary responses to these second-generation questions, these areas of research have also generated additional questions we wish to address in future research. First, the findings on our funding allocation measure suggest that this measure may serve as an effective nonreactive approach to assessing one form of discriminatory behavior directed against gay men and lesbians. Of course, it would be beneficial to develop other nonreactive measures that are potentially more hostile in nature. For instance, a nonreactive measure designed to assess an individual's willingness to hire and promote gay and lesbian employees would provide valuable information, as would a measure designed to assess the extent to which respondents would physically harm a gay individual.

A second area that requires additional attention concerns the construct of perceived value dissimilarity and its potential to increase our understanding of antigay prejudice. Our initial work assessing the impact of perceived value dissimilarity suggests that it plays an integral part in antigay prejudice. Additional research assessing perceived value dissimilarity is necessary in order to determine its effects on attitudes toward other out-groups (e.g., Struch & Schwartz, 1989). As well, a more complete understanding of the content of these differences is required. For instance, perceived value dissimilarity can be conceptualized as containing two components: actual differences in values, and inaccuracy in the perception of others' values. Thus, one can examine the extent to which perceived dissimilarity is determined by actual differences in values, as compared with inaccurate perceptions, and also determine whether the relation between RWA and perceived value dissimilarity is mediated by larger actual differences in values, greater perceptual inaccuracy on the part of high authoritarians, or both.

Third, our research that has attempted to change high and low RWA males' attitudes toward gay men by modifying either subjects' stereotypes or subjects' symbolic beliefs about gay men has generated some promising findings. However, this avenue of investigation is clearly at an early stage of development. In this study, subjects simply read about individuals who disconfirmed consensually held negative beliefs about gay men. In the future, it would be worthwhile to examine the effects on attitudes of interacting with individuals who disconfirm these beliefs.

A final area for future research involves a more specific assessment of attitudes toward lesbians. In our initial research, participants were asked to provide their evaluations of the group *homosexuals*. We used this label in order to determine how subjects interpreted the term. Generally, more than 80% of our respondents used the term *homosexuals* to refer to gay men, suggesting that it is possible that our results may not necessarily generalize to an understanding of attitudes toward lesbians. As well, past research that has assessed the favorability of heterosexuals' attitudes toward lesbians has revealed conflicting results with respect to the interaction between gender of respondent and gender of target (Whitley & Kite, 1995). Thus, these findings suggest that future research should examine with greater specificity the structure of attitudes toward lesbians.

Overall, our research has revealed that attitudes toward gay men and lesbians result from multiple sources of information, and that changing these attitudes might require more than simply developing techniques designed to modify the content of individuals' stereotypes. Specifically, subjects' perceptions of the extent to which homosexuals promote or hinder the attainment of values that are important to the subjects appear to play an extremely important role in antigay attitudes. It is our hope that our research will contribute to the development of strategies that will reduce the prevalence of antigay prejudice and discrimination.

Notes

1. In the first study described in this chapter, we examined the relative importance of cognitive and affective responses in predicting attitudes, consistent with most other research that has assessed the underlying structure of prejudice (e.g., Eagly et al., 1994; Esses et al., 1993; Stangor et al., 1991). A measure of the behavioral component has been included in other research (see Haddock et al., 1993, Study 2).

2. We used this label, rather than *gay men and lesbians*, to determine how individuals construe the term *homosexuals*. We have found that more than 80% of subjects interpret *homosexuals* as referring to gay men, and that the pattern of findings in our research is not affected by different interpretations of the term *homosexuals*.

3. The consideration of gender differences in attitudes was not a primary purpose of the present study. In both studies, males expressed less favorable attitudes than did females. For a comprehensive review on the issue of gender differences and antigay attitudes, see Kite and Whitley (Chapter 3, this volume).

4. We elected not to assess subjects' sexual orientation, a decision consistent with other research in the field (see Kite & Whitley, Chapter 3, this volume). Accordingly, although the majority of our subjects were likely heterosexual, the sample probably also included gay respondents. Thus, it is not entirely appropriate to conclude that our data on attitude structure reflect solely the attitudes of heterosexuals.

5. For the purposes of our regression analyses, subjects were assigned to high and low RWA groups on the basis of a tertile split of our sample. High RWAs were those individuals who scored greater than 54 on the RWA scale, whereas low RWAs were operationalized as those scoring less than 42. Mean attitudes toward homosexuals for high and low RWAs were 27.06 (SD = 24.16) and 51.67 (SD = 22.15), respectively.

6. This funding measure is more than a simple evaluative measure, in the sense that subjects were led to believe that their responses might influence important budgetary decisions. Accordingly, it might be most appropriate to think of this measure as somewhat similar to the concept of behavioroid measures, described by Aronson, Brewer, and Carlsmith (1985).

7. The 11 value types assessed were self-direction, stimulation, hedonism, achievement, power, security, conformity, tradition, spirituality, benevolence, and universalism. In recent work, Schwartz and colleagues (e.g., Schwartz & Huismans, 1995) have not assessed the type *spirituality*. Removal of this type from our data did not noticeably change our results.

8. Because control group subjects did not take part in the impression formation task, analyses on the attitude measure take the form of a 2×2 ANOVA.

9. Male subjects were exclusively used for two reasons. First, our earlier research had revealed that males expressed the most negative attitudes. Second, because the descriptions were of gay men, we decided it might be best, in this first study, to not consider the effects of matching or mismatching gender of subject and the gender of the individuals depicted in the descriptions.

10. Although there were six targets, impressions of each target were highly correlated, allowing us to create a composite measure of attitude.

11. The contrast weights were as follows: low RWA stereotype (+1), high RWA stereotype (–1), low RWA symbolic (–2), high RWA symbolic (+2), low RWA control (+1), high RWA control (–1).

References

Altemeyer, B. (1988). *Enemies of freedom: Understanding right-wing authoritarianism.* San Francisco: Jossey-Bass.

Aronson, E., Brewer, M., & Carlsmith, J. M. (1985). Experimentation in social psychology. In G. Lindzey & E. Aronson (Eds.) *The handbook of social psychology* (3rd ed., Vol. 1, pp. 441-486). New York: Random House.

Ashmore, R. D., & Del Boca, F. K. (1981). Conceptual approaches to stereotypes and stereotyping. In D. L. Hamilton (Ed.), *Cognitive processes in stereotyping and intergroup behavior* (pp. 1-35). Hillsdale, NJ: Lawrence Erlbaum.

Chaiken, S., Pomerantz, E. M., & Giner-Sorolla, R. (1995). Structural consistency and attitude strength. In R. E. Petty & J. A. Krosnick (Eds.), *Attitude strength: Antecedents and consequences* (pp. 387-412). Hillsdale, NJ: Lawrence Erlbaum.

Eagly, A. H., & Chaiken, S. (1993). *The psychology of attitudes.* Fort Worth, TX: Harcourt Brace Jovanovich.

Eagly, A. H., Mladinic, A., & Otto, S. (1994). Cognitive and affective bases of attitudes toward social groups and social policies. *Journal of Experimental Social Psychology, 30,* 113-137.

Esses, V. M., Haddock, G., & Zanna, M. P. (1993). Values, stereotypes, and emotions as determinants of intergroup attitudes. In D. M. Mackie & D. L. Hamilton (Eds.), *Affect, cognition, and stereotyping: Interactive processes in group perception* (pp. 137-166). New York: Academic Press.

Haddock, G., & Zanna, M. P. (1993). [Right-wing authoritarianism and the importance of human values]. Unpublished raw data.

Haddock, G., & Zanna, M. P. (1994). Preferring "housewives " to "feminists": Categorization and the favorability of attitudes toward women. *Psychology of Women Quarterly, 18,* 25-52.

Haddock, G., Zanna, M. P., & Esses, V. M. (1993). Assessing the structure of prejudicial attitudes: The case of attitudes toward homosexuals. *Journal of Personality and Social Psychology, 65,* 1105-1118.

Herek, G. M. (1991). Stigma, prejudice, and violence against lesbians and gay men. In J. C. Gonsiorek & J. D. Weinrich (Eds.), *Homosexuality: Research implications for public policy* (pp. 60-80). Newbury Park, CA: Sage.

Hewstone, M. (1994). Revision and change of stereotypic beliefs: In search of the elusive subtyping model. In W. Stroebe & M. Hewstone (Eds.), *European review of social psychology* (Vol. 5, pp. 69-109). London: Wiley.

McConahay, J. B. (1986). Modern racism, ambivalence, and the modern racism scale. In J. F. Dovidio & S. L. Gaertner (Eds.), *Prejudice, discrimination, and racism* (pp. 84-105). New York: Academic Press.

Rohan, M. J., & Zanna, M. P. (1996). Value transmission in families. In C. Seligman, J. M. Olson, & M. P. Zanna (Eds.), *The psychology of values: The Ontario Symposium* (Vol. 8, pp. 253-276). Hillsdale, NJ: Lawrence Erlbaum.

Rokeach, M. (1968). *Beliefs, attitudes, and values: A theory of organization and change.* San Francisco: Jossey-Bass.

Schwartz, S. H. (1992). Universals in the content and structure of values: Theoretical advances and empirical tests in 20 countries. In M. P. Zanna (Ed.), *Advances in experimental social psychology* (Vol. 25, pp. 1-65). San Diego, CA: Academic Press.

Schwartz, S. H., & Huismans, S. (1995). Value priorities and religiosity in four Western religions. *Social Psychology Quarterly, 58,* 88-107.

Sears, D. O. (1988). Symbolic racism. In P. A. Katz & D. A. Taylor (Eds.), *Eliminating racism* (pp. 53-84). New York: Plenum.

Stangor, C., Sullivan, L. A., & Ford, T. E. (1991). Affective and cognitive determinants of prejudice. *Social Cognition, 9,* 359-391.

Struch, N., & Schwartz, S. H. (1989). Intergroup aggression: Its predictors and distinctness from in-group bias. *Journal of Personality and Social Psychology, 56,* 364-373.

Whitley, B. E., Jr., & Kite, M. E. (1995). Sex differences in attitudes toward homosexuality: A comment on Oliver and Hyde (1993). *Psychological Bulletin, 117,* 146-154.

Zanna, M. P., & Rempel, J. K. (1988). Attitudes: A new look at an old concept. In D. Bar-Tal & A. W. Kruglanski (Eds.), *The social psychology of knowledge* (pp. 315-334). Cambridge, England: Cambridge University Press.

6

Civil Liberties, Civil Rights, and Stigma

Voter Attitudes and Behavior in the Politics of Homosexuality

DOUGLAS ALAN STRAND

A sizable body of literature has helped us understand why heterosexuals stigmatize gay people. But how do citizens decide on their responses to stigma in the political realm? Are their preferences for the legal treatment of gays based largely on the level of stigma they attach to this group, or are other considerations also very important? How far can we go in characterizing people as likely to be either "pro-gay rights" or "anti-gay rights," and "tolerant" or "intolerant" across the range of policy questions concerning the treatment of gays? In particular, how do heterosexual citizens view civil liberties compared with how they view civil rights for gays? What do the answers to these questions suggest about prospects for the future of gay politics?

In this chapter, I address these questions and reach two main conclusions. First, my analysis of public preferences for the legal treatment of gays shows that there is a good deal more than stigma underlying these

AUTHOR'S NOTE: I would like to thank George E. Marcus, Kenneth Sherrill, Laura Stoker, and Joan Tronto for their invaluable advice in the preparation of this chapter. These scholars, of course, bear no responsibility for any errors in fact, analysis, or interpretation that manage to appear nonetheless in the final product.

attitudes. A pair of abstract political values can influence these preferences to a degree rivaling stigma. In addition, the way a gay-relevant issue is framed can importantly affect how heterosexuals want the law to treat gays.[1] My second main conclusion emerges as a fundamental instance of these framing effects. I argue that it is a mistake to identify people as either more or less likely to be "pro-gay rights" or "anti-gay rights," "tolerant" or "intolerant." Instead, potential public coalitions of likely supporters and opponents of policies supporting gays will vary substantially depending on whether the issue at hand takes on the character of civil liberties or civil rights. These two main sets of findings suggest that the continued advancement of public support for policies supporting gays faces more difficult prospects as the primary battleground shifts from civil liberties to civil rights.

Theoretical Expectations and Hypotheses

Stigma attaches to a wide variety of individuals and groups in society. By *stigma*, I mean "a characteristic of persons that is contrary to a norm of a social unit. The characteristic might involve what people do (or have done), what they believe, or who they are (owing to physical or social characteristics)" (Stafford & Scott, 1986, p. 80). When an out-group is stigmatized, how do in-group members decide how to treat that group in the realms of politics and law?

Some scholarship has argued or suggested that the stigma attached to an out-group can be the leading determinant of how members of the public reach their preferences concerning its political treatment. Converse (1964) found this to be the case with race policy views. Typically, views about diverse racial policies "would tend to boil down for many respondents to the same single question: 'Are you sympathetic to Negroes as a group, are you indifferent to them, or do you dislike them?' The responses would be affected accordingly" (p. 235). More generally, as Sears (1993) has noted, a reader of social psychology will often encounter the view that "groups are . . . the most 'central' of political attitude objects, so that political parties are perceived in terms of which groups they favor or oppose" (p. 126). Nelson and Kinder (1996) have recently argued that in the case of issues such as government assistance to the poor, federal spending on the fight against AIDS, and affirmative action, politics "lends itself to group-centric thinking. By their nature, each [policy] invites citizens to reach an opinion primarily by drawing on their thoughts and feelings toward the group in question, and the evidence is abundant that citizens do just that" (pp. 1058-1059).

If an in-group member's policy preferences for dealing with a stigmatized out-group are based largely on the level of stigma that he or she attaches to the group, then variations in the type of policy related to the out-group should not greatly affect those preferences. When policy battlegrounds shift, if the stigmatized group affected by the policy remains the same, combatants should continue to know roughly where they can find their friends and enemies in the mass public. Sears and Citrin (1985) have provided an empirical example of what such attitudinal predictability might look like. In their investigation of the underpinnings of support for government spending programs during California's Proposition 13 tax battle, they found that about the same mix of partisan identification, self-designated ideology, and symbolic racism predicted government spending attitudes regardless of whether the spending would go for education, health care, or welfare.

On the other hand, Sniderman, Tetlock, Carmines, and Peterson (1993) surprised themselves when they discovered that people's views of race policy showed three different structures. According to their research, Americans think differently about nondiscrimination policies, affirmative action policies, and race-targeted welfare policies (see also Sniderman & Piazza, 1993). The researchers have pointed out that their persistent tendency to find "issue pluralism" (p. 212) in mass attitudes toward race entailed "swimming upstream" (p. 234) against the prevailing conclusions in the race literature. In his review of the literature, Sears (1993, p. 130) noted that there were mixed findings on whether varying the political framing of an issue changed the bases of support and opposition.[2]

In my view, we make a serious mistake when we fail to draw a sharp distinction between stigma and preferences for the legal treatment of the stigmatized. We should expect people to approach the two attitudes quite differently. Stigma is likely to be an easier judgment, because in-group members may well be able to draw on personal experience, early socialization, or basic ethical or religious principles. Politics, in contrast, is more distant from personal experiences and social development. Thus, although the attachment of stigma to a group might be an "easy" reaction for many Americans, guidelines for the appropriate legal treatment of the group may well be much more elusive.

One should expect this to be the case with lesbians and gay men. Many heterosexuals seem to acquire the opinion that gays are "sinful," "un- natural," or "disgusting," and that it might be best to avoid their close company. Yet these same citizens might have little idea as to whether gays should be imprisoned, tolerated, or protected against discrimina- tion by the government.

In conducting the research reported here, I hypothesized that many Americans do not maintain general "pro-gay rights" or "anti-gay rights" positions. Instead, I expected to find important distinctiveness in how members of the public see different gay-relevant issues. I predicted that this distinctiveness would take at least one basic form: The public would respond differently to gay civil liberties issues than to gay civil rights issues. Thus, I expected that it would be wrong to characterize members of the public as either "tolerant" or "intolerant" in how they prefer to treat gays in general across both the civil liberties and civil rights do- mains.

Civil Liberties and Civil Rights

Philosophical and conceptual discussions have typically differenti- ated civil liberties from civil rights. Although there is no canonical com- parison, certain major definitions and distinctions stand out in the litera- ture (see, e.g., Grey, 1991). In this section I will very briefly highlight the key features that distinguish civil liberties from civil rights. The discus- sion draws mainly on the work of Grey (1991), who has defined and contrasted the two concepts.

The civil liberties perspective has been "centrally concerned with pro- tecting freedom of expression" (Grey, 1991, p. 82). At least since the semi- nal U.S. Supreme Court decisions on marriage and contraception rights, the meaning of freedom of expression has expanded to imply some kind of right to privacy, though heated argument rages over its particular applications (McClosky & Brill, 1983; Sandel, 1989). An important part of the controversy stems from differences over the definition of private versus public.

From the civil liberties perspective, the leading danger is excessive *state* power over individuals and social life. At least until recently, civil libertarians "have not spent much of their time or energy seeking ways to positively empower dissenters, deviants, and nonconformists against the pressures brought on them by unorganized public opinion, or by private employers or landlords" (Grey, 1991, p. 82). Moreover, the civil liberties tradition seeks to preserve or advance state neutrality toward ideas and toward individual behaviors that do not harm others (Grey, 1991; Stoker, 1997).

The civil rights perspective, in contrast, focuses on fundamentally different concerns. Instead of freedom, equality is the central emphasis. As Grey (1991) has noted,

> The civil-rights approach, with its roots in anti-discrimination law and social policy, is centrally concerned with injuries of stigma and humiliation to those who are victims of discrimination. . . . The point is not [as with civil liberties] to protect a sphere of autonomy or personal security from *intrusion* as to protect potentially marginal members of the community from *exclusion*—from relegation, that is, to the status of second-class citizens. (p. 82, emphasis in original)

In the quest to end the kind of second-class status that arises from discrimination, state power becomes a friend rather than a potential threat. Preserving freedom from government constraint in individual life and social relations is much less important, if not irrelevant, in the civil rights mentality. Not only government, but all of civil society is potentially subject to being purged of the second-class status that arises from discrimination.

This mission intrinsically obviates the kind of state ideological neutrality that the civil liberties perspective favors. The civil rights perspective involves the use of state power essentially to advance an ideological crusade throughout civil society. The state must disempower "false" ideologies that promote second-class status for some citizens.

Philosophers, judges, and possibly other political elites will see fundamental differences between civil liberties and civil rights. But how does the mass public perceive them? Do they see the distinction when they reach specific policy preferences? Or can we rank people by their likelihood of supporting a gay rights measure without attending to whether the frame is civil liberties or civil rights? How safe is it to generalize across civil liberties and civil rights and label people as "pro-gay rights" or "anti-gay rights," "tolerant" or "intolerant"?

Scholars of public opinion have seemed to expect people to react in about the same way to civil liberties and civil rights. Nunn, Crockett, and Williams (1978) casually assumed that their findings on civil liberties would shed light on people's views of civil rights laws protecting gays. In their exhaustive investigation, McClosky and Brill (1983) treated classic civil liberties issues (such as free speech rights) along with civil rights issues (such as gay antidiscrimination laws and the Equal Rights Amendment) in a way that suggested they are more or less the same. The work of Sniderman, Tetlock, Glaser, Green, and Hout (1991) argued for a "principled tolerance" that not only rises above stigma toward particular groups but also covers both civil liberties and civil rights (p. 128). Without explicitly invoking the research of Sniderman and his associates, Dennis Chong (1994) has taken a similar position. He has lamented the lack of any unified theory on tolerance that would apply to civil liberties for politically unpopular groups (e.g., Communists and neo-Nazis), racial and gender civil rights, and the political treatment of "lifestyle differences." Given the traditional view, noted above, wherein the public sees political issues mainly in terms of the group in question rather than the political treatment proposed, we should expect to find scholars assuming, suggesting, or claiming that the American public does not make a major distinction between civil liberties judgments and civil rights judgments. Yet rarely if ever has any scholar actually compared public responses to these two types of policies, as I do below.

In this chapter, I assess the distinctiveness of how the public views gay civil liberties, as opposed to gay civil rights, in three main ways. First, after defining issues as matters of either civil liberty or civil rights, I look at how sociodemographic groups lined up on one set of opinions compared with the other. Then I examine exit polls of those who voted in state conflicts over gay-relevant policies and see how varying the frame to increase the relevance of a civil libertarian perspective affected the behavior of different demographic groups. Finally, I move from demographics to attitudinal correlates, focusing on two values that should matter differently to civil liberties and civil rights preferences: freedom of speech and humanitarianism.

Demographic correlates. My comparisons of gay civil liberties and gay civil rights opinion controlled for antigay stigma by holding it constant *across* the two basic types of issues: Gays were the target group in all cases. Because none of the separate equations that I estimated in these comparative analyses included stigma as a variable, we should expect to find education and age-related effects on the political dependent variables simply by virtue of the strong associations they have each shown with antigay stigma in previous research (Herek, 1991).

Even taking stigma into account, previous research has uncovered education's importance in attitudes toward general civil liberties (Bobo & Licari, 1989; Marcus, Sullivan, Theiss-Morse, & Wood, 1995) and civil liberties for gays (Gibson & Tedin, 1988). Scholars theorize that formal education promotes civil liberties for two main reasons: (a) It promotes an openness to new ideas, and (b) it socializes people to accept prevailing elite norms favoring free expression and some right to privacy (Bobo & Licari, 1989; McClosky & Brill, 1983).

Previous research has given us mixed messages on the connection between education and civil rights attitudes. Some scholars have reported finding that education promotes a "principled tolerance" that covers both civil liberties and civil rights protections for stigmatized groups (Sniderman et al., 1991). By contrast, other scholars have found theoretical and empirical reasons to doubt education's contribution to civil rights support. They have argued that the individualistic and meritocratic ethos of education undercuts support for government-mandated egalitarianism (Jackman & Muha, 1984). There is reason, therefore, to expect a more limited role for education in promoting gay civil rights.

Another basic demographic factor that should have an important effect on gay-relevant policy opinion is age. Older people are substantially less supportive of civil liberties than are younger people (Gibson & Duch, 1993, p. 313; McClosky & Brill, 1983). Scholars have suggested that this difference results both from aging's promotion of dogmatism (Sullivan, Pierson, & Marcus, 1982) and from the socialization of new generations in the context of revised social norms more supportive of civil liberties (Jennings & Niemi, 1981; Sullivan, Shamir, Walsh, & Roberts, 1985). When the stigmatized group is gays and lesbians, massive generational differences in socialization environments should produce considerably more friendliness toward gay civil liberties among younger Americans. After all, they were raised in an era when gays seemed to have little trouble getting permits to parade down Main Street in many towns, gay bars operated openly in most metropolitan areas, and sympathetic or neutral portrayals of gays and lesbians sometimes got past censors and appeared on television. Older Americans, by contrast, grew up in an era when gays were officially banned from work in the federal civil service and news about gays mainly took the form of occasional stories about bar raids by vice cops.

Based on findings in the race literature (Dowden & Robinson, 1993; Schuman, Steeh, & Bobo, 1985), I also expected to find a relationship between age and opposition to gay civil rights. However, I expected that the degree of association should be weaker for civil rights than for civil liberties. This is because the environment in which new generational cohorts have been socialized has changed less with respect to gay civil rights than it has with respect to gay civil liberties. Nonetheless, younger people should still be more favorable toward civil rights because they were raised after women, Blacks, and other minorities had gained legal protections against discrimination. We should expect that these developments would have fostered some additional inclination to accept non-discrimination laws protecting gays.

Values. I assess the distinctiveness of attitudes on gay civil liberties and gay civil rights not only by looking at how sociodemographic groups align themselves but also by seeing if values help differentiate the two kinds of politics in the public mind. As noted above, one of these value tests will look at how much gay civil liberties and civil rights preferences line up with an instance of classic civil libertarianism, namely, the priority someone gives to the protection of free speech in general. If civil rights tolerance resembles civil liberties tolerance, then the importance attached to protecting free expression should predict both types of gay-relevant policy attitudes to at least a modest degree.

One other important value that should distinguish political preferences on civil liberties and civil rights is humanitarianism. Humanitarianism is typically defined as a general concern for the well-being of others (those who are not relatives or friends) and a desire to give them assistance (Steenbergen, 1996). One reason to expect the public as a whole to react differently to gay civil liberties and gay civil rights is that support for the latter should require more humanitarianism than support for the former. Civil rights protections for a stigmatized group requires more sacrifice from mainstream citizens. Such laws go beyond the civil libertarian's "live and let live" approach and instead constrain the stigmatizer's freedom to engage in social and occupational exclusion. In addition, some people might perceive that civil rights laws protecting a minority group would mean that members of the majority might suffer a relative deprivation (Runciman, 1966) of government protection and attention: Government is helping "them" when there are plenty more things that government should be doing for "us" or "me." The plausibility of this perception is suggested by the "special rights" slogan proclaimed by opponents of gay civil rights laws (Schacter, 1994). I expected that those showing higher levels of humanitarianism would be more

concerned about the discrimination suffered by a member of a stigmatized group and more willing to pay a political price to support governmental assistance to a minority they might dislike.

The analysis of key attitudinal differences between civil liberties and
civil rights, together with the demographic tests, shows how much more
there is to gay-relevant policy attitudes than simply the level of stigma.
Framing an issue in terms of civil liberties or, alternatively, civil rights
has an important effect on how people react—who supports and who
opposes particular policies concerning gays. I conclude this chapter by
looking at the underpinnings of civil rights attitudes in more depth. I
examine how stigma's influence on political preferences compares with
the influence of an expanded set of abstract political values, and show
how these values can rival stigma as underpinnings of the response of
Americans to the politics of homosexuality.

Data, Measures, and Method

Data for the study discussed below came from several surveys of national adult populations. The analysis of gay civil liberties opinion drew
on data from the General Social Survey (GSS), an in-person survey conducted in most years since 1972 for the National Data Program for the
Social Sciences at the National Opinion Research Center of the University of Chicago (Davis & Smith, 1997). The analysis of gay civil rights and
other gay-relevant opinion used data from the 1992-1993 panel of the
American National Election Study, or NES (Miller, Kinder, Rosenstone,
& the National Election Studies, 1993; Rosenstone, Kinder, Miller, & the
National Election Studies, 1994), and the 1996 pre- and postelection survey of the NES (Rosenstone, Kinder, Miller, & the National Election
Studies, 1997). The NES has been conducted since 1952 by the University
of Michigan's Center for Political Studies. In the 1992-1993 NES panel,
approximately 770 people who were first surveyed in person in the fall
of 1992 were reinterviewed by telephone a year later for the 1993 Pilot
Study. In the 1996 NES, about three fourths of the 1,714 respondents had
also participated in the 1992 NES, 1994 NES, or both. The GSS and NES
respondents constitute an approximately random sample of the national
adult population. (Some biases may have arisen from panel mortality in
the 1992-1993 and 1996 NES, and from the loss of the 5% of households
that lacked telephones at the time of the 1992-1993 NES.) The analysis of

voting on state initiatives used data gathered in self-administered surveys of voters leaving polling places. Voter News Service (formerly Voter Research and Surveys) conducted these "exit polls" in the 1992 and 1994 November elections in relevant states (Voter News Service, 1995; Voter Research and Surveys, 1993).

All tables presented here show the results of ordinary least squares regressions, using unstandardized coefficients (*b*), standardized coefficients (*beta* weights), or both; the data are unweighted. Where they might have been especially useful (in Tables 6.1 and 6.2), logistic regressions did not yield substantially different results from ordinary least squares. The tables focus just on voters, because I expect that the portion of the public especially likely to influence the course of gay politics is the subset that actually votes. Variable construction and coding are described in the appendix to this chapter.

Results

Sociodemographic Factors

The analysis presented in Table 6.1 compares civil liberties policies and civil rights policies in terms of their relationships with sociodemographic factors. Except for the dummy variables for gender, race, and family income, each unstandardized coefficient in Table 6.1 represents the change in the dependent variables associated with a movement from one extreme on an independent variable to the other extreme. The comparison base for the dummy variables are males, non-Hispanic Whites, and those with annual family income between $15,000 and $50,000.

Civil liberties policies are represented by the dependent variables in the first two columns of Table 6.1. They are based on questions in the 1993-1994 General Social Survey that ask (a) whether a library should remove any book written by a man who is homosexual, and (b) whether a man who is homosexual should be allowed to teach in a university. The dependent variables in the third and fourth columns of the table are based on questions in the 1993 National Election Study that ask (a) whether homosexuals should be allowed to serve in the U.S. military, and (b) whether there should be laws protecting homosexuals against job discrimination. I categorize these last two as civil rights policies.

Table 6.1 Gay Civil Liberties Versus Gay Civil Rights: Policy Opinions

	Policy Opinion Dependent Variables[a]			
	Allow Gay Book in Library (GSS)	Allow Gay Teach in University (GSS)	Allow Gay Serve in Military (NES)	Gay Discrimination Protection (NES)
Independent Variables	b	b	b	b
Age	−.208***	−.266***	−.082	.077
Education	.257***	.279***	.110	.216**
Female	.045*	.059**	.176***	.141***
Black	−.072*	−.009	.102	.084
Other race	−.012	.071	−.228†	−.028
Family income < $15,000	−.046†	−.028	.034	.031
Family income $50,000-75,000	.076**	.041	−.099†	−.021
Family income > $75,000	.064*	.051†	−.004	−.050

NOTE: GSS is 1993-1994 combined ($N = 1,854$ voters). NES is 1993, from 1992-1993 panel ($N = 545$ voters). Entries are unstandardized coefficients (b).
a. Scores ranged from 0 (oppose) to 1 (support). See the appendix to this chapter for detailed explanations of the variables.
†$p < .10$, two-tailed; *$p < .05$, two-tailed; **$p < .01$, two-tailed; ***$p < .001$, two-tailed.

The status of the first two policy questions as civil liberties issues should not be very controversial. The GSS question on removing a library book has been used in the civil liberties literature as a standard question addressing the freedom of a wide variety of unpopular groups and individuals. The question touches on themes that are central to civil liberties: freedom of expression and the free circulation of ideas. Thus, it is a paradigmatic civil liberties policy.

The teaching question has played a similar role in the civil liberties literature (e.g., Bobo & Licari, 1989; Gibson & Tedin, 1988). It raises the issue of the right to personal privacy. The question does not talk about hiring a teacher who would teach students that homosexuality is a good thing. It merely asks whether someone who says he is gay should be hired as a professor. The question thus invites one particular reaction from those with a civil libertarian inclination: "What they do in the privacy of their bedrooms is their own business, not the government's."

The question of whether government should prohibit job discrimination against gays, by contrast, is a paradigmatic issue of civil rights. There, the question is not about whether members of a stigmatized group should be left alone to express themselves, pursue happiness in their intimate private lives, or have jobs for which their private lives are of questionable relevance. Instead, the question is concerned with whether the freedom of the stigmatizers in what some might see as a private realm should be constrained by government action in the interest of promoting the equality of the stigmatized. Essentially, it would be another instance of the kind of law embodied in the 1964 Civil Rights Act, which prohibits discrimination on the basis of race, national origin, gender, and religion.

It is less clear that the gays-in-the-military issue is more a matter of civil rights than of civil liberties. I consider it more in the civil rights than in the civil liberties domain for two reasons. First, the dispute over gays in the military has centrally involved the civil rights concern for equality. Second, the relevance of a civil libertarian's privacy concern was called into question by the unique military context of this issue. Privacy is not a major norm in the military, to say the least. If anything, a concern for the privacy rights of the mainstream group, rather than the stigmatized group, seemed to dominate in the public debate on allowing gays to serve in the military. Heterosexual soldiers seemed to garner no small amount of public sympathy for having to shower, change clothing, and sleep in close proximity to gays or lesbians. In a battery of agree/disagree statements in a January 29-31, 1993, Gallup/CNN/*USA Today* poll, one of the more popular objections to allowing gays in the military was "It is not right to require non-gay men and women to share living quarters with gays" (58% agreed and 38% disagreed). Based on these considerations, I treat the issue of gays in the military as one of civil rights instead of civil liberties, although its status in this regard is far less clear-cut than the case of employment antidiscrimination law.[3]

As shown in Table 6.1, the civil liberties category appeared to garner support somewhat more easily than did the civil rights issues. In the national samples of voters examined here, 71% opposed removing a library book written by a gay (versus 26% who wanted to remove it) and 73% thought that a gay person should be allowed to teach in a university (versus 24% who stood in opposition). Support for laws protecting gays against discrimination was only 63% (versus 34% opposed), whereas support for allowing gays into the military reached just 61% (versus 36% opposed).

More important to demonstrating the public's distinction between civil liberties and civil rights is the difference in the sociodemographic correlates of opinion on the two types of policies. A gender difference plainly appeared on civil rights, but not at all on civil liberties. Formal education was notably less consequential for civil rights than for civil liberties when the civil rights issue was gays in the military ($p < .05$, one-tailed). Such a difference showed up only to a small degree, however, when antidiscrimination law was in the comparison. Thus, the prediction was only partially fulfilled in the analysis of education in Table 6.1.

In the case of age, the contrast between civil liberties and civil rights is more arresting because of the size, consistency, and nature of the difference. The association of age with civil liberties opinions was what one would expect from the positive association of age with antigay stigma (Herek, 1991), and from the association of age with a heightened opposition to civil liberties for unpopular groups in general. The difference here translated to roughly 25% less support for gay civil liberties among the oldest age group (aged 60 and up) than among the youngest cohort (18-24 years old).

Yet when the policy question fell within the civil rights domain, the age association either disappeared or reversed direction. When there was any age-related difference over civil rights for gays, as on the question of antidiscrimination laws, it was the *younger* groups who showed more opposition. (In all comparisons here, $p < .01$. For those concerned that the analyses in Tables 6.1 and 6.2 might have obscured any important nonlinear age relationships, I should note that the findings here held up well when age was treated as a set of dummy variables.)

This is especially surprising given that gays and homosexuality tended to carry less stigma for the younger groups, and their antigay stigma seemed to incorporate less tangible danger. Among all voters in this NES sample, the *beta* weight for the association between age and lower feeling thermometer scores for gays,[4] after the sociodemographic factors in the table were controlled for, was less than one would expect: $\beta = .08$. But younger groups were also less likely to see gays as posing threats to nongays through casual disease contagion and sexual harassment: The partial correlation between age and position on an index combining these two threat assessments was $\beta = .18$. Finally, younger adults were substantially less likely to find anything wrong with homosexuality per se. For example, in the GSS for 1993-1994, among high school educated voters (thus controlling for education), 81% of those older than 60 said that homosexuality is "always wrong"; only 11% said that there is nothing wrong with it. Compare that with the evaluation of homosexuality by those with a high school diploma who are under 30 years of age: 56% found it always wrong, whereas 36% thought that homosexuality was not wrong at all.

As this chapter went to press, the 1996 NES and 1996 GSS data sets were released. The results in Table 6.1 for education, age, and gender held up at least as well when I replicated the analysis using the 1996 data (for GSS, N = 1,085 voters; for NES, N = 1,002 voters). In the replication, education was substantially and consistently more associated with civil liberties than with civil rights. All education, age, and gender differences between the civil liberties and civil rights opinions reached significance at $p < .10$, and the age and education differences continued to support expectations clearly (analysis not shown).

The attitudinal results from Table 6.1 showing how Americans differentiate between civil liberties and civil rights find additional support in the analyses in Table 6.2 of voting behavior on citizen initiatives concerning the treatment of gays. In Table 6.2, the dependent variables are reported vote choices on initiatives in Oregon and Colorado in 1992 and in Oregon and Idaho in 1994. All four ballot measures not only would have repealed any civil rights protections based on sexual orientation that existed at the time in any governmental unit in each state, but would have prohibited the future enactment of such civil rights laws.

In addition, the 1992 Oregon initiative—Measure 9—proposed something more that distinctively framed this particular vote choice as both a civil liberties and a civil rights matter: Its language instructed governmental units in Oregon to actively promote the idea that homosexuality is, in the words of the initiative, "immoral, unnatural, and perverse" (quoted in Ness, 1992, p. A19). In other words, the policy in question called for the government to take action to, in effect, enhance the stigmatization of gays. No other state initiative has explicitly done such a thing. This added a unique civil liberties angle to the conflict in Oregon in 1992. At issue was whether the government should assume an official orthodoxy attacking what some would see as the private life of an unpopular minority of its citizens. The other cases in Table 6.2 were predominantly disputes over civil rights, without the heightened civil liberties consideration that Oregon voters faced in 1992.

Measure 9 lost, with a vote of 56% to 44%. For the other state initiatives, which lacked any stigmatizing provision such as Measure 9's, the results were very close: losing with a vote of 52% to 48% in Oregon in 1994 and 50.4% to 49.6% in Idaho in 1994; and winning with a vote of 53% to 47%

Table 6.2 Gay Civil Liberties Versus Gay Civil Rights: Voting on State Initiatives Concerning Gays

	Dependent Variables = Vote by State[a]						
	Independent Variable = Age				Independent Variables = All Demographics		
	Oregon 1992 (n = 980)	Colorado 1992 (n = 1,010)	Oregon 1994 (n = 934)	Idaho 1994 (n = 800)	Oregon 1992 (n = 980)	Oregon 1994 (n = 934)	Idaho 1994 (n = 800)
Independent Variables	b	b	b	b	b	b	b
Age	−.103†	−.014	−.054	.084	−.098†	−.028	.103†
Education					.408***	.250***	.166*
Female					.112***	.108**	.109**
Black					.105	−.088	−.102
Hispanic					.196	−.028	.304†
Other race					−.064	.122	.057
Family income < $15,000					.076†	.116*	.071
Family income $50,000-75,000					.118**	.049	.086†
Family income > $75,000					.081	.029	.014

a. Scores range from 0 (pro-initiative/antiprotection) to 1 (anti-initiative). See the appendix to this chapter for detailed explanations of the variables.
†$p < .10$, two-tailed; *$p < .05$, two-tailed; **$p < .01$, two-tailed; ***$p < .001$, two-tailed.

in Colorado in 1992. As in the case of the public opinion results cited above, gay civil rights garnered less support than did gay civil liberties.[5]

The sociodemographic independent variables in Table 6.2 are the same ones that appear in Table 6.1. The education variable and the dummy variables for race/ethnicity had to be slightly modified from the previous table. The dependent variables—reported vote choice on the initiatives—also have a scoring that is similar to that of the policy opinions in Table 6.1. For the 1992 Colorado vote analysis, the data set did not permit multivariate analysis of the sociodemographic variables because the exit pollsters omitted any question about the voter's educational background. Consequently, Colorado is included only in a first set of analyses (the first four columns) that looks at the bivariate relationship between age and vote choice in all four cases.

Results in Table 6.2 show that a salient civil liberties angle to an initiative produced sociodemographic bases of support and opposition that differed from those that emerged when civil rights was the dominant frame. When civil libertarianism was challenged, as with the threat of state stigmatization of gays in Oregon's Measure 9, age showed the negative association with support for gays that one would expect from the civil liberties literature. This appeared in both the bivariate and the multivariate analyses. Even when education and other sociodemographic variables are controlled for, the oldest group voted in favor of Measure 9 by about 10 percentage points more than did the 18- to 24-year-old group. But when this distinctive and salient civil liberties frame disappeared, and the dispute focused predominantly on civil rights instead, either the age groups voted approximately the same or the younger groups became the more likely opponents of policies protecting gays. (For the difference between Oregon in 1992 and Oregon in 1994 in the multivariate analyses, $p < .20$; for the difference between Oregon in 1992 and Idaho in 1994, $p < .01$.)

Education shows its classic civil libertarian bent in Table 6.2, and with no subtlety. Even when age, ethnicity, and income are controlled for, those with a graduate education reacted to Measure 9 with about 40 percentage points more opposition than did those who did not finish high school. Where there was no such salient civil liberties frame, however, education was much less associated with opposition to initiatives that barred legal protections specifically intended to help gays (for both comparisons, $p < .05$).

One finding from the analysis of attitudes in Table 6.1 is not confirmed in the analysis of behavior in Table 6.2: Similar gender differences appeared in voting on the initiatives regardless of whether the frame highlighted civil rights alone or both civil rights and civil liberties. The fact that all four state initiatives raised a fundamental civil rights question probably made any true civil liberties versus civil rights distinctions less likely to appear in a comparison of these vote choices. In any event, men were consistently and substantially more likely than women to vote yes on state initiatives hostile to government protections concerning sexual orientation. However, as with Table 6.1, results here showed no clear patterns with respect to race, ethnicity, or economic class.

Values

Freedom of speech. The basic difference between civil liberties and civil rights for gays becomes even clearer when we go beyond the sizable sociodemographic differences in Tables 6.1 and 6.2 and, returning to the

GSS and NES survey data, focus instead on attitudinal predictors. In the first of a series of analyses, I compared policy preferences for gay civil liberties and gay civil rights in terms of their association with a person's attitude toward one key civil liberty in general, to wit, free speech. To do this, I took the equations from Table 6.1 and added a measure of support for free speech protection that appeared in both the NES and GSS questionnaires. This measure is Ronald Inglehart's often-used "postmaterialism" question (see Abramson & Inglehart, 1995), which asks respondents to rank the first and second most important national goals out of the following four options: (a) maintaining order, (b) fighting rising prices, (c) making sure people have a say in how the government is run, and (d) protecting freedom of speech.

Controlling for sociodemographics, those who ranked the preservation of free speech as either their highest or second-highest national priority opposed removing a library book written by a homosexual by a margin of 12 percentage points over those who did not pick the preservation of free speech as one of their top two priorities (analysis not shown). The comparable margin was 8 percentage points with respect to allowing a homosexual to teach in a university. But avid free-speech preservationists showed absolutely no enhanced likelihood of supporting laws to protect gays against discrimination, the paradigmatic gay civil rights issue. Treasuring free speech went along with an 8-point enhancement of support for allowing gays into the military, but, as shown in Table 6.3, this partial correlation disappeared under multivariate controls. Thus, it appears that a classic form of general civil libertarianism showed a substantial relationship with the two gay civil liberties, as expected, but no relationship at all with one of the gay civil rights and an evanescent relationship with the other. (For the difference between the nondiscrimination law and library book opinions, $p <$ .10; for the difference between nondiscrimination law and gay professor opinions, $p < .25$.)

Humanitarianism. As explained above, humanitarianism is another attitude that should fundamentally distinguish gay civil liberties from gay civil rights positions. Unlike the NES data set, the GSS included no direct operationalization of humanitarianism. For the comparison of civil liberties and civil rights across the data sets, therefore, I used two partial indicators of humanitarianism, namely, the inclination to spend government money on aid to "the poor" and the level of support for spending on "welfare."[6]

Table 6.3 Modeling Gay Civil Rights Opinion: Stigma Versus Political Values

| | 1993 Policy Opinion Dependent Variables[a] | | | |
| | Gays in the Military | | Gay Discrimination Protection | |
Selected Independent Variables[b]	b	β	b	β
Thermometer gay-White positives	.139	.024	.214	.040
Thermometer gay-White negatives	−.502**	−.361	−.242**	−.186
Education	−.055	−.031	.143*	.087
Age	.054	.038	.184**	.137
Female	.196**	.228	.127**	.159
Partisan identification	.059**	.106	.046*	.090
Military/defense index	.387**	.152	.085	.036
Racial/ethnic superiority view	−.072	−.012	−.053	−.010
Moral relativism	.084†	.071	.069	.063
Free speech protection	.055	.047	−.033	−.031
"Big Government" power	.090*	.078	.152**	.143
Humanitarianism	.036	.018	.269**	.148
Bible fundamentalism × church attendance	−.172†	−.121	.002	.002
Bible fundamentalism × personal religiosity	−.022	−.015	−.260*	−.182
R^2		.399		.295

NOTE: N = 467 White non-Hispanic voters.
a. Scores ranged from 0 (strongly oppose) to 1 (strongly support). See the appendix to this chapter for explanations of the variables and undisplayed control variables.
b. Gay thermometer scores are from 1993. All other variables are from 1992.
†$p < .10$, two-tailed test; *$p < .05$, two-tailed test; **$p < .01$, two-tailed test.

Each indicator of humanitarianism showed a strong connection with gay civil rights opinion but either much less or no connection at all with views on gay civil liberties. With controls for sociodemographics, a person who supported more spending on aiding "the poor" favored allowing a gay-authored book in a library by a margin of 9 percentage points over someone who wanted to spend less on the poor (analysis not shown). Support was higher by the same margin in the case of employing a gay professor. For the two gay civil rights preferences, however, the difference was much greater: 17% for gays in the military and 30% for antidiscrimination laws. Similarly, preferences for "welfare" spending corresponded to a 3-point difference in support for each of the civil liberties preferences. Yet such spending desires corresponded to a 20-point difference on the two civil rights opinions (for six of the eight civil rights differences, $p < .01$).[7]

Values versus stigma. In sum, the analysis found sizable differences between gay civil liberties and gay civil rights in terms of their comparative associations with age and education, and with free speech and humanitarianism values. These findings lead to the conclusion that the public judges civil rights matters quite differently from civil liberties issues. The following analyses focus more in depth on attitudes in the area of civil rights for gays. The primary aim is to determine the importance of values compared with stigma in Americans' judgments about gay civil rights. Is stigma the predominant factor? Or is there evidence to suggest that scholars who conflate stigma and the political treatment of the stigmatized can miss the important role of abstract political values?

Table 6.3 shows the results of this investigation. Respondents did not base their civil rights attitudes solely on the stigma they associated with lesbians and gays. At least on the paradigmatic civil rights issue—laws protecting gays against discrimination—people appeared to be at least as likely to reach their policy preference in accordance with their basic, abstract political values.

The civil rights dependent variables in Table 6.3 are the same as those in Table 6.1, except that in Table 6.3 they include the full variance measured by the 1993 NES questions, ranging from strong disapproval of each policy to strong approval.[8] In addition to the sociodemographic variables that show predictive potency in Table 6.1, the independent variables here include those that operationalized both key political values and stigma. Control variables included general ethnocentrism, party identification, and religious variables.

I measured antigay stigma by the degree to which respondents gave a relatively negative feeling thermometer rating to gays and lesbians. Overall affect toward gays was divided into "gay-positive" and "gay-negative" sides—that is, two different variables. The former varied the degree to which respondents rated gays higher than Whites on the respective feeling thermometers, and the latter varied the degree to which respondents rated gays lower than Whites. I limited the analyses presented in Table 6.3 to adults who were both self-reported voters and non-Hispanic Whites. This allowed an analysis of how the majority or dominant ethnic group decided to legally treat one particular stigmatized minority group, namely, gays.[9] About 72% of the majority group rated homosexuals to some degree lower than their own ethnic group. It is this relative homonegativism that captured stigma in the analysis.

Table 6.3 compares the influence of stigma with the influence of a set of three key political values. The discussion above dealt with two of these values, the importance of free speech and humanitarianism. The analysis in Table 6.3 incorporated a more extensive measure of humanitarianism than the one I used in the comparison of civil rights with civil liberties attitudes (which was constrained by the need for item comparability across the GSS and NES data sets). Here, I used a multiple-item index based on spending preferences for six federal programs aimed at the needy (see the appendix to this chapter).

The analysis in Table 6.3 also could add a third key value that could not be used in the comparison of civil rights with civil liberties (because the GSS did not measure it in 1993 or 1994): fear of government power. Whereas intrusive governmental power is the main threat from the civil liberties perspective, civil rights requires an active state vigorously rooting out discrimination, whether public or private. The race literature has posited and tested the idea that such a fear of "Big Government" accounts for the prominent gap between people's support for racial equality in principle and their support for laws and government policies aimed at promoting racial equality in practice (Schuman et al., 1985). This suspicion has found only limited empirical support (Carmines & Merriman, 1993; Stoker, in press). In my analysis, aversion to governmental power was operationalized with the NES question "Is the government in Washington getting too powerful for the good of the country and the individual person, or is the government not getting too strong?"[10]

Table 6.3 shows that abstract civil rights values did not play much of a role in people's preferences in the military case. Opposition to allowing gays in the military came more from those who expressed a greater willingness to support the use of military force and those who wanted the United States to spend what it would take to remain the world's leading military power. The "military readiness" argument seems to have resonated with Americans independent of their feelings about gay people. Fear of government power carried some weight, at least in part, I suspect, because opponents of gays in the military argued that the proposal amounted to government-instigated social experimentation. Antigay stigma, however, seems to have played the leading role in helping people decide their positions on gays in the military.

The impression is much different, however, in the case of the paradigmatic civil rights issue, employment antidiscrimination laws. Military values did not matter for this nonmilitary policy opinion. As theory predicted, the civil libertarian goal of preserving free speech continued to be irrelevant for taking a stand on either antidiscrimination laws or gays in the military. But the civil rights values that I discussed above were the leading predictors of opinion about laws protecting gays from job discrimination. Humanitarianism and concern about governmental power together showed more influence than antigay stigma. This inference derives from a consideration of the *beta* weights for the two values taken together in comparison with the *beta* weight for antigay stigma.[11] Both civil rights values showed this influence even after the analysis took into account a respondent's partisanship, ethnocentrism, religiosity, and degree of moral relativism.[12] Concern about excessive governmental power and humanitarianism should have mattered more here than in the case of gays in the military because Americans are probably more likely to believe that antidiscrimination laws require both widespread government involvement in social life and some sacrifice of personal or social freedom.

Of course, it is possible that reverse causality produced an exaggeration of the apparent impact of humanitarianism and aversion to Big Government. Future investigations on the underpinnings of civil rights opinions might benefit from experimental manipulations that can directly address questions of causal direction. However, it seems unlikely that opinion on antidiscrimination laws exerted strong causal influences on opinion about governmental power in the abstract. Gay civil rights proposals were probably too low in salience to the national public in 1992 to affect response to the NES government power question. Charges of Big Government, on the other hand, have been a central theme in politics across the country for decades. It is much more reasonable to assume that a direct empirical connection between fear of government and antidiscrimination law arose because respondents heard "laws protecting gays against job discrimination" and thought, "There goes Big Government again," rather than the reverse. It seems even less plausible that the humanitarianism measure, based as it was on questions about government spending on the needy, was influenced by how individuals thought about gay civil rights policy. By contrast, it makes good theoretical sense that people would be more likely to want the government to protect a stigmatized group when they are also somewhat more likely to be showing humanitarianism in their willingness to sacrifice (by paying higher taxes or giving up other government spending) to provide more aid to the needy.

Discussion

In the politics of homosexuality and sexual orientation, opinions in the mass public appear to involve much more than just antigay stigma. General political values, especially humanitarianism and fear of government power, can matter just as much and maybe more so. How a gay-relevant issue is framed can also make an important difference in who is more or less likely to be a supporter or an opponent. The issue pluralism that Sniderman, Tetlock, Carmines, and Peterson (1993) found in public opinion about race policy also describes how Americans think about policies concerning the treatment of lesbians and gay men.

A fundamental instance of the importance of substantive framing is the distinction that the public makes between civil liberties and civil rights issues. Attitudes on these two matters are not part of the same continuum of opinion. It is a mistake to conflate them and suggest that people are inclined to either support or oppose "gay rights" in general, to show a broad "tolerance" or "intolerance." More than a few people will be tolerant from the perspective of civil liberties and not so tolerant from the perspective of civil rights, and vice versa. Contrary to what some public opinion scholars suggest (Sniderman et al., 1991), this variation is not necessarily an unprincipled inconsistency. Indeed, principles encourage citizens to see issues differently across the two basic domains.

The findings presented here have important implications for gay politics. What is more, the results of this investigation probably shed light on the politics of stigma in general. Because gay civil liberties and gay civil rights both continue to be controversial, they might well allow a fresh reading on how the public would react to any new civil liberties or civil rights proposals that might arise and affect a potentially wide range of stigmatized groups.

For their part, however, gay political groups seem to face more formidable odds as the primary battleground has generally shifted from civil liberties to civil rights. The findings above suggest that any increase in the public's level of "postmaterialism," with its characteristic support for personal freedom (Abramson & Inglehart, 1995), would not help advance gay civil rights in the way that it might foster gay civil liberties. In addition, because of generational replacement and aggregate educational increases, the age and education correlates of civil liberties in general have historically offered the possibility of increased support over time (Sniderman, Tetlock, & Carmines, 1993). But with much lower correlations of this sort in the case of gay civil rights, the passage of time in itself does not seem to offer the possibility of much increased support. Instead of enjoying some benefit from ongoing historical trends, a more dominant factor in the fate of gay civil rights might be a national mood that seems to approve of cutbacks in government aid to the poor and seems to accept the idea, prominently articulated by President Bill Clinton, that the era of big government is over.

Appendix: Question Wording, Variable Construction, and Control Variables for Tables

Tables 6.1-6.3
Age:
    A 6-category variable, ranging from 0 = 18-24 to 1 = 60 and older. Categories are 18-24, 25-29, 30-39, 40-49, 50-59, and 60 and older.

Table 6.1
Allow gay book in library:
    A response to the GSS question (part of a battery that also included similar questions about communists, racists, and atheists), "If some people in your community suggested that a book that a man who admits he is a homosexual wrote in favor of homosexuality should be taken out of your public library, would you favor removing this book, or not?" Possible scores are 0 (remove), 0.5 (don't know), and 1 (don't remove).

Allow gay teach in university:
    A response to the GSS question, "Should a man who admits he is a homosexual be allowed to teach in a college or university, or not?" Possible scores are 0 (don't allow), 0.5 (don't know), and 1 (allow).

Allow gay serve in military:
    Based on responses to the NES question, "Do you think homosexuals should be allowed to serve in the United States Armed Forces, or don't you think so?" Possible scores are 0 (oppose), 0.5 (don't know), and 1 (support).

Gay discrimination protection:
    Based on responses to the NES question, "Do you favor or oppose laws to protect homosexuals against job discrimination?" Possible scores are 0 (oppose), 0.5 (don't know), and 1 (support).

Education:
   Possible scores are 0 (non-high school graduate), 0.25 (high school diploma),
   0.50 (junior college degree), 0.75 (college degree), and 1 (graduate degree).

Table 6.2

Education:
   Possible scores are 0 (non-high school graduate), 0.25 (high school diploma),
   0.50 (some college, no degree), 0.75 (college degree), and 1 (postgraduate
   study).

Table 6.3

In order to minimize case loss, "don't knows" and not ascertained responses
were scored at the midpoints for the attitude questions listed below (but not for
the gay stigmatization variables or the two dependent variables). Gay-White
thermometer difference scores were omitted if respondent did not give both
groups a rating. For the dependent variables, cases where responses were not
ascertained were eliminated from the analysis.

Gays in the military:
   Same item as in Table 6.1 except that this version uses the follow-up question
   asking how strongly the respondent holds any pro or con position. Possible
   scores are 0 (oppose strongly), 0.25 (oppose, not strongly), 0.5 (don't know),
   0.75 (support, not strongly), and 1 (support strongly).

Gay discrimination protection:
   Same item as in Table 6.1 except that this version uses the follow-up question
   asking how strongly the respondent holds any pro or con position. Possible
   scores are 0 (oppose strongly), 0.25 (oppose, not strongly), 0.5 (don't know),
   0.75 (support, not strongly), and 1 (support strongly).

Thermometer gay-White positives:
   1993 feeling thermometer rating for gays minus 1992 feeling thermometer
   rating for Whites. Scores ranged from 0 (no difference or gays less favorable
   than Whites) to 1 (maximum gays more favorable than Whites).

Thermometer gay-White negatives:
   1993 feeling thermometer rating for gays minus 1992 feeling thermometer
   rating for Whites. Scores ranged from 0 (no difference or gays more favorable
   than Whites) to 1 (maximum gays less favorable than Whites).

Education:
   Possible scores are 0 (less than 8 years of education completed), 0.2 (9-11 years),
   0.4 (12 years), 0.6 (13-15 years), 0.8 (16 years), and 1 (17 or more years).

Partisan identification.
   Possible scores are 0 (Republican), 0.5 (Independent), and 1 (Democrat).

Military/defense index:
   An additive index summing responses to (a) a Likert item stating that the
   United States should stay the leading military power, regardless of the cost,
   and (b) a question asking how willing the United States should be to use force

to solve international problems. Scores ranged from 0 (maximum promilitary; "hawkish") to 1 (maximum antimilitary; "dovish").

Racial/ethnic superiority view:

An additive index composed of two parts: (a) the differences in the feeling thermometer ratings of Whites, on the one hand, and Blacks and Hispanics, on the other hand; and (b) the differences between ratings of Whites versus Blacks and Hispanics on the qualities of lazy/hardworking, violent/peaceful, and unintelligent/intelligent. Scores ranged from 0 (maximum White superiority) to 1 (maximum Black/Hispanic superiority).

Free speech protection:

Based on response to question that asked for the two top choices in response to the following: "For a nation, it is not always possible to obtain everything one might wish. On page ten of the booklet, several different goals are listed. If you had to choose among them, which one [seems most desirable to you/would be your second choice]? 1. Maintaining order in the nation; 2. Giving people more say in important political decisions; 3. Fighting rising prices; and 4. Protecting freedom of speech." Possible scores are 0 (freedom of speech not picked as either first or second priority), 0.5 (freedom of speech picked as second priority), and 1 (freedom of speech picked as top priority).

Moral relativism:

Based on responses to a Likert item stating: "The world is always changing and we should adjust our view of moral behavior to those changes." Possible scores are 0 (strongly disagree), 0.25 (disagree somewhat), 0.5 (neutral/don't know/not ascertained), 0.75 (agree somewhat), and 1 (strongly agree).

"Big Government" power:

Based on response to the question, "Is the government in Washington getting too powerful for the good of the country and the individual person, or is the government not getting too strong?" Possible scores are 0 (getting too powerful), 0.5 (it depends/don't know/not ascertained), and 1 (not getting too strong).

Humanitarianism:

An additive index composed of responses to the question, "Should federal spending be increased, decreased, or kept the same on . . . ?" asked about child care, food stamps, assistance to the unemployed, poor people, welfare, and the homeless. Scores ranged from 0 (cut spending on all) to 1 (increase spending on all).

Bible fundamentalism × church attendance:

Multiplicative interaction. The former component is belief about whether the Bible is the words of men (0), inspired by God but not literally true word for word (0.5), or the literal word of God (1). The latter variable was coded as 0 = never go to church, 0.2 = a few times a year, 0.4 = once or twice a month, 0.6 = almost weekly, 0.8 = once a week, 1 = more than once a week.

Bible fundamentalism × personal religiosity:

Multiplicative interaction. The former component is the same as in the previous interaction. The latter component is an additive index based on a response to how often respondent prays and the importance of religion in guiding the respondent's daily life. Scores ranged from 0 (never pray and not important) to 1 (pray several times daily and a great deal of importance).

Rural upbringing (not displayed in table):
Possible scores are 1 (grew up in country/small town) and 0 (all others).

Marital status (not displayed in table):
Possible scores are 1 (never married) and 0 (all others).

Have children (not displayed in table):
Possible scores are 1 (have or care for children under 18) and 0 (all others).

Notes

1. To avoid confusion between the general category conventionally called *gay rights* and one subcategory that I discuss extensively, namely, *gay civil rights*, I use somewhat awkward substitutes for gay rights, such as *gay-relevant policies*.

2. A *frame* here means "a central organizing idea or story line that provides meaning to an unfolding strip of events, weaving a connection among them. The frame suggests what the controversy is about, the essence of the issue" (Gamson & Modigliani, 1987, p. 143).

3. Those who disagree with the categorization of the gay teacher or the gays-in-the-military items will still be able to see the points I make in Table 6.1 and elsewhere by paying attention to the findings just on the paradigmatic civil liberties and civil rights issues, that is, the book-in-the-library and the antidiscrimination law, respectively.

4. The feeling thermometer in the NES is presented as follows: "I'll read the name of a [person/group] and I'd like you to rate that [person/group] using something called the feeling thermometer. You can choose any number between 0 and 100. The higher the number, the warmer or more favorable you feel toward that [person/group]; the lower the number, the colder or less favorable. You would rate the [person/group] at the 50 degree mark if you feel neither warm nor cold toward them."

5. Another statewide vote not analyzed in Table 6.2 (because no independent exit poll data are publicly available) took place in Maine in 1995. It amounted to another narrow defeat: 53% to 47%. These four states fairly well span the ideological spectrum, based on my comparison of state opinion distributions on ideological self-designation, governmental spending preferences, and opinion about abortion law. (State-level data came from the 1988-1990-1992 National Election Study's Senate Election Study.) Even in states with an opinion climate that is generally moderate to liberal—such as Oregon and Colorado—opinion on gay civil rights legislation seemed about evenly divided between supporters and opponents. Thus, the more supportive attitudes toward gay civil rights that are expressed in the survey data reported above give a false impression that such rights would get the endorsement of a sizable majority in an actual political conflict.

6. Some readers might be unwilling to believe that these spending measures could have helped differentiate respondents with respect to their level of humanitarianism. Instead, they might have just measured the level of welfare state liberalism. But even if that were true, the variable could still have served to show how attitudes on gay civil liberties were substantially different from attitudes on gay civil rights: If the test succeeds, the latter

was connected in people's minds with welfare state liberalism, the former was not. That would be a fundamental difference. Yet I think there is good reason to think that for the average respondent, the spending measures I used here partially capture the broader value of humanitarianism. Getting a valid measure of humanitarianism is likely to be problematic. But in the 1994-1995 NES data set (Rosenstone, Kinder, Miller, & the National Election Studies, 1995; Rosenstone, Miller, Kinder, and the National Election Studies, 1995), a 2-item index composed of the preferences for governmental aid used here (spending on "the poor" and "welfare") covaried ($r = .22$) with one seemingly key measure of humanitarianism that NES added that year, namely, agreement or disagreement with the statement, "One should always find ways to help others less fortunate than oneself."

7. Results remained approximately the same when the analyses were replicated on the 1996 NES and GSS data sets.

8. In Table 6.1 they were dichotomized as *disapprove* versus *approve*, in order to match the values of the GSS civil liberties measures there as well as the "yes-no" votes in Table 6.2.

9. I use a relative measure here for two reasons. First, I do not believe that aversion to gays is limited to those who rate gays in what is defined by the NES survey interviewer as the unfavorable part of the scale, the range below 50. This is based on the fact that only 8% of non-Hispanic White adults in the United States will rate Blacks in this zone, together with my strong suspicion that substantially more than 8% of American non-Hispanic Whites attach at least some stigma to Blacks as a group. A rating relative to that given one's own racial group would seem more appropriately sensitive to any actual stigmatization. Second, stigmatization is usually thought to mean "disvaluing" others (Stafford & Scott, 1986, p. 79), and a relative measure indicates that a group is rated as inferior to one's "own people."

10. Unfortunately, the 1996 GSS data set was released too late for me to include full analysis of it in this chapter. The wording of the "Big Government" question that appeared in the 1996 GSS was somewhat different from the one NES used in 1992. The GSS asked, "And what about the federal government, does it have too much or too little power?" ("About the right amount of power" was volunteered by many respondents.) Still, it now seems possible for me to perform at least a rough test of how well a fear of "Big Government" predicted opinion on gay civil liberties in comparison with gay civil rights. The results strongly support the theoretical expectations. When sociodemographics are controlled for, voters who thought that the federal government had too much power essentially did not differ in their civil liberties opinions from those who saw no excess of governmental power. (The differences in both cases—the gay-authored book and the gay professor—were less than 4%, and neither showed statistical significance.) In the case of gay civil rights, however (using NES 1992-1993), concern about "Big Government" showed a sizable relationship with both opinions. Those who saw too much government power were more likely to oppose allowing gays into the military by a margin of 17 percentage points over those who did not see too much government power. Voters fearing "Big Government" were more likely to oppose nondiscrimination laws by a 21% margin. (All civil liberties versus civil rights differences reached statistical significance, $p < .05$.)

11. Results with respect to government power hold up even if one uses the other measures of attitude toward government that appeared in the 1992 NES survey, but that seemed to me on their face less likely to measure a generalized fear of government's threat to individual freedom. For example, a 4-item index that includes the measure I use here plus the 3-item battery on the role and size of government (variables 5730, 5731, and 5732) showed essentially the same direct relationship with nondiscrimination law opinion as did the single-item measure that I used for the analysis presented in Table 6.3.

12. For a discussion of the role of moral relativism and moral objectivism in public opinion, see Stoker (1997).

References

Abramson, P. R., & Inglehart, R. (1995). *Value change in global perspective*. Ann Arbor: University of Michigan Press.

Bobo, L., & Licari, F. C. (1989). Education and political tolerance: Testing the effects of cognitive sophistication and target group affect. *Public Opinion Quarterly, 53,* 285-308.

Carmines, E. G., & Merriman, W. R. (1993). The changing American dilemma: Liberal values and racial policies. In P. M. Sniderman, P. E. Tetlock, & E. G. Carmines (Eds.), *Prejudice, politics, and the American dilemma* (pp. 237-255). Stanford, CA: Stanford University Press.

Chong, D. (1994). Tolerance and social adjustment to new norms and practices. *Political Behavior, 16,* 21-53.

Converse, P. E. (1964). The nature of belief systems in the mass public. In D. E. Apter (Ed.), *Ideology and discontent* (pp. 206-261). New York: Free Press.

Davis, J. A., & Smith, T. W. (1997). *General Social Surveys, 1972-1996* [Machine-readable data file]. Chicago: National Opinion Research Center [Producer]. Storrs, CT: University of Connecticut, Roper Center for Public Opinion Research [Distributor].

Dowden, S., & Robinson, J. P. (1993). Age and cohort differences in American racial attitudes: The generational replacement hypothesis revisited. In P. M. Sniderman, P. E. Tetlock, & E. G. Carmines (Eds.), *Prejudice, politics, and the American dilemma* (pp. 86-104). Stanford, CA: Stanford University Press.

Gamson, W. A., & Modigliani, A. (1987). The changing culture of affirmative action. *Research in Political Sociology, 3,* 137-177. Greenwich, CT: JAI.

Gibson, J. L., & Duch, R. M. (1993). Political intolerance in the USSR: The distribution and etiology of mass opinion. *Comparative Political Studies, 26,* 286-329.

Gibson, J. L., & Tedin, K. L. (1988). The etiology of intolerance of homosexual politics. *Social Science Quarterly, 69,* 587-604.

Grey, T. C., Jr. (1991). Civil rights versus civil liberties: The case of discriminatory verbal harassment. In E. F. Paul, F. D. Miller, Jr., & J. Paul (Eds.), *Reassessing civil rights* (pp. 81-108). Cambridge, MA: Basil Blackwell.

Herek, G. M. (1991). Stigma, prejudice, and violence against lesbians and gay men. In J. C. Gonsiorek & J. D. Weinrich (Eds.), *Homosexuality: Research implications for public policy* (pp. 60-80). Newbury Park, CA: Sage.

Jackman, M. R., & Muha, M. J. (1984). Education and intergroup attitudes: Moral enlightenment, superficial democratic commitment, or ideological refinement? *American Sociological Review, 49,* 751-769.

Jennings, M. K., & Niemi, R. G. (1981). *Generations and politics: A panel study of young adults and their parents*. Princeton, NJ: Princeton University Press.

Marcus, G. E., Sullivan, J., Theiss-Morse, E., & Wood, S. L. (1995). *With malice toward some: How people make civil liberties judgments*. New York: Cambridge University Press.

McClosky, H., & Brill, A. (1983). *Dimensions of tolerance: What Americans believe about civil liberties*. New York: Russell Sage.

Miller, W. E., Kinder, D. R., Rosenstone, S., & the National Election Studies. (1993). *American National Election Study, 1992: Pre- and Post-Election Survey* [enhanced with 1990 and

1991 data] [Computer file]. Ann Arbor: University of Michigan, Center for Political Studies, and Inter-university Consortium for Political and Social Research [Producers]. Ann Arbor: Inter-university Consortium for Political and Social Research [Distributor].

Nelson, T. E., & Kinder, D. R. (1996). Issue frames and group-centrism in American public opinion. *Journal of Politics, 58,* 1055-1078.

Ness, C. (1992, October 1). Oregon battleground for anti-gay measure. *San Francisco Examiner,* pp. A1, A19.

Nunn, C. Z., Crockett, H. J., Jr., & Williams, J. A., Jr. (1978). *Tolerance for nonconformity.* San Francisco: Jossey-Bass.

Rosenstone, S., Kinder, D. R., Miller, W. E., & the National Election Studies. (1994). *American National Election Study: 1992-1993 Panel Study on Securing Electoral Success/1993 Pilot Study* [Computer file]. Ann Arbor: University of Michigan, Center for Political Studies [Producer]. Ann Arbor: Inter-university Consortium for Political and Social Research [Distributor].

Rosenstone, S., Kinder, D. R., Miller, W. E., & the National Election Studies. (1995). *American National Election Study, 1994: Post-election survey* [enhanced with 1992 and 1993 data] [Computer file]. Ann Arbor: University of Michigan, Center for Political Studies, and Inter-university Consortium for Political and Social Research [Producers]. Ann Arbor: Inter-university Consortium for Political and Social Research [Distributor].

Rosenstone, S., Kinder, D. R., Miller, W. E., & the National Election Studies. (1997). *American national election study, 1996: Pre- and post-election survey* [Computer file]. Ann Arbor: University of Michigan, Center for Political Studies [Producer]. Ann Arbor: Inter-university Consortium for Political and Social Research [Distributor].

Rosenstone, S., Miller, W. E., Kinder, D. R., & the National Election Studies. (1995). *American National Election Study: 1995 pilot study* [Computer file]. Ann Arbor: University of Michigan, Center for Political Studies [Producer]. Ann Arbor: Inter-university Consortium for Political and Social Research [Distributor].

Runciman, W. (1966). *Relative deprivation and social justice.* London: Routledge & Kegan Paul.

Sandel, M. J. (1989). Moral argument and liberal toleration: Abortion and homosexuality. *California Law Review, 77,* 521-538.

Schacter, J. S. (1994). The gay civil rights debate in the states: Decoding the discourse of equivalents. *Harvard Civil Rights-Civil Liberties Law Review, 29,* 283-317.

Schuman, H., Steeh, C., & Bobo, L. (1985). *Racial attitudes in America: Trends and interpretations.* Cambridge, MA: Harvard University Press.

Sears, D. O. (1993). Symbolic politics: A socio-psychological theory. In S. Iyengar & W. J. McGuire (Eds.), *Explorations in political psychology* (pp. 113-149). Durham, NC: Duke University Press.

Sears, D. O., & Citrin, J. (1985). *Tax revolt: Something for nothing in California.* Cambridge, MA: Harvard University Press.

Sniderman, P. M., & Piazza, T. (1993). *The scar of race.* Cambridge, MA: Belknap.

Sniderman, P. M., Tetlock, P. E., & Carmines, E. G. (1993). Prejudice and politics: An introduction. In P. M. Sniderman, P. E. Tetlock, & E. G. Carmines (Eds.), *Prejudice, politics, and the American dilemma* (pp. 1-31). Stanford, CA: Stanford University Press.

Sniderman, P. M., Tetlock, P. E., Carmines, E. G., & Peterson, R. S. (1993). The politics of the American dilemma: Issue pluralism. In P. M. Sniderman, P. E. Tetlock, & E. G. Carmines (Eds.), *Prejudice, politics, and the American dilemma* (pp. 212-236). Stanford, CA: Stanford University Press.

Sniderman, P. M., Tetlock, P. E., Glaser, J., Green, D., & Hout, M. (1991). Democratic values and mass publics. In P. M. Sniderman, R. A. Brody, & P. E. Tetlock (Eds.), *Reasoning and choice: Explorations in political psychology* (pp. 120-149). New York: Cambridge University Press.

Stafford, M. C., & Scott, R. R. (1986). Stigma, deviance, and social control: Some conceptual issues. In S. C. Ainlay, G. Becker, & L. M. Coleman (Eds.), *The dilemma of difference: A multidisciplinary view of stigma* (pp. 77-91). New York: Plenum.

Steenbergen, M. (1996). *Compassion and American public opinion: An analysis of the NES humanitarianism scale.* Ann Arbor: University of Michigan, Center for Political Studies.

Stoker, L. (1997). *The moral basis of political choice.* Unpublished manuscript.

Stoker, L. (in press). Understanding White resistance to affirmative action: The role of principled commitments and racial prejudice. In J. Hurwitz & M. Peffley (Eds.), *Perception and prejudice: Race and politics in the United States.* New Haven, CT: Yale University Press.

Sullivan, J. L., Pierson, J., & Marcus, G. E. (1982). *Political tolerance and American democracy.* Chicago: University of Chicago Press.

Sullivan, J. L., Shamir, M., Walsh, P., & Roberts, N. S. (1985). *Political tolerance in context: Support for unpopular minorities in Israel, New Zealand and the United States.* Boulder, CO: Westview.

Voter News Service. (1995). *Voter research and surveys general election polls, 1994* [Computer file]. New York: Author [Producer]. Ann Arbor, MI: Inter-university Consortium for Political and Social Research [Distributor].

Voter Research and Surveys. (1993). *Voter research and surveys general election polls, 1992* [Computer file]. New York: Author [Producer]. Ann Arbor, MI: Inter-university Consortium for Political and Social Research [Distributor].

7

Minority Stress Among Lesbians, Gay Men, and Bisexuals

A Consequence of Heterosexism, Homophobia, and Stigmatization

JOANNE DiPLACIDO

L esbians, gay men, and bisexuals face much discrimination, stigmatization, and violence. They must deal with enormous amounts
of stress as a result of living in a heterosexist and homophobic society.
Moreover, often they are tolerated by society only when they remain
"closeted." Lesbians, gay men, and bisexuals represent a sexual
minority, and like other minorities, they are often treated by the
majority with much disdain and discrimination. Yet, unlike most other
minority groups, they are often not recognized as a legitimate minority
group deserving of constitutional protections against discrimination.

In this chapter, I focus on the *minority stress* experienced by sexual
minorities. I present a review of the existing literature on stress among
lesbians, gay men, and bisexuals, and then offer a new conceptualization
for studying stress among sexual minorities that draws from research on

AUTHOR'S NOTE: This research was supported in part by a National Research Service
Award in Health Psychology from the National Institute of Mental Health
(08F2MH11153A) and by grants from the Lesbian Health Fund of the Gay and Lesbian
Medical Association and the Wayne F. Placek Fund of the American Psychological
Foundation.

external and internal stressors in other populations. I begin with a discussion of traditional stress research, then focus on stress among sexual minorities, with an emphasis on possible psychological and physical health consequences resulting from experiences of heterosexism, homophobia, racism, and sexism. I then report on the results of a pilot study among lesbian and bisexual women that suggest a link between minority stress and well-being.

Minority Stress

Sexual minorities experience stress as a result of stigmatization. Virginia Brooks (1981), in her study of stress among lesbians, has explained lesbian stress as a type of "minority stress":

> The initial cause of minority stress is the cultural ascription of inferior status to particular groups. This ascription of defectiveness to various categories of people, particularly categories based on sex, race, and sociosexual preference, often precipitates negative life events for the minority member over which the individual has little control. (p. 71)

Brooks has argued that lesbians, due to their double minority status (as both women and lesbians), experience proportionally more negative life events as a result of living in a sexist, homophobic, and heterosexist society.

Minority stress could potentially lead to negative health outcomes among some members of sexual minorities, however, not all members of sexual minorities experience negative health consequences as a result of their minority status. Many lesbians, for example, have been found to live extremely happy, healthy, and productive lives (Bradford, Ryan, & Rothblum, 1994). Moreover, lesbians and gays on average do not differ from heterosexuals in psychological adjustment (Gonsiorek, 1991). In fact, there may be times when there are advantages to a same-sex orientation or identity (Garnets & Kimmel, 1993). It is clear, therefore, that many people learn to cope successfully with minority stress, whereas others have more difficulty. Determining which factors are related to *both* positive and negative health outcomes could provide future directions for therapeutic interventions with lesbians, gay men, and bisexuals who are having difficulty dealing with their minority status.

Stress and Health Outcomes

Life Events and Daily Hassles

Before focusing specifically on stress experienced by lesbians, gay men, and bisexuals, I want to discuss what we have learned from traditional stress research. Research with other populations has typically operationalized stress in two ways. One approach has been to assess the number of major life events (e.g., using Holmes & Rahe's, 1967, life events checklist), with more life events assumed to indicate greater stress on the individual. More recent work has focused specifically on negative life events, with a greater number of negative life events considered to be indicative of greater stress. Links have been found between negative life events and depression (Benjamin, 1981; Brown, Ahmed, Gary, & Milburn, 1995; Lu, 1995), premenstrual symptoms (Mitchell, Woods, & Lentz, 1994), headache pain (Kowal & Pritchard, 1990), coronary heart disease (Hinkle, 1974), cancer (Jacobs & Charles, 1980), and other physical and psychological symptoms (Cui & Vaillant, 1996; Dohrenwend & Dohrenwend, 1978).

The measurement of daily hassles represents the second common conceptualization of stress (DeLongis, Coyne, Dakof, Folkman, & Lazarus, 1982). The cumulative effects of small negative daily events, or hassles, are assumed to lead to greater stress. Daily hassles have been found to have a stronger relationship with psychological and somatic health (Banks & Gannon, 1988; Chan & Lee, 1992; Landreville & Vezina, 1992; Ruffin, 1993), chronic headaches (deBenedittis & Lorenzetti, 1992), schizophrenic symptomatology (Malla & Norman, 1992), and negative mood (Wolf, Elston, & Kissling, 1989) than has the experience of major life events.

Referring back to Brooks's (1981) assertion that minority status leads to more negative life events for the minority member, we can see how the life events and daily hassles approaches can be applied to a study of the stress experienced by lesbians, gay men, and bisexuals. In the context of their sexual minority status, lesbians, gay men, and bisexuals experience homophobia and stigmatization, which put them at risk for experiencing negative life events, especially gay-relevant events (e.g., loss of employment, home, custody of children; antigay violence and discrimination due to their sexual orientation), as well as more chronic daily hassles (e.g., hearing antigay jokes, always being on guard). Badgett (1995), for example, found that both gay and bisexual male and female workers earn less than their same-sex counterparts, indicating a possible role of sexual orientation discrimination in their lower wages.

Lesbians and bisexual women, because of their minority status as women, also experience sex discrimination that can lead to stressors (e.g., pay unequal to that of men, lower-status jobs, restricted opportunities). These greater numbers of stressors may lead to greater distress (e.g., depression). Racial and ethnic minority lesbians, gay men, and bisexuals also have a multiple minority status. The limited research that has examined racial and ethnic minority gays and lesbians suggests that stress may be even greater for these minority groups (e.g., Chan, 1989; Espin, 1987; Greene, 1994; Icard, 1986; Loiacano, 1989). The combined effects of racism, heterosexism, and sexism may create intense stressors for racial and ethnic sexual minorities (Greene, 1994).

Research on Minority Stress
Among Lesbians, Gay Men, and Bisexuals

Most of the research on the impact of stress on health among sexual minorities has focused on either gay men and HIV infection or sexual minority youth. Very little work has focused on the relationship between stress and well-being among lesbian and bisexual women.

Gay Men

Meyer (1995), in a study of minority stress among gay men, found discrimination and experiences of negative treatment in society to be related to greater mental health problems (see also Meyer & Dean, Chapter 8, this volume). Similarly, Ross (1990) found life events related to stigmatization to be related to emotional distress among gay men. These two studies represent the only research on gay-related stressors and well-being among gay men that has not focused on HIV infection.

Research has found evidence for a link between HIV stressors and health outcomes. Negative events have been found to be related to greater distress among asymptomatic HIV-positive gay men (Blaney et al., 1991). Nott and Vedhara (1995), using a measure of stressful life events for HIV-positive gay men, found positive associations between HIV-related stressors and emotional distress. In another study, perceived stress in several domains was reported to be associated with depressive mood a year later among HIV-positive and HIV-negative gay men (Folkman, Chesney, Pollack, & Coates, 1993). Moreover, Martin, Dean, Garcia, and Hall (1989) found that stress resulting from AIDS-related bereavement and having HIV-positive status were related to increased drug use and psychological distress among gay men. In terms of physical health, Antoni, LaPierriere, Schneiderman, and Fletcher (1991) found a link between stress and immunity in both HIV-negative and HIV-positive gay men.

Lesbian, Gay, and Bisexual Youth

For many lesbians, gay men, and bisexuals, the coming-out process is very stressful. Because many first experience questions about their sexual orientation during their identity struggles in adolescence, often compounded by feelings of isolation, sexual minority youth may be the most vulnerable to gay-related stressors. Because of this vulnerability, risk behaviors have been most often examined in regard to the negative effects of stress among sexual minority youth.

One study found that gay-related stressors were significantly more common among adolescent gay and bisexual males who had attempted suicide compared with those who had not (Rotheram-Borus, Hunter, & Rosario, 1994). Moreover, coping with high levels of stress has been related to high-risk sexual behavior among gay and bisexual youth (Folkman, Chesney, Pollack, & Phillips, 1992; Rotheram-Borus, Reid, Rosario, & Kasen, 1995) and to delinquent behaviors among Black and Hispanic gay and bisexual youth (Rotheram-Borus, Rosario, Van-Rossem, Reid, & Gillis, 1995). Verbal and physical abuse as stressors have been associated with school problems, substance abuse, running away, prostitution, and suicide among lesbian, gay, and bisexual youth (Savin-Williams, 1994). All of these risk behaviors may potentially compromise the physical and psychological health of sexual minority youth (see also D'Augelli, Chapter 9, this volume).

The generalizability of these findings is limited, however, because all of the research conducted to date on stressors among gay, lesbian, and bisexual youth has included only youth from clinical populations and those recruited from shelters, clinics, and other organizations serving problem and runaway youth. We do not know how nontroubled youth deal with these same stressors. Many gay, lesbian, and bisexual young people may be coping effectively with such stressors.

Lesbian and Bisexual Women

Unlike research on stress among gay men and sexual minority youth, empirical research on stress and health among lesbians and bisexual women has been virtually nonexistent. Most of the research on lesbian health has focused on lesbian health care, including access and satisfaction with medical care (for good reviews of the lesbian health care literature, see Banks & Gartrell, 1996; Rankow, 1995). In general, because of heterosexism and homophobia on the part of medical care providers, lesbians have been found to be less likely than heterosexual women to seek routine medical care, and are often afraid to disclose their sexual orientation to health providers. Little attention, however, has been paid directly to studying health in lesbians' lives and, in particular, to exploring the psychosocial factors (e.g., stressors) related to health.

Although stress among lesbians is described in the literature, most articles have been descriptive in nature. This anecdotal evidence has important heuristic value and represents an important first step in the investigation of the effects of lesbian stress. However, we know very little about the stressors that lesbians and bisexual women experience. As Riddle and Sang (1978) have noted, the handling of stress has been one of the most overlooked aspects of lesbian identity. Stress among lesbian families is one area that has received some attention (Levy, 1992; Lott-Whitehead & Tully, 1993; Pagelow, 1980; Slater & Mencher, 1991). In general, research on lesbian families has found support for the important role of social networks in buffering the negative effects of stress. All of these studies, however, have been qualitative in nature and have been unable to test systematically the possible connections between stress and well-being.

Because stress has not been measured directly among lesbian and bisexual women, focusing on negative health behaviors may allow us to explore indirectly the role of stress on health outcomes. Radecic (1993) reviewed four large-scale descriptive surveys (the Los Angeles Lesbian Health Needs Assessment, the National Lesbian Health Care Survey, the Iowa Survey on Bisexual Women and Lesbians, and the Michigan Lesbian Health Survey) and concluded that lesbians and bisexual women engage in a number of negative health behaviors that put them at risk for developing certain illnesses, including cancer and heart disease. Cigarette smoking, heavy alcohol consumption, and being overweight were present at fairly high rates among the women in these surveys.

Similarly, other researchers have found evidence among lesbians and bisexual women for high rates of smoking (Biddle, 1993), excessive weight (Biddle, 1993; Brand, Rothblum, & Solomon, 1992), higher rates of moderate drinking (McKirnan & Peterson, 1989), intravenous drug use (Cohen, Hauer, & Wofsky, 1989), sharing needles (Lemp et al., 1993; Young, Weissman, & Cohen, 1992), and high-risk sexual practices with women (Stuntzner-Gibson, 1991) and with gay and bisexual men (Kinsey, 1987, cited in Young et al., 1992).

Although it is not yet known whether the above-mentioned health behaviors are more prevalent among lesbian and bisexual women compared with heterosexual women, it appears from preliminary research that these negative health behaviors show up enough to cause concern, and therefore warrant further research. Some lesbian and bisexual women may be coping with stressors resulting from their multiple minority status in maladaptive and unhealthy ways.

Stress-Buffering Factors

As I mentioned earlier, many lesbians, gay men, and bisexuals deal successfully with minority stress, so that it does not lead to negative health outcomes. If one is trying to predict health outcomes, then, it is important to examine what moderating variables buffer the negative health consequences resulting from minority stress.

A great deal of research evidence suggests that social support and certain personality characteristics moderate the effects of stress. Researchers have found, for example, that individuals who experienced high levels of stress but received adequate social support and plenty of resources were less likely to get sick than were individuals who experienced high levels of stress but did not receive adequate social support (Cohen & Hoberman, 1983; Cohen & Wills, 1985). In terms of personal dispositions, the personality construct of *hardiness* has received a great deal of attention. Hardiness is the ability to face new situations with feelings of challenge, control, and commitment. In one study, individuals who scored high on hardiness were less likely to become ill under high levels of stress (Kobasa, 1979). In a study that examined both social support and dispositional factors, DeLongis, Folkman, and Lazarus (1988) found that respondents who had nonsupportive relationships *and* low self-esteem were more likely to experience increases in psychosomatic and psychological problems after stressful days than were individuals high in self-esteem and social support.

Social support among lesbians, gay men, and bisexuals. Social support from family members, from relationship partners, and from the lesbian, gay, and bisexual community can help to fend off the negative consequences of stress resulting from stigmatization, homophobia, and heterosexism. To date, except for one study that found family support to buffer the negative effects of victimization among lesbian, gay, and bisexual youths (Hershberger & D'Augelli, 1995), the only quantitative studies that have examined social support as a stress buffer among sexual minorities have focused on HIV infection and coping with AIDS. These studies have found social support to play a moderating role (e.g., Hays, Turner, & Coates, 1992; Nott, Vedhara, & Powers, 1995; Turner, Hays, & Coates, 1993). As mentioned earlier, two qualitative studies have found social support to buffer stress among lesbian mothers (Levy, 1992; Lott-Whitehead & Tully, 1993).

For many lesbians, gay men, and bisexuals, the major or sole source of social support is the lesbian, gay, and bisexual community. The community can offer emotional support (e.g., group meetings, social events) as well as information about practical daily living issues, such as what an individual's rights are as a gay person, what neighborhoods are safe to live in as an openly gay person, and what medical services are available to members of the gay community.

Relationships with family members (e.g., parents, siblings) may also be pivotal. Upon disclosure of a family member's sexual orientation, there is often upheaval, and usually negative reactions, from family members (Strommen, 1993). In extreme cases, some lesbians and gay men are disowned by disapproving parents and other family members (Muller, 1987). Others, however, after a period of family mourning, eventually gain acceptance, support, and love from family members, which can help them to deal with stress resulting from their minority status. A poor familial relationship, on the other hand, can lead to greater stress and contribute to inadequate coping for the gay family member.

Relationships with significant others may also be important in buffering the negative effects of stress. For both homosexuals and heterosexuals, relationship status has been linked to well-being (Kurdek, 1994). Compared with individuals not in relationships, homosexual persons in relationships report greater well-being (Bell & Weinberg, 1978). Moreover, relationship breakups among homosexual couples have been perceived by these couples as one of their most stressful life events (Kurdek, 1991). For a lesbian, gay, or bisexual in a primary relationship, the status of that relationship is bound to affect how she or he handles stress. If an individual's relationship is going well—giving support, love, security, and happiness—it will probably help her or him to deal with the stress that results from stigmatization, homophobia, and heterosexism. However, if the relationship is fraught with problems, this in and of itself may become a source of stress, leading to inadequate coping and poorer health outcomes.

Personal resources. In spite of the enormous stressors that lesbians, gay men, and bisexuals must endure, many are living very productive and fulfilling lives. For these individuals, personal strength in the face of adversity may be more characteristic of their personalities than is the case for those who do not fare as well under the same situations. O'Leary and Ickovics (1995), for example, have proposed the need for a major paradigm shift in women's research to focus on resilience, "women's strengths and their ability to thrive in the face of adversity" (p. 121).

Qualitative studies have indicated that the experience of infection among some HIV-positive gay men can be a catalyst for growth, a new appreciation of life (Schwartzberg, 1994), and positive shifts of meaning of their HIV status (Schaefer & Coleman, 1992; Schwartzberg, 1993). Moreover, these men felt that they had the power and control "to shape the meaning of their own HIV infection" (Schwartzberg, 1994, p. 599).

Litzenberger's (1994) two case studies of lesbian priests have come closest to examining resilience or *inner strength* among lesbians. Facing stereotypes about being gay, female, and priests, "these women have challenged and been challenged by these stereotypes" (p. 275). An important component of their inner strength has come from their ability to see the importance of growth, and how the challenges of living in a hostile society can enable personal growth.

Given the obstacles put forth by a homophobic, heterosexist, sexist, and racist society, lesbians, gay men, and bisexuals must draw on whatever personal resources they have to help them overcome these difficulties. Being resilient, staying challenged, and having feelings of control despite their minority status can possibly help individuals to cope and even thrive under stressful circumstances, leading to better emotional and physical health.

Future Directions

Thus far, I have emphasized how an individual's social status can lead to what I refer to as *external stressors*, such as negative events and daily hassles. These stressors originate in the social environment. The picture is incomplete, however, without the inclusion of a more psychological perspective. In order to understand how stress may be related to health outcomes among lesbians, gay men, and bisexuals, we must also focus on internal processes—that is, stressors from within the individual.

Internalized Homophobia

Cultural stereotypes can become very hazardous when internalized (McLean & Link, 1994). In these instances, social conditions can lead to what I refer to as *internal stressors*. These stressors, manifested within the individual, often represent more chronic strains, such as the internalization of negative attitudes toward lesbians, gay men, and bisexuals.

Individuals internalize idealized values learned from their society and culture; when these idealized values fail to match reality, internal conflict can ensue (Pearlin, 1993). Internalized homophobia presents a major roadblock to well-being for many lesbians, gay men, and bisexuals. From the time American children are very young, they are socialized with the antihomosexual biases that are sanctioned by Western culture (Gonsiorek, 1993). Upon realizing that they are different from the social norms and are negatively regarded by society, lesbians, gay men, and bisexuals incorporate these negative feelings into their self-image, which results in internalized homophobia. Internalized homophobia can range from self-doubt to overt self-hatred (Gonsiorek, 1993). These negative attitudes and feelings toward homosexuality in oneself and in others have been found to be related to depression (Meyer, 1995; Shidlo, 1994), alcoholism (Finnegan & Cook, 1984) and other substance abuse (Glaus, 1988), eating disorders (Brown, 1986), and suicide (Rofes, 1983).

Self-Concealment and Emotional Inhibition

A major limitation of traditional stress research has been the sole focus on external life events and daily hassles as stressors. To understand the relationship between stress and health outcomes among sexual minorities, we need a new conceptualization of stress, one that takes into consideration the hidden nature of sexual orientation. Research outside the traditional stress literature has shown how the constructs of self-concealment and emotional inhibition can be conceptualized as important internal stressors for many sexual minorities.

Operationalizing stress as life events and daily hassles may be particularly relevant to sexual minorities who are out of the closet. Because others know their sexual orientation, their stigma is more visible. Being out puts them at risk of experiencing a greater number of negative life events, such as discrimination, rejection (Bradford et al., 1994), and violence (D'Augelli, 1989; Duncan, 1990; Garnets, Herek, & Levy, 1992; Herek, 1991; Savin-Williams, 1994). Moreover, verbal abuse and physical abuse, significant stressors for gays and lesbians, have been found to affect psychological health and adjustment (Garnets et al., 1992; Savin-Williams, 1994).

But what about lesbians, gay men, and bisexuals who are not out, or who are out only in some aspects of their lives? Their stigma is more invisible. They may experience fewer negative life events because people do not know their sexual orientation. But do they experience less stress? Probably not. Operationalizing stress solely as coming from external sources (i.e., life events) is of limited value in this case. Other possible sources of stress, particularly internal sources of stress manifested in aspects of the person, may be more relevant for sexual minorities who are less out.

Jourard (1971) theorized that self-disclosure of one's true self leads to better psychological *and* physical health. Pennebaker, in a number of studies, has found that emotional inhibition (the suppression of feelings and thoughts) is related to reports of physical symptoms (Pennebaker, Kiecolt-Glaser, & Glaser, 1988), visits to the doctor (Pennebaker & O'Heeron, 1984), and specific physiological responses (Pennebaker & Chew, 1985). Larson and Chastain (1990) similarly have found self-concealment (the keeping of secrets) to be related to increased physical and psychological symptoms. These findings suggest that actively holding back the expression of feelings and thoughts requires physiological work. Cumulative inhibition of thoughts and feelings produces wear and tear on the body and reduces resistance to disease.

The inhibition of feelings and thoughts is a very important stressor among lesbians, gay men, and bisexuals. Many live their daily lives in the closet, or at least constantly monitor situations to determine whether or not they can be open about their sexual orientation. Unlike members of racial and ethnic minorities and those who are physically disabled, lesbians, gay men, and bisexuals possess a stigma that is usually not visible until they choose to reveal it. Internalized and societal homophobias lead to what Gonsiorek (1988) calls a *cost-benefit* analysis for each situation in which a lesbian or gay man considers coming out. Choosing to negotiate two different worlds (gay and heterosexual) adds potential stress. Therefore, lesbians, gay men, and bisexuals must constantly decide whether or not to tell, whom to tell, and when to tell.

Social situations can be a constant challenge and struggle for those who feel the need to hide their identities. In one study, lesbian mothers emphasized the importance of *passing* in order to avoid being fired from their jobs, being evicted from their homes, or having problems with child custody (Pagelow, 1980). For many, deception can become a way of life for which they may pay a high price, both physically and psychologically. Research has indicated that there are psychological benefits to coming out and not hiding one's identity (for a review, see Garnets & Kimmel, 1993).

Moreover, many must constantly monitor their emotional responses in order not to reveal their true feelings. Members of sexual minorities often must be careful not to demonstrate too much affection toward their same-sex lovers in public (Gartrell, 1981). In cases where lesbians, gay men, and bisexuals are not closeted, they still may hold back public displays of affection toward their lovers out of fear for their safety. Heterosexuals do not have to deal with the stress of self-concealment and emotional inhibition in the same way. They are usually free to express their feelings toward their lovers or spouses openly, whether by holding hands, hugging, kissing, verbally expressing love for one another, or gazing lovingly at each other.

Lesbian physical educators (Woods & Harbeck, 1992) and lesbians in corporate occupations (Hall, 1986) have reported anecdotally on the costs resulting from chronic daily self-concealment and emotional inhibition. In order not to lose their jobs, these women engaged in identity management strategies to hide their lesbianism, such as passing as heterosexual, and distanced themselves from others. Keeping a distance from others entailed maintaining an image of being stern, businesslike, efficient, and task oriented, regardless of the individuals' true personalities. For lesbians in corporate occupations, this necessary distance often jeopardized their future advancement (Hall, 1986). They all paid a high price for their self-distancing behavior; many felt misunderstood, isolated, and dishonest. Personally and professionally, they paid a toll in emotional energy, self-esteem, self-hatred, frustration, nonacceptance of their lesbianism, fear, and isolation.

From these qualitative interview data, it appears that internal stressors such as emotional inhibition and self-concealment can be linked to psychological health. In the studies cited here, self-concealment and emotional inhibition were described as precursors to feelings of self-hatred, fear, isolation, and nonacceptance of one's sexual orientation (Hall, 1986; Woods & Harbeck, 1992). It is essential, however, that researchers studying stress find better ways to define and operationalize these stress variables, and test empirically with more quantitative methods the possible relationships between these stressors and well-being.

Proposed Research Questions

Lesbians, gay men, and bisexuals have ample reasons to hide their sexual orientation. Many feel that they are at major risk of losing their jobs, homes, families, friends, children, safety, and economic security if their sexual orientation is disclosed. These are all very realistic fears. Some choose to take the risk and come out to others, thus reducing the stress of self-concealment but increasing potential stress from negative life events. Closeted individuals, on the other hand, are forced to lead double lives, constantly denying who they really are and whom they really love. This way of living contributes to their experiencing more internal stressors (e.g., self-concealment, emotional inhibition).

In trying to understand the roles of internal and external stressors, I propose three important questions:

1. Do lesbians, gay men, and bisexuals who are more closeted (and are likely to experience more internal stressors) have better or worse psychological and physical health than those who are more out of the closet (and probably experience more external stressors)?
2. Do lesbians, gay men, and bisexuals who are more closeted cope with minority stress in ways that are different from those who are more out (e.g., do they engage in different health behaviors)?
3. Are there social and personality influences that buffer the negative effects of minority stress on health outcomes?

Lesbian and Bisexual Women Stress Project

I am exploring these three questions in my current research, the Lesbian and Bisexual Women Stress Project. I am empirically measuring external stressors (general and gay-related life events and daily hassles), internal stressors (self-concealment, emotional inhibition, internalized homophobia), social and personality moderating variables (hardiness, locus of control, social support, relationship satisfaction), health behaviors, and physical and psychological health outcomes.

Pilot Study on Stress and Well-Being

In the project's first phase, a pilot study was conducted with 17 lesbian and bisexual women who were recruited through professional and personal contacts. Respondents completed questionnaires measuring various stressors and health outcomes. Although this sample is very homogeneous, small, and not at all representative of all lesbian and bisexual women, a number of findings offer support to the notion that internal stressors are related to well-being among lesbians and bisexual women. Therefore, further research with a larger, more diverse sample is warranted.

Demographics. The women in the pilot study were on average 32 years of age, had 1 year of graduate education, and reported average annual income between $30,000 and $39,000. Most (88%) were White; 12% were from ethnic or racial minority groups. These demographics are very similar to statistics found in other lesbian health studies.

Internal stressors: self-concealment, emotional inhibition, internalized homophobia. In this sample, a large proportion of the women were closeted about their sexual orientation to some degree: 41% reported themselves to be at least halfway or more in the closet; 71% reported holding back public displays of affection toward their partners within the past month; and 41% in the past month did not discuss a gay-related topic in public for fear of disclosing their sexual orientation.

Findings from the pilot study suggest a link between internal stressors and well-being. The number of instances of concealing one's sexual orientation was positively correlated with negative affect ($r = .49, p < .05$) and scores on the Center for Epidemiological Studies and Disease Control Depression Scale (CES-D; Radloff, 1977) ($r = .58, p < .05$). Internalized homophobia was positively associated with negative affect ($r = .46, p < .06$). The disclosure subscale of the Nungesser Homosexuality Attitudes Inventory (NHAI, as modified by Shidlo, 1994) was positively associated with CES-D depression scores ($r = .54, p < .05$), indicating that the more the women felt the need to conceal their sexual orientation, the more depressive symptoms they reported. Moreover, general self-concealment was positively associated with CES-D depression scores ($r = .61, p < .01$).

External stressors: gay-related life events. A large percentage of women in this pilot study had experienced negative gay-related life events: 18% reported experiencing disruption of ties with their families in the past year due to their sexual orientation; 18% reported verbal harassment; 77% reported someone's telling an antigay joke in their presence; and 35% reported living, working, or socializing with someone who is homophobic. There were, however, no significant relationships between gay-related life events and psychological or physical health outcomes. This lack of association may be attributed to the very small sample size, as well as the relatively low number of occurrences of major life events in the sample. A larger sample with ample statistical power should be able to detect the existence of such a relationship.

Moreover, none of the women reported any major forms of antigay victimization. Herek, Gillis, and Cogan (1996) found significant relationships between antigay criminal victimization and psychological symptoms for crimes against the person (e.g., assault, rape), but not for property crimes or relatively minor forms of harassment. It may be that most lesbians, gay men, and bisexuals are usually able to take most minor forms of harassment in stride, without damage to their overall psychological or physical well-being. It is possible that with more reported person crimes (from a larger sample), a significant relationship between major life events and physical and psychological symptoms will emerge.

Health behaviors. There were similar percentages for smoking and alcohol consumption in the pilot study sample compared with other studies of lesbians: 53% reported drinking alcohol two to three times a week or more, and 23.5% currently smoked. Amount of alcohol consumed was positively related to reported stress attributed to sexual lifestyle ($r = .39$,

$p < .07$), number of instances of concealing one's sexual orientation ($r = .43$, $p < .06$), internalized homophobia ($r = .54$, $p < .05$), the disclosure subscale of the NHAI ($r = .59$, $p < .05$), and general self-concealment ($r = .50$, $p < .05$). Amount of alcohol consumption was negatively related to reported outness ($r = -.54$, $p < .05$).

Large-Scale Study on Stress and Well-Being

Earlier reference was made to lesbians' double minority status (as both lesbians and women), but it should be noted that many lesbians have a triple minority status, because of their racial and ethnic identities. I am very interested in studying the multiple levels of stressors among women who partner with women. Unfortunately, most research on lesbians has focused on young adult self-identified lesbians from White, well-educated backgrounds. Lesbians, gay men, and bisexuals do not constitute a homogeneous group. Their heterogeneity necessitates the inclusion in research of lesbian, gay, and bisexual individuals from divergent backgrounds.

After finding preliminary support for my stress model in the pilot study's homogeneous sample, I have now moved ahead to collect data from a much more diverse population of women. In the Lesbian and Bisexual Women Stress Project, I am collecting survey data from 500 lesbian and bisexual women in the New York City area. At least 50% of the women in the study will be from racial or ethnic minority groups. I am also targeting women from late adolescence to later adulthood, and from all education and income levels, as well as those who may not self-identify as lesbian or bisexual yet have sexual relationships with women.

Concluding Remarks

In this chapter I have focused on the stress experienced by lesbians, gay men, and bisexuals as a result of their minority status (in some cases, their double or triple minority status). Sexual minorities in the United States live in a homophobic society where they must deal with prejudice resulting from living a lifestyle that does not fit in with societal norms. As a result of homophobia, many search for a safe path—which often means staying in the closet to some degree. Importantly, lesbians, gay

154 | STIGMA AND SEXUAL ORIENTATION

men, and bisexuals have choices about whether or not to make their stigma visible. Each choice, however, leads to its own kind of stress.

I have made an important distinction in this discussion regarding gay-related external and internal stressors. I have argued that gay-related external stressors are more relevant for those lesbians, gay men, and bisexuals who are more open about their sexual orientation. This disclosure opens the door for negative life events to occur, such as discrimination and antigay violence. On the other hand, internal stressors—such as self-concealment, emotional inhibition, and internalized homophobia—may play a more significant role for those who are less out. Researchers need to include both conceptualizations of stress in any studies designed to elucidate the connections between stress and well-being among sexual minorities.

References

Antoni, M. H., LaPierriere, A., Schneiderman, N., & Fletcher, M. A. (1991). Stress and immunity in individuals at risk for AIDS. *Stress Medicine, 7*, 35-44.

Badgett, M. V. L. (1995). The wage effects of sexual orientation discrimination. *Industrial and Labor Relations Review, 48*, 726-739.

Banks, A., & Gartrell, N. K. (1996). Lesbians in the medical setting. In R. P. Cabaj & T. S. Stein (Eds.), *Textbook of homosexuality and mental health* (pp. 659-671). Washington, DC: American Psychiatric Press.

Banks, J. K., & Gannon, L. R. (1988). The influence of hardiness on the relationship between stressors and psychosomatic symptomatology. *American Journal of Community Psychology, 16*, 25-37.

Bell, A. P., & Weinberg, M. S. (1978). *Homosexualities: A study of diversity among men and women.* New York: Simon & Schuster.

Benjamin, S. (1981). Stressful life events preceding the onset of neurotic depression. *Psychotic Medicine, 11*, 369-378.

Biddle, B. S. (1993). *Health status indicators for Washington area lesbians and bisexual women: A report on the Lesbian Health Clinic's first year.* Washington, DC: Whitman-Walker Clinic.

Blaney, N. T., Goodkin, K., Morgan, R. O., Feister, D., Millon, C., Szapocznik, J., & Eisdorfer, C. (1991). A stress-moderator model of distress in early HIV-1 infection: Concurrent analysis of life events, hardiness, and social support. *Journal of Psychosomatic Research, 35*, 297-305.

Bradford, J., Ryan, C., & Rothblum, E. D. (1994). National lesbian health care survey: Implications for mental health care. *Journal of Consulting and Clinical Psychology, 62*, 228-242.

Brand, P. A., Rothblum, E. D., & Solomon, L. J. (1992). A comparison of lesbians, gay men, and heterosexuals on weight and restrained eating. *International Journal of Eating Disorders, 11*, 253-259.

Brooks, V. R. (1981). *Minority stress and lesbian women.* Lexington, MA: D. C. Heath.

Brown, D. R., Ahmed, F., Gary, L. E., & Milburn, N. G. (1995). Major depression in a community sample of African Americans. *American Journal of Psychiatry, 152,* 373-378.

Brown, L. S. (1986). Confronting internalized oppression in sex therapy with lesbians. *Journal of Homosexuality, 12*(3-4), 99-107.

Chan, C. S. (1989). Issues of identity development among Asian-American lesbians and gay men. *Journal of Counseling and Development, 68,* 16-20.

Chan, D. W., & Lee, H. C. B. (1992). Hassles, life events, and health status among Chinese college students in Hong Kong. *International Journal of Psychosomatics, 39,* 44-55.

Cohen, J. B., Hauer, L. B., & Wofsky, C. B. (1989). Women and IV drugs: Parenteral and heterosexual transmission of human immunodeficiency virus. *Journal of Drug Issues, 19,* 39-56.

Cohen, S., & Hoberman, H. M. (1983). Positive life events and social supports as buffers of life change stress. *Journal of Applied Social Psychology, 13,* 99-125.

Cohen, S., & Wills, T. A. (1985). Stress, social support, and the buffering hypothesis. *Psychological Bulletin, 98,* 310-357.

Cui, X., & Vaillant, G. E. (1996). Antecedents and consequences of negative life events in adulthood: A longitudinal study. *American Journal of Psychiatry, 153,* 21-26.

D'Augelli, A. R. (1989). Lesbians' and gay men's experiences of discrimination and harassment in a university community. *American Journal of Community Psychology, 17,* 317-321.

deBenedittis, G., & Lorenzetti, A. (1992). The role of stressful life events in the persistence of primary headache: Major events vs. daily hassles. *Pain, 51,* 35-42.

DeLongis, A., Coyne, J. C., Dakof, G., Folkman, S., & Lazarus, R. S. (1982). Relationship of daily hassles, uplifts, and major life events to health status. *Health Psychology, 1,* 119-136.

DeLongis, A., Folkman, S., & Lazarus, R. S. (1988). The impact of daily stress on health and mood: Psychological and social resources as mediators. *Journal of Personality and Social Psychology, 54,* 486-495.

Dohrenwend, B. P., & Dohrenwend, B. S. (1978). Some issues in research on stressful life events. *Journal of Nervous and Mental Disease, 165,* 403-417.

Duncan, D. F. (1990). Prevalence of sexual assault victimization among heterosexual and gay/lesbian university students. *Psychological Reports, 66,* 65-66.

Espin, O. M. (1987). Issues of identity in the psychology of Latina lesbians. In Boston Lesbian Psychologies Collective (Eds.), *Lesbian psychologies: Explorations and challenges* (pp. 35-55). Urbana: University of Illinois Press.

Finnegan, D. G., & Cook, D. (1984). Special issues affecting the treatment of male and lesbian alcoholics. *Alcoholism Treatment Quarterly, 1,* 85-98.

Folkman, S., Chesney, M. A., Pollack, L., & Coates, T. J. (1993). Stress, control, coping and depressive mood in human immunodeficiency virus-positive and negative gay men in San Francisco. *Journal of Nervous and Mental Disease, 181,* 409-416.

Folkman, S., Chesney, M. A., Pollack, L., & Phillips, C. (1992). Stress, coping, and high-risk sexual behavior. *Health Psychology, 11,* 218-222.

Garnets, L. D., Herek, G. M., & Levy, B. (1992). Violence and victimization of lesbians and gay men: Mental health consequences. In G. M. Herek & K. T. Berrill (Eds.), *Hate crimes: Confronting violence against lesbians and gay men* (pp. 207-226). Newbury Park, CA: Sage.

Garnets, L. D., & Kimmel, D. C. (1993). Introduction: Lesbian and gay male dimensions in the psychological study of human diversity. In L. D. Garnets & D. C. Kimmel (Eds.), *Psychological perspectives on lesbian and gay male experiences* (pp. 1-51). New York: Columbia University Press.

Gartrell, N. K. (1981). The lesbian as a "single" woman. *American Journal of Psychotherapy, 35,* 502-509.

Glaus, O. K. (1988). Alcoholism, chemical dependency and the lesbian client. *Women and Therapy, 8,* 131-144.

Gonsiorek, J. C. (1988). Mental health issues of gay and lesbian adolescents. *Journal of Adolescent Health Care, 9,* 114-122.

Gonsiorek, J. C. (1991). The empirical basis for the demise of the illness model of homosexuality. In J. C. Gonsiorek & J. D. Weinrich (Eds.), *Homosexuality: Research implications for public policy* (pp. 115-136). Newbury Park, CA: Sage.

Gonsiorek, J. C. (1993). Mental health issues of gay and lesbian adolescents. In L. D. Garnets & D. C. Kimmel (Eds.), *Psychological perspectives on lesbian and gay male experiences* (pp. 469-485). New York: Columbia University Press.

Greene, B. (1994). Ethnic-minority lesbians and gay men: Mental health and treatment issues. *Journal of Consulting and Clinical Psychology, 62,* 243-251.

Hall, M. (1986). The lesbian corporate experience. *Journal of Homosexuality, 12*(3-4), 59-75.

Hays, R. B., Turner, H., & Coates, T. J. (1992). Social support, AIDS-related symptoms, and depression among gay men. *Journal of Consulting and Clinical Psychology, 60,* 463-469.

Herek, G. M. (1991). Stigma, prejudice, and violence against lesbians and gay men. In J. C. Gonsiorek & J. D. Weinrich (Eds.), *Homosexuality: Research implications for public policy* (pp. 60-80). Newbury Park, CA: Sage.

Herek, G. M., Gillis, J. R., & Cogan, J. C. (1996, August). *Hate crimes against gay men, lesbians, and bisexuals: Psychological consequences.* Symposium presented at the annual meeting of the American Psychological Association, Toronto.

Hershberger, S. L., & D'Augelli, A. R. (1995). The impact of victimization on the mental health and suicidality of lesbian, gay, and bisexual youths. *Developmental Psychology, 31,* 65-74.

Hinkle, L. E., Jr. (1974). The effect of exposure to cultural change, social change, and changes in interpersonal relationships on health. In B. S. Dohrenwend & B. P. Dohrenwend (Eds.), *Stressful life events: Their nature and effects* (pp. 9-44). New York: John Wiley.

Holmes, T. H., & Rahe, R. H. (1967). The Social Readjustment Rating Scale. *Journal of Psychosomatic Research, 11,* 213-218.

Icard, L. (1986). Black gay men and conflicting social identities: Sexual orientation versus racial identity. *Journal of Social Work and Human Sexuality, 4,* 83-93.

Jacobs, T. J., & Charles, E. (1980). Life events and the occurrence of cancer in children. *Psychosomatic Medicine, 42,* 11-24.

Jourard, S. M. (1971). *The transparent self.* New York: Van Nostrand Reinhold.

Kobasa, S. C. (1979). Stressful life events, personality, and health: An inquiry into hardiness. *Journal of Personality and Social Psychology, 37,* 1-11.

Kowal, A., & Pritchard, D. W. (1990). Psychological characteristics of children who suffer from headache: A research note. *Journal of Child Psychology and Psychiatry and Allied Disciplines, 31,* 637-649.

Kurdek, L. A. (1991). The dissolution of gay and lesbian couples. *Journal of Personal and Social Relationships, 8,* 265-278.

Kurdek, L. A. (1994). The nature and correlates of relationship quality in gay, lesbian, and heterosexual cohabitating couples: A test of the individual difference, interdependence, and discrepancy model. In B. Greene & G. M. Herek (Eds.), *Lesbian and gay psychology: Theory, research, and clinical applications* (pp. 133-155). Thousand Oaks, CA: Sage.

Landreville, P., & Vezina, J. (1992). A comparison between daily hassles and major life events as correlates of well-being in older adults. *Canadian Journal on Aging, 11,* 137-149.

Larson, D. G., & Chastain, R. L. (1990). Self-concealment: Conceptualization, measurement, and health implications. *Journal of Social and Clinical Psychology, 9,* 439-455.

Lemp, G., Jones, M., Kellogg, T., Nieri, G., Martinez, T., Lakhana, P., & Storey, S. (1993). *HIV seroprevalence and risk behaviors among lesbians and bisexual women: The 1993 San Francisco/ Berkeley women's survey.* San Francisco: San Francisco Department of Public Health, AIDS Office.

Levy, E. F. (1992). Strengthening the coping resources of lesbian families. *Families in Society, 73,* 23-31.

Litzenberger, B. W. (1994). Struggle and strength in the lives of two lesbian priests. In C. E. Franz & A. J. Stewart (Eds.), *Women creating lives: Identities, resilience, and resistance* (pp. 273-288). Boulder, CO: Westview.

Loiacano, D. K. (1989). Gay identity issues among Black Americans: Racism, homophobia, and the need for validation. *Journal of Counseling and Development, 68,* 21-25.

Lott-Whitehead, L., & Tully, C. T. (1993). The family lives of lesbian mothers. *Smith College Studies in Social Work, 63,* 265-280.

Lu, L. (1995). Life events, social support, and depression among Taiwanese female homemakers. *Journal of Social Psychology, 135,* 185-190.

Malla, A. K., & Norman, R. M. (1992). Relationship of major life events and daily stressors to symptomatology in schizophrenia. *Journal of Nervous and Mental Disease, 180,* 664-667.

Martin, J. L., Dean, L., Garcia, M., & Hall, W. (1989). The impact of AIDS on a gay community: Changes in sexual behavior, substance use, and mental health. *American Journal of Community Psychology, 17,* 269-293.

McKirnan, D. J., & Peterson, P. L. (1989). Alcohol and drug use among homosexual men and women: Epidemiology and population characteristics. *Addictive Behaviors, 14,* 545-553.

McLean, D. E., & Link, B. G. (1994). Unraveling complexity: Strategies to refine concepts, measures, and research designs in the study of life events and mental health. In W. R. Avison & I. H. Gotlib (Eds.), *Stress and mental health: Contemporary issues and prospects for the future* (pp. 15-42). New York: Plenum.

Meyer, I. H. (1995). Minority stress and mental health in gay men. *Journal of Health and Social Behavior, 7,* 9-25.

Mitchell, E. S., Woods, N. F., & Lentz, M. J. (1994). Differentiation of women with three premenstrual symptom patterns. *Nursing Research, 43,* 25-30.

Muller, A. (1987). *Parents matter.* Tallahassee, FL: Naiad.

Nott, K. H., & Vedhara, K. (1995). The measurement and significance of stressful life events in a cohort of homosexual HIV positive men. *AIDS Care, 7,* 55-69.

Nott, K. H., Vedhara, K., & Powers, M. J. (1995). The role of social support in HIV infection. *Psychological Medicine, 25,* 971-983.

O'Leary, V. E., & Ickovics, J. R. (1995). Resilience and thriving in response to challenge: An opportunity for a paradigm shift in women's health. *Women's Health: Research on Gender, Behavior, and Policy, 1,* 121-142.

Pagelow, M. D. (1980). Heterosexual and lesbian single mothers: A comparison of problems, coping, and solutions. *Journal of Homosexuality, 5*(3), 189-204.

Pearlin, L. I. (1993). The social context of stress. In L. Goldberger & S. Breznitz (Eds.), *Handbook of stress: Theoretical and clinical aspects* (pp. 303-315). New York: Free Press.

Pennebaker, J. W., & Chew, C. H. (1985). Behavioral inhibition and electrodermal activity during deception. *Journal of Personality and Social Psychology, 49,* 1427-1433.

Pennebaker, J. W., Kiecolt-Glaser, J. K., & Glaser, R. (1988). Disclosure of traumas and immune function: Health implications for psychotherapy. *Journal of Consulting and Clinical Psychology, 56,* 239-245.

Pennebaker, J. W., & O'Heeron, R. C. (1984). Confiding in others and illness rate among spouses of suicide and accidental death victims. *Journal of Abnormal Psychology, 93,* 473-476.

Radecic, P. J. (1993). *Lesbian health issues and recommendations.* Washington, DC: National Gay and Lesbian Task Force.

Radloff, L. S. (1977). The CES-D Scale: A self-report depression scale for research in the general population. *Applied Psychological Measurement, 1,* 385-401.

Rankow, E. J. (1995). Lesbian health issues for the primary care provider. *Journal of Family Practice, 40,* 486-493.

Riddle, D. I., & Sang, B. (1978). Psychotherapy with lesbians. *Journal of Social Issues, 34*(3), 84-100.

Rofes, E. E. (1983). *I thought people like that killed themselves: Lesbians, gay men and suicide.* San Francisco: Grey Fox.

Ross, M. W. (1990). The relationship between life events and mental health in homosexual men. *Journal of Clinical Psychology, 46,* 402-411.

Rotheram-Borus, M. J., Hunter, J., & Rosario, M. (1994). Suicidal behavior and gay-related stress among gay and bisexual male adolescents. *Journal of Adolescent Research, 9,* 498-508.

Rotheram-Borus, M. J., Reid, H., Rosario, M., & Kasen, S. (1995). Determinants of safer sex patterns among gay/bisexual male adolescents. *Journal of Adolescence, 18,* 3-15.

Rotheram-Borus, M. J., Rosario, M., Van-Rossem, R., Reid, H., & Gillis, R. (1995). Prevalence, course, and predictors of multiple problem behaviors among gay and bisexual male adolescents. *Developmental Psychology, 31,* 75-85.

Ruffin, C. L. (1993). Stress and health: Little hassles vs. major life events. *Australian Psychologist, 28,* 201-208.

Savin-Williams, R. C. (1994). Verbal and physical abuse as stressors in the lives of lesbian, gay male, and bisexual youths: Associations with school problems, running away, substance abuse, prostitution, and suicide. *Journal of Consulting and Clinical Psychology, 62,* 261-269.

Schaefer, S., & Coleman, E. (1992). Shifts in meaning, purpose, and values of human immunodeficiency virus (HIV) infection among gay men. *Journal of Psychology and Human Sexuality, 5,* 13-29.

Schwartzberg, S. S. (1993). Struggling for meaning: How HIV-positive gay men make sense of AIDS. *Professional Psychology: Research and Practice, 24,* 483-490.

Schwartzberg, S. S. (1994). Vitality and growth in HIV-infected gay men. *Social Science and Medicine, 38,* 593-602.

Shidlo, A. (1994). Internalized homophobia: Conceptual and empirical issues in measurement. In B. Greene & G. M. Herek (Eds.), *Lesbian and gay psychology: Theory, research, and clinical applications* (pp. 176-205). Thousand Oaks, CA: Sage.

Slater, S., & Mencher, J. M. (1991). The lesbian family life cycle: A contextual approach. *American Journal of Orthopsychiatry, 61,* 372-382.

Strommen, E. F. (1993). "You're a what?": Family member reactions to the disclosure of homosexuality. In L. D. Garnets & D. C. Kimmel (Eds.), *Psychological perspectives on lesbian and gay male experiences* (pp. 248-266). New York: Columbia University Press.

Stuntzner-Gibson, D. (1991). Women and HIV disease: An emerging social crisis. *Social Work, 36,* 22-28.

Turner, H. A., Hays, R. B., & Coates, T. J. (1993). Determinants of social support among gay men: The context of AIDS. *Journal of Health and Social Behavior, 34,* 37-53.

Wolf, T. M., Elston, R. C., & Kissling, G. E. (1989). Relationship of hassles, uplifts, and life events to psychological well-being of freshman medical students. *Behavioral Medicine, 15,* 37-45.

Woods, S. E., & Harbeck, K. M. (1992). Living in two worlds: The identity management strategies used by lesbian physical educators. *Journal of Homosexuality, 22*(3-4), 141-166.

Young, R. M., Weissman, G., & Cohen, J. B. (1992). Assessing risk in the absence of information: HIV risk among women injection drug users who have sex with women. *AIDS and Public Policy Journal, 7,* 175-183.

8

Internalized Homophobia, Intimacy, and Sexual Behavior Among Gay and Bisexual Men

ILAN H. MEYER
LAURA DEAN

Antihomosexual attitudes and the stigmatization of homosexuality in Western society shape a sociocultural environment characterized by rejection of and discrimination against the gay person (Herek, 1986, 1992). As a result, gay men and lesbians are subjected to social stressors ranging from general antihomosexual attitudes and rejection by family and friends to violent assaults and discrimination in housing, employment, entitlements, and basic civil rights (Dean, Wu, & Martin, 1992).

Such a social environment is bound to have mental health effects on gay and lesbian people. In addressing the effects of prejudice on mental health, Allport (1954) has noted, "One's reputation, whether false or true, cannot be hammered, hammered, hammered, into one's head without doing something to one's character" (p. 142). Clinicians agree that negative societal attitudes are related to adverse mental health (e.g., Gonsiorek, 1988; Isay, 1989; Malyon, 1982; Marmor, 1980a; McHenry & Johnson, 1993; Stein & Cohen, 1984; Weinberg, 1972). Based on clinical

AUTHORS' NOTE: An earlier version of this chapter was presented at the annual meeting of the American Psychological Association, New York, August 1995. The study was supported by grants from the National Institute of Mental Health (MH39557), the Aaron Diamond Foundation (CU508227), and the New York Community Trust (CU508287, Laura Dean, principal investigator). The first author was supported by a National Research Service Award postdoctoral research training in health psychology at the Graduate School at the City University of New York (5T32MH19382).

conceptions, gay-affirmative psychotherapeutic approaches have been developed that are aimed at helping the individual examine psychological issues in the context of negative societal attitudes (e.g., Cohen & Stein, 1986).

Following Brooks (1981), Meyer (1995) has referred to this social environment as a source of *minority stress* and has described its effects on mental health. At the core of minority stress is some kind of conflict or disharmony between the minority member and the dominant social environment. For gay men and lesbians, this conflict is expressed in discordant values and norms regarding sexuality, intimacy, and, more generally, human existence and purpose. Meyer has defined specific minority stress processes as internalized homophobia, expectations of rejection and discrimination, and actual events of antigay violence and discrimination. Internalized homophobia, the most insidious of the minority stress processes, is the gay person's direction of negative social attitudes toward the self, leading to a devaluation of the self and resultant internal conflicts and poor self-regard.

Internalized homophobia has been described as a source of stress for gay men and lesbians in clinical settings, but little mental health research has been done in nonclinical populations. In this chapter, we review theoretical and research evidence on internalized homophobia and briefly describe our findings from different investigations of internalized homophobia in a community sample of New York City gay and bisexual men. We assess the relationships between internalized homophobia and intimacy, sexual behavior, and AIDS-related risk taking.

Because the study presented here, the Longitudinal AIDS Impact Project, was concerned with gay and bisexual men, we limit our discussion to men. But clearly, internalized homophobia is an important factor in lesbian mental health as well (Sophie, 1987; see also DiPlacido, Chapter 7, this volume). Generalizations from gay and bisexual men to lesbians should be made with caution, however, because findings from one group may not always be applicable to the other (de Monteflores & Schultz, 1978). For example, lesbians are subject to social stress and oppression, as well as affiliative opportunities, related to both the homosexual and gender portions of their identities (Brooks, 1981). Men and women are socialized very differently, especially with regard to intimacy and sexuality, so it is reasonable to assume that the effects of internalized homophobia on intimacy and sexuality are different for men and women.

Identity Development
and Internalized Homophobia

Homosexually oriented persons are most often raised by heterosexual parents and socialized as heterosexuals in environments that frequently promote antihomosexual attitudes. Unlike members of stigmatized ethnic minority groups, most homosexually oriented persons are not exposed to self-protecting, supportive attitudes in their families (see Crocker & Major, 1989). Thus, until they come out, most homosexually oriented people lack access to an affirmative reference group (the gay community) and to mentors and role models to help in the development of healthy sociosexual identity (Hetrick & Martin, 1984; Warren, 1980).

How do prevalent social attitudes, such as homophobia, affect individuals? Lazarus and Folkman (1984) have maintained that in order to affect an individual psychologically, general societal attitudes must become personally relevant. They have described social structures and attitudes as "distal concepts whose effects on an individual depend on how they are manifested in the immediate context of thought, feeling, and action—the proximal social experiences of a person's life" (p. 321). Distal social attitudes gain psychological importance through cognitive appraisal and become proximal concepts with psychological importance to the individual. For the gay person, societal antihomosexual attitudes gain psychological importance as the individual begins to label himself or herself as gay.

Long before they begin to realize their own homosexuality, homosexually oriented people internalize societal antihomosexual attitudes to varying degrees. When, as adolescents or adults, they recognize their own same-sex attraction, they begin to question their presumed heterosexuality and apply the label *homosexual* or *gay* to themselves. Such self-labeling often occurs before any interpersonal disclosure of their homosexual longings or behavior. But as self-labeling begins, the psychologically injurious effects of societal homophobia can take effect. Link (1987) described a similar process in individuals who become labeled as mental patients. He noted that societal negative attitudes that "once seemed to be an innocuous array of beliefs . . . now become applicable personally and [are] no longer innocuous" (p. 97). Even if disclosure is avoided and the individual is spared any condemnation because of his or her sexual orientation (as may be the case for a closeted individual who passes as heterosexual), he or she often begins to apply the learned antigay attitudes to himself or herself. Thoits (1985) has described such a process of self-stigmatization as *self-labeling*, explaining, "Role-taking abilities enable individuals to view themselves from the imagined perspective of others. One can anticipate and respond in advance to others' reactions regarding a contemplated course of action" (p. 222).

Thus, along with the recognition of same-sex attraction, a deviant identity (Goffman, 1963) begins to emerge that can threaten the psychological well-being of the homosexually oriented person (Hetrick & Martin, 1984; Stein & Cohen, 1984). At the same time, however, an adaptational process of resocialization (*coming out*) toward self-acceptance typically begins. Nevertheless, internalized antihomosexual attitudes pose potential threats to the coming-out process and often play an important role in the individual's psychic conflict around sexual identity (Cass, 1984; Cohen & Stein, 1986; Coleman, 1982; Troiden, 1989).

The term *internalized homophobia* has been used by clinicians to refer to the internalization of societal antihomosexual attitudes (e.g., Malyon, 1982). In a gay person, it signifies the failure of the coming-out process to thoroughly overcome negative self-perceptions and attitudes. Although internalized homophobia is likely to be most acute early in the coming-out process, it may persist even when the person appears to accept his or her homosexuality (Cass, 1984; Coleman, 1982; Gonsiorek, 1991; Troiden, 1989). Because of the strength of early socialization experiences, and because of continued exposure to negative attitudes, internalized homophobia remains an important factor in gay men's psychological adjustment throughout life (Malyon, 1982). That is, many gay people maintain varying degrees of residual antihomosexual attitudes that are integrated into their self-perceptions (Hetrick & Martin, 1984; Malyon, 1982; Nungesser, 1983). Gonsiorek (1988) has referred to residual internalized homophobia in lesbians and gay men who have come out as "covert internalized homophobia," and stated, "Covert forms of internalized homophobia are the most common. Affected individuals appear to accept themselves, yet sabotage their own efforts in a variety of ways" (p. 117).

Ego-Dystonic Homosexuality
and Internalized Homophobia

In an extreme case, a person who has failed to accept his or her homosexual orientation will experience persistent distress over homosexual feelings and will be unable to adjust to a gay sociosexual identity. The third edition of the *Diagnostic and Statistical Manual of Mental Disorders* (*DSM-III*; American Psychiatric Association, 1980) referred to this pattern as *ego-dystonic homosexuality* (EDH) and recognized that "the factors that predispose to ego-dystonic homosexuality are those negative societal attitudes toward homosexuality which have become internalized" (p. 282). Associated with EDH, according to *DSM-III*, are loneliness, guilt, shame, anxiety, and depression.

The addition of the diagnosis of EDH to *DSM-III* was opposed by gay-affirmative psychiatrists and psychologists for many reasons, primarily because of its misuse by clinicians who advocated reversal of homosexual orientation for their patients. EDH was eventually eliminated as a diagnostic category from the revised *DSM-III* (*DSM-III-R*; American Psychiatric Association, 1987; see Bayer, 1981; Spitzer, 1981). Ironically, however, the basic concept behind EDH is consistent with the gay-affirmative perspective in that it identifies the cause of psychological distress in societal antihomosexual attitudes.

Despite this seeming conceptual similarity, there are important differences between the constructs. EDH was described as a static condition, and therapeutic interventions aimed at either reversing sexual orientation or helping the person accept homosexual orientation were suggested, based on the patient's preference. This seemingly sensible, client-centered approach to treatment is misleading, however. Patients who present with high levels of internalized homophobia are likely to seek to become heterosexual exactly because they cannot envision satisfying lives as gay persons. Reversal or reparative therapies may be applied, but these are doomed to failure (Haldeman, 1991; Martin, 1984); such failure will likely further damage the individual's self-image and mental health.

In contrast to EDH, internalized homophobia is viewed by gay-affirmative therapists as an early stage of a developmental process. As coming out unfolds, the gay person is expected to move toward a healthier adjustment and a lower level of internalized homophobia. Reflecting this basic conceptual difference, the recommended therapeutic intervention for internalized homophobia is directed at helping patients achieve greater self-acceptance and healthier adjustment to homosexual orientation.

Internalized Homophobia and Intimacy

One of most common stereotypes of gay men is that they are incapable of intimate relationships, do not have families and children, and die (or kill themselves) desperate and lonely. Gay men who internalize such beliefs may feel inferior to heterosexuals and unworthy or incapable of achieving goals that conflict with stereotypical proscriptions regarding what gay people can achieve. For example, they may not attempt to develop satisfying intimate relationships or to create alternative family units (Cohen & Stein, 1986; Duberman, 1991; Garnets & Kimmel, 1991; Weston, 1991).

Merton's (1957) formulations on the *opportunity structure* may help in this discussion. According to Merton, minority groups are socially disadvantaged in attaining monetary success because social structures are stacked against them, leading minority group members to experience a disjunction between culturally prescribed goals and institutionally legitimate means of achieving those goals. Merton developed his theory in the context of opportunities for economic success, but indicated that the same processes are also applicable to other spheres of life where the success theme in American culture posits unattainable goals.

We can apply Merton's concepts to the goal of attaining intimacy as it affects gay people. Gay people who internalize societal values about the centrality of family life for the attainment of intimacy and happiness are, by societal standards, doomed to failure because their sexual orientation cannot be accommodated by what may be termed the *heterosexist opportunity structure*: norms and institutions that promote opposite-sex relationships and devalue and discourage same-sex intimate relationships. This is because the achievement of intimacy and love is often "internalized as something which is unexpected or prohibited for gay people" (Cohen & Stein, 1986, p. 37). For example, in an autobiographical account of his coping with internalized homophobia, Duberman (1991) described how for years intimacy and love seemed incompatible with his homosexuality because of such heterosexist assumptions. Weston (1991), in a study of gay and lesbian kinship, found that for many people the acquisition of a gay identity was initially associated with the renunciation of access to kinship. As one of her respondents said, "My image of gay life was very lonely, very weird, no family" (p. 25).

In order to expand the opportunity structure that defines interpersonal intimacy and familial success and happiness, gay people have to adopt alternative values and norms. Merton (1957) referred to this type of adaptation as rebellion, which involves rejection of prevailing values and their substitution with new values. Rebellion presupposes alienation from reigning goals and standards, and "involves a genuine transvaluation, where the direct or vicarious experience of frustration leads to full denunciation of previously prized values" (p. 210). Gay culture had to reformulate norms and values within which intimacy and family will be attainable for gay people. Gay people thus developed a value system that promotes alternative family compositions and institutionalized intimate relationships among people of the same sex (Berzon, 1988; Weston, 1991).

In coming out, gay men who can connect with a gay community may find friends and role models. Such a connection can help them redefine social values, find alternative opportunities for intimacy and family, and develop a healthy sociosexual identity (Warren, 1980; Weston, 1991). Gay men who overcome heterosexist attitudes and have lower levels of internalized homophobia are able to recognize—and be critical of—heterosexism from an empowered position and are more capable of adopting alternative values and norms (Weston, 1991). McCombs (1992), a former director of counseling services at the Los Angeles Gay and Lesbian Community Services Center, has described a sense of abundant opportunities for gay people who successfully adopt gay culture:

> One of my favorite advantages to surviving the heterosexist, homophobic illness of our culture is the richness of the opportunity to define one's own rightness. Part of accepting ourselves as gay people means we have learned to expand the boundaries of "good" beyond the fallacies of "appropriate." The life experience of accepting oneself against such hateful odds prepares one to choose self-satisfaction over the empty categories of acceptability. (p. 54)

But gay men who have high levels of internalized homophobia have not yet been able to counter social attitudes and values regarding homosexuality, and may have greater difficulties in developing same-sex intimate relationships.

Research Evidence on Internalized Homophobia in Gay and Bisexual Men

Although systematic research on the effects of internalized homophobia on mental health is scarce, psychologists have implicated internalized homophobia in many adverse mental health outcomes (Cabaj, 1988; Forstein, 1988; Gonsiorek, 1988; Hanley-Hackenbruck, 1988; Malyon, 1982). For example, Cabaj (1988) has claimed that "the major factor that plays a role in psychotherapy with gay men and women, no matter what the presenting complaints may be . . . is [internalized as well as external] homophobia" (p. 14). Similarly, in his discussion of the effects of internalized homophobia on gay men, Malyon (1982) concluded that "it influences identity formation, self-esteem, the elaboration of defenses, patterns of cognition, psychological integrity, and object relations" (p. 60). In fact, Malyon viewed internalized homophobia as so pervasive and central that he found it necessary to warn psychotherapists not to succumb to reductionist inclinations to overlook other important dynamics when treating gay men.

These clinical observations have been supported in studies with non-clinical populations as well. Several studies have found internalized homophobia to be related to psychological distress, lowered self-esteem, and lower levels of community integration and social support (Herek & Glunt, 1995; Shidlo, 1994). Other studies of mental health in gay and bisexual men also provide corroborative evidence that is consistent with the internalized homophobia predictions described above. For example, Weinberg and Williams (1974) assessed gay men's "normalization," which they defined as "seeing homosexuality as 'normal' and not as an illness or mental illness," and "commitment," which they defined as "the respondent's unwillingness to give up his homosexuality" (p. 160). These authors found that men who normalized more and who were more committed to homosexuality (who presumably also had lower levels of internalized homophobia) reported less psychological distress, including fewer depressive and psychosomatic symptoms, and less loneliness, guilt, shame, and anxiety regarding their homosexuality.

Studies on AIDS-related risk-taking behavior have shown complex and inconsistent relationships among internalized homophobia, community affiliation, and risk behavior (Sandfort, 1995). Neither Shidlo (1994) nor De Wit, De Vroome, Sandfort, Van Grinsven, and Tielman (as cited in Sandfort, 1995) found an association between self-acceptance and risk-taking behavior. Herek and Glunt (1995), however, found an indirect relationship: Respondents who scored high on internalized homophobia had lower levels of self-efficacy for safe sex and reported more barriers to practicing safe sex. Low self-efficacy and high barriers to safe sex, in turn, were related to increased risk-taking behavior. Herek and Glunt concluded that "to the extent that men are out of the closet, have positive feelings about their sexual orientation, and feel a sense of connection to other gay and bisexual men, they are more likely to perceive social support for safe-sex practices and to feel empowered to practice safe sex with their partners" (p. 69).

Other studies of gay men's coping with AIDS have stimulated research on the concept of internalized homophobia. For example, Nicholson and Long (1990) studied the relationships among self-esteem, social support, internalized homophobia, and coping strategies used by HIV-positive gay men. They found that internalized homophobia was significantly correlated with self-esteem and mood disturbance. In addition, internalized homophobia was associated with the use of less effective coping strategies (avoidant versus proactive coping) regarding diagnosis of HIV infection. Similarly, Wolcott, Namir, Fawzy, Gottlieb, and Mitsuyasu (1986), in a study of gay and bisexual men with AIDS, reported that internalized homophobia was associated with mood disturbance as well as subjective (but not objective) measures of health status.

The Longitudinal
AIDS Impact Project

To examine some of the issues related to internalized homophobia, we used data from the Longitudinal AIDS Impact Project, a study of a large, nonclinical sample of gay and bisexual men in New York City. Overall, more than 1,000 gay and bisexual men over age 18 took part in the project. The original cohort was recruited in 1985 and followed for 7 years. A second cohort, consisting entirely of young men (ages 18-24), was recruited in 1990 and followed for 2 years. The results presented here come primarily from cross-sectional analyses of Wave 3 (1987) of the original sample ($N = 738$), the first year that internalized homophobia was assessed, and from Wave 1 (1990) of the young men's cohort (*N* = 174).

Respondents were recruited from a variety of sources within the gay community. Men were enrolled in the study through a stratified random sampling of gay organizations and systematic snowball sampling to include unaffiliated men. Respondents were interviewed in annual face-to-face sessions. Respondents in the original cohort were 18 to 75 years old, with a mean age of 36 in 1985. They were primarily White (13% were not White), had a mean education of 16 years, and had a median income of $35,000 in 1987. Respondents in the second cohort were 18 to 24 years old, with a mean age of 22 in 1990; 71% were White, 16% were Black, and 13% were Latino; and 45% were full-time students. Their median income was $10,000 in 1990. The recruitment techniques, samples, and measures have been described in greater detail elsewhere (Dean & Meyer, 1995; Martin & Dean, 1990).

Internalized Homophobia

A measure of internalized homophobia was designed to assess the extent to which gay and bisexual men are uneasy about their homosexuality and seek to avoid homosexual feelings (Dean, 1996). Examples of items in the 9-item scale (α = .79) include "How often have you wished you weren't gay?"; "Have you thought that being gay was a personal shortcoming?"; and "How often have you tried to become sexually attracted to women in general?" Respondents rated the frequency with which they experienced such thoughts in the year prior to the interview on a 4-point Likert scale ranging from 4 (*often*) to 1 (*never*). A total score of 9, therefore, represents no internalized homophobia on the scale. The total scores in the original cohort ranged from 9 to 33, the mean (*M*) was 12.1, and the standard deviation (*SD*) was 3.9. The total score in the young cohort ranged from 9 to 33 (*M* = 13.1, *SD* = 4.3). As expected for a nonclinical sample of gay and bisexual men—most of whom were out of the closet—the distribution of internalized homophobia scores was positively skewed, indicating that most men had low scores of internalized homophobia. Nevertheless, in both cohorts an overwhelming majority of the men (about 70%) reported some (i.e., a total score of 10 or more) level of internalized homophobia.

Internalized Homophobia, Demographic
Characteristics, and Religiosity

Internalized homophobia was not significantly associated with ethnicity, income, or educational level (but, as described above, our sample may have been limited in variability in these demographics).

Based on the clinical observations described earlier in this chapter, we expected internalized homophobia to decrease with age as the men became more self-accepting along the coming-out process. But we did not find a significant correlation between internalized homophobia and age. Age may not be a good predictor of internalized homophobia because the men began to come out at different ages; therefore, men of similar ages may have had different amounts of time to arrive at self-acceptance. We therefore examined the relationship between internalized homophobia and time since coming out. For this analysis we considered coming out to a friend a milestone in the coming-out process and used it as our predictor variable. Men in the original cohort varied in the ages that they first came out to a friend ($M = 21$, $SD = 5.2$). Consistent with our hypothesis, we found a significant association between time since coming out to a friend and level of internalized homophobia—the more time, the less internalized homophobia ($r = -.09$, $p = .01$). This relationship was weaker than we expected. We hypothesized a posteriori that a ceiling effect may have attenuated the correlation we found; that is, time since coming out may help to predict internalized homophobia up to a point, beyond which increase in time is not related to further decrease in internalized homophobia. We confirmed this by fitting a polynomial regression ($F = 5.42$, $p < .005$), indicating that the association of time since coming out to a friend and internalized homophobia is better fitted in a curvilinear plot consistent with the ceiling effect hypothesis. Among respondents who had come out fewer than 15 years earlier (the sample median), time since first coming out was significantly correlated with internalized homophobia ($r = -.17$, $p < .001$). Among respondents who had been out for more than 15 years, however, the correlation was not significant ($r = -.01$).

Because most mainstream religious organizations condemn homosexuality, we suspected that religious men may have internalized more negative attitudes toward homosexuality than have nonreligious men. In contrast to most religious organizations, gay-affirmative religious organizations (e.g., Metropolitan Community Church, Dignity) have been created for the purpose of countering the condemnation of mainstream religious organizations. We therefore expected that gay or bisexual men who belonged to gay-affirmative religious organizations would have lower levels of internalized homophobia than would men in mainstream religious organizations. As expected, analyses in the original cohort showed that religious men who were not associated with gay churches or synagogues (*n* = 253) had higher levels of internalized homophobia than did the nonreligious men (*n* = 374), *M*s = 12.5 (*SD* = 3.9) and 11.7 (*SD* = 3.9), respectively; *t* = 2.51, *p* = .01. Men who were religious but who participated in gay-affirmative churches or synagogues (*n* = 55) had levels of internalized homophobia very similar to those of nonreligious men, *M* = 11.8 (*SD* = 3.7).

Community and Intimacy

Despite the relatively low level of internalized homophobia in this sample, it was an important predictor of participation in the gay community and establishment of same-sex intimacy. We assessed gay identity by asking respondents to what extent they were in or out of the closet. We assessed participation in the gay community by asking respondents whether they read gay newspapers regularly and whether they were members of gay or bisexual groups or organizations. Men in the original cohort who had higher levels of internalized homophobia were characterized by less involvement in the gay community and a weaker gay identity. Table 8.1 shows that they were less likely to disclose their homosexuality, less likely to read gay newspapers regularly, and less likely to belong to gay groups and organizations. Men with higher levels of internalized homophobia were also less likely to be coupled with partners.

Similarly, men in the original cohort who had higher levels of internalized homophobia were about twice as likely to report sex problems, including inhibited sexual desire, excitement, or orgasm, in the year prior to the interview (*r* = .12, *p* < .01). The odds ratio gives a more tangible impression of the magnitude of this association. The odds ratio of 3.6 (confidence interval = 1.4, 9.4) suggests that men with high levels of internalized homophobia (defined as above the sample's mean) were almost four times more likely to report sex problems than men with low levels of internalized homophobia.

In the subgroup of coupled men (*n* = 332 in the original cohort), internalized homophobia was related to stability of the relationship, as measured by length of the relationship, cohabitation, and relationship dis-

Table 8.1 Differences in Internalized Homophobia by Gay Identity Items
(original cohort; $N = 738$)

Gay Identity Items	Internalized Homophobia Mean (SD)	t^a
Explicitly "out" to others about homosexuality		
Yes 85%	11.6 (3.4)	6.08***
No 15%	14.8 (5.4)	
Gay newspaper reader		
Yes 48%	11.5 (3.3)	4.09***
No 52%	12.6 (4.3)	
Gay group member		
Yes 50%	11.6 (3.3)	3.30***
No 41%	12.7 (4.6)	
Coupled (has a life partner)		
Yes 45%	11.5 (3.3)	3.24***
No 55%	12.4 (4.3)	

a. Separate variance estimates were used in all analyses because variance in the group with higher internalized homophobia was significantly larger than the variance in the comparison group.
***$p < .001$.

cord. Coupled men who had higher levels of internalized homophobia had been in relationships for less time ($r = -.16$, $p < .05$), were less likely to live with their partners (*chi-square* $[1, N = 317] = 5.5$, $p < .05$; internalized homophobia score was dichotomized at the sample mean), reported more problems in their relationships ($r = -.11$, $p < .05$), and had thought about breaking up their relationships more often ($r = .11$, $p < .05$). Although of low magnitude, these relationship are noteworthy because, as a group, coupled men had lower levels of internalized homophobia than did the total sample (see Table 8.1), thereby reducing variability and making it difficult to detect correlations.

Mental Health

Based on the clinical and theoretical literature cited above, we hypothesized that internalized homophobia would be related to numerous mental health problems. We examined the association of internalized homophobia and four measures of psychological distress (Meyer, 1995). Mental health measures included the following scales from the Psychiatric Epidemiology Research Instrument (PERI; Dohrenwend, Shrout, Egri, & Mendelsohn, 1980): (a) demoralization, a generalized measure of distress that includes symptoms of anxiety and depression (27 items, α = .92); (b) guilt feelings (4 items, α = .79); and (c) suicidal ideation and behavior (4 items, α = .52). We also used a measure of AIDS-related traumatic stress response, a posttraumatic stress measure that includes symptoms of avoidance and intrusion regarding the AIDS epidemic (17 items, α = .89).

The hypothesis was confirmed: Separate multiple regression analyses (using data from the original cohort) confirmed that internalized homophobia was associated with each of these mental health measures (Meyer, 1995). To assess the clinical significance of these associations, and to give a more tangible description of these results, we also estimated the risk of having mental health problems for people with high versus low internalized homophobia. We divided the sample into men with high versus low levels of internalized homophobia and into men with high versus low levels of psychological distress by dichotomizing these measures at the sample's mean. The results indicate that men who reported high levels of mental health problems were two to three times more likely than their counterparts to have reported high levels of internalized homophobia (see Table 8.2). This suggests that internalized homophobia is associated with a two- to threefold increase in risk for high levels of psychological distress.

In addition to assessing the hypothesis about the direct effect of internalized homophobia on mental health outcomes, we examined whether internalized homophobia may exacerbate mental health problems by stripping individuals of defenses against external assaults on their sense of identity. Such assaults are most clearly manifested as antigay violence and discrimination. We expected that men who experienced antigay violence and discrimination and who had high levels of internalized homophobia would lack psychological resources for coping with these antigay events. Rather than blaming the perpetrators of the antigay violence or discrimination, such men may blame themselves, thus exacerbating their psychological distress.

We assessed whether respondents had experienced antigay violence or discrimination in the year prior to the interview (see Dean et al., 1992, for a more detailed account of antigay violence and discrimination). Men who had experienced at least one such event received a score of 1 on a combined measure of *prejudice events*. To test the proposition that inter-

Table 8.2 Relationship Between Internalized Homophobia and Mental Health (original cohort; N = 738)

Mental Health Measure	Odds Ratio	95% Confidence Interval
Demoralization	2.3	(1.6, 3.1)
Guilt	3.3	(2.4, 4.5)
Suicidal ideation	1.9	(1.3, 2.7)
AIDS-related traumatic stress	2.2	(1.6, 3.1)

nalized homophobia exacerbates mental health outcomes in the face of prejudice events, we introduced the interaction term of internalized homophobia by prejudice events to regression equations testing the effect of prejudice events on psychological distress (using data from the original cohort; Meyer, 1993). We assessed the significance of this interaction in a multivariate analysis of variance (MANOVA) that tested the effects of prejudice events on all the mental health outcomes described above considered as a block. The interaction term was significant (Pillai's value = .0212, F = 2.69, p < .05). Separate regressions for each of the mental health outcomes showed that the interaction term of internalized homophobia by prejudice events significantly predicted demoralization (β = .28, p < .05) and guilt feelings (β = .27, p < .05) and that there was a trend for prediction of suicidal thoughts and behavior (β = .21, p = .09).

As an example, the significant interaction of internalized homophobia by prejudice events in predicting demoralization is depicted in Figure 8.1, which shows that the association of prejudice events and demoralization is more profound in the face of high levels of internalized homophobia than in the face of low levels of internalized homophobia. That is, in men with low levels of internalized homophobia, an experience of prejudice events was not related to psychological distress, but in men with high levels of internalized homophobia, an experience of prejudice events was related to increased levels of psychological distress. This finding is consistent with the explanation that victimization by events of discrimination or violence is more painful when one agrees with the homophobic attitudes conveyed in the victimization event. Men with high internalized homophobia may lack resources to cope with having been victims of violence or discrimination. By stigmatizing their own condition, these gay men identify with the perpetrators of the prejudice events and suffer further pain—feeling more guilty and more demoralized than men with lower levels of internalized homophobia. Looked at another way, it seems that men with lower levels of internalized homophobia were able to avoid the negative mental health impacts of prejudice events, perhaps by countering the perpetrators' actions with self-affirming beliefs.

Self-affirming beliefs are likely to increase with stronger affiliation with the gay community. We expected that affiliation with the gay community may lead to exposure to affirmative values and norms and may help counter antigay attitudes. We hypothesized that stronger affiliation with the gay community would have an ameliorative effect on mental health. To test this hypothesis, we assessed the role of sense of cohesiveness with the gay community in predicting the same mental health outcomes discussed above (using data from the original cohort). Against the negative effects of internalized homophobia, we looked at the ameliorative effect of a sense of cohesiveness with the gay community. In each of the 12 items measuring sense of cohesiveness (scale $\alpha = .78$), respondents chose one of two statements that characterized the extent of their sense of cohesiveness with the gay community in the context of the AIDS epidemic. In each pair, one statement indicated more cohesion and the other indicated less cohesion. Sample items are "I feel a stronger [weaker] sense of community among gay men because of the AIDS epidemic" and "I prefer to involve myself with [distance myself from] the gay community now that AIDS is here." Community cohesiveness acted as a buffer against the negative effects of internalized homophobia (Meyer, 1993). For example, sense of cohesiveness reduced level of demoralization in the presence of internalized homophobia ($\beta = -.17$, $p < .001$). Figure 8.2 depicts this relationship, showing that the effect of internalized homophobia on distress became weaker as sense of cohesiveness increased.

AIDS-Related Risk Behavior

If internalized homophobia is related to intimacy, sexual problems, and other adjustment problems, we suspected that it may be associated with AIDS-related risk-taking behavior. We were initially surprised to find that among men in the original cohort, those who were diagnosed with AIDS or AIDS-related complex ($n = 43$ in 1987) had significantly *lower* levels of internalized homophobia than did men who were not so diagnosed ($n = 695$), $Ms = 11.2$ ($SD = 2.6$) and 12.1 ($SD = 4.0$), respectively;

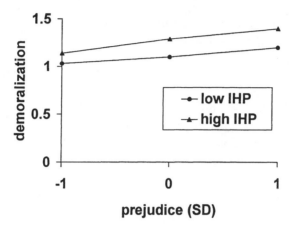

Figure 8.1. Interaction of Internalized Homophobia by Prejudice Events on Demoralization (original cohort; $N = 738$)

$t = 2.09$, $p < .05$, separate variance estimate. Plausible explanations for this finding are that the diagnosis of AIDS mobilized these gay and bisexual men to become more involved with the gay community and more self-accepting and that lower internalized homophobia was related to higher rates of past sexual activity and, consequently, to increased risk for HIV infection.

It is important to note, however, that this relationship might be different for younger gay men. Most of the men in the original cohort were infected with HIV before risk for AIDS was known, and before AIDS prevention efforts were initiated in the gay community. Currently, however, higher levels of internalized homophobia—through their association with less identification with the gay community and less exposure to educational materials directed at gay men—may be more likely to be related to increased risk for HIV infection (Peterson & Marin, 1988). To test this hypothesis, we looked at the group of young gay and bisexual men (ages 18-24) who came of age during the AIDS epidemic. Although our sample is too small to permit definitive conclusions, the results give some support to this hypothesis. Contrary to the finding in the original cohort of gay and bisexual men, the young gay and bisexual men who tested HIV-positive ($n = 8$) had higher levels of internalized homophobia ($M = 15.1$) than did those who tested negative ($n = 79$, $M = 12.5$), $t = 1.66$, $p = 0.10$.

We also looked at sexual risk-taking behavior among these young gay and bisexual men (Dean & Meyer, 1995; Meyer & Dean, 1995). The fol-

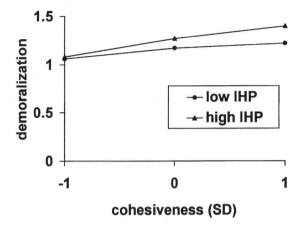

Figure 8.2. Interaction of Internalized Homophobia by Sense of Community Cohesiveness on Demoralization (original cohort; $N = 738$)

lowing results relate to the first wave of the cohort, measured in 1990. Sexual risk behavior was defined as any receptive anal intercourse with or without condoms, but we differentiated among levels of risk (Figure 8.3). A total of 107 (61%) of the young men engaged in receptive anal intercourse (Levels 1-4). Most did so with condoms only (Level 1: 63 men or 59%), and those who had unprotected anal intercourse did so primarily with one partner (Levels 2 and 3: 34 men or 32%), although a substantial number of them (Level 3: 23 men or 21%) engaged in additional protected receptive anal intercourse with other partners during the year. A small but clinically important group of men engaged in what seems to be recklessly risky behavior, by having had unprotected receptive anal sex with multiple partners (Level 4: 10 men or 9%). These men constituted about 6% of the total sample.

Internalized homophobia and other mental health problems did not predict receptive anal intercourse with condoms or unprotected receptive anal intercourse without condom if limited to one partner (Levels 1-3). Men who took this type of risk seemed to have engaged in decision making—implicit or explicit—to manage their risk. Men in Levels 1 through 3 were more likely than men in Level 4 to be in coupled relationships and to know their sex partners' HIV status, for example.[1]

By contrast, the very high risk takers (Level 4) seemed qualitatively different. As Table 8.3 shows, they reported more mental health problems, including more problems due to drug use (consistent with drug abuse

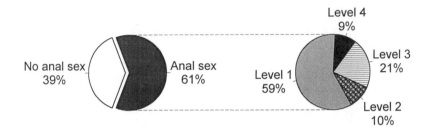

Figure 8.3. HIV-Related Risk-Taking Behaviors According to Level of Risk
($N = 174$)

NOTE: Level 1 = protected receptive anal intercourse only; Level 2 = unprotected receptive anal intercourse with one partner only; Level 3 = unprotected receptive anal intercourse with one partner, but additional protected receptive anal intercourse with multiple partners; Level 4 = unprotected receptive anal intercourse with multiple partners.

Table 8.3 Mental Health Predictors of Very High Sexual Risk Taking (young cohort; $N = 174$)

Mental Health Measures	Odds Ratio	95% Confidence Interval
Internalized homophobia	8.7	(3.4, 33.2)
Drug problems	8.4	(1.7, 40.1)
AIDS-related traumatic stress	2.1	(0.6, 7.4)

or dependence), and higher levels of internalized homophobia and AIDS-related traumatic stress response. The convergence of internalized homophobia, drug problems, and AIDS-related traumatic stress response suggests that the mechanism for high risk taking may be a process of denial and escape. These men, who suffered because of both their difficulty in accepting their homosexuality *and* their fear of AIDS, seemed to have alleviated this stress by engaging in sex while denying its risk for AIDS and, perhaps, by denying their homosexuality.

Discussion

The importance that theory and clinical observations ascribe to internalized homophobia led us to expect high levels of internalized homophobia among gay and bisexual men. Clinical evidence, however, tends to overestimate the prevalence of mental health problems in nonclinical populations (Cohen & Cohen, 1984). In our study, the distribution of internalized homophobia was skewed, suggesting that gay and bisexual men sampled from nonclinical settings, unlike men studied in clinical settings, typically have few negative attitudes about their homosexuality. This suggests that clinical observations may have led psychologists to overstate the extent to which gay men at later stages of the coming-out process are troubled by internalized homophobia.

It is important to remember that generalizations from our sample should be made with caution. Problems in sampling make it difficult to assemble samples that represent a wide range of gay and bisexual men. For example, men in the early stages of coming out and men who have sex with men but have not accepted their homosexuality are likely to have higher levels of internalized homophobia than their counterparts. But sampling problems in studies of gay and bisexual men make it difficult to reach such men because they may not identify themselves as gay, may not be willing to disclose their sexual behavior, or may not want to volunteer as study respondents (Harry, 1986; Martin & Dean, 1990; Meyer, in press). Samples such as the one we studied, consisting of self-identified gay and bisexual men, are probably biased in that they underrepresent men with high levels of internalized homophobia. This selection problem, which is inherent in community studies of gay and bisexual men, biases against detecting the hypothesized relationship of internalized homophobia and adjustment problems.

Nevertheless, more than two thirds of both the original cohort and the young cohort of New York City gay and bisexual men reported some levels of internalized homophobia. This leads us to conclude that, although often of low level, internalized homophobia is common among many gay and bisexual men who have apparently accepted their homosexual orientation. Our finding corroborates the observations of others that internalized homophobia continues to be manifested in gay and bisexual men even after they have come out (Herek & Glunt, 1995; McDonald, 1982; Nungesser, 1983; Wolcott et al., 1986).

Moreover, despite the possible underrepresentation of men with high internalized homophobia in our sample and the lower level of internalized homophobia in community compared with clinical samples, we found internalized homophobia to be a predictor of mental health problems, intimacy problems, and AIDS-related risk-taking behavior. Gay and bisexual men with higher levels of internalized homophobia seemed to suffer greater adjustment problems and more psychological distress, and were less likely to be in a coupled relationship.

Our findings further suggest that internalized homophobia acts as an insidious self-oppressor in the face of external homophobia. As Garnets, Herek, and Levy (1990) have noted, following antigay events,

> one's homosexual orientation . . . may be experienced as a source of pain and punishment rather than intimacy, love, and community. . . . Attempts to make sense of the attack, coupled with the common need to perceive the world as a just place, may lead to feelings that one has been justifiably punished for being gay. (p. 370)

Having been victimized, men with higher levels of internalized homophobia may not be able to mount self-enhancing defenses, leading to worse mental health outcomes compared with men who have lower levels of internalized homophobia. It seems that men with higher levels of internalized homophobia need help in reinterpreting such events in a self-enhancing rather than self-blaming manner.

Such self-protective reinterpretations of social stigma may be achieved through affiliation with one's minority community (see Crocker & Major, 1989). Consistent with this view, we found an ameliorative role for sense of cohesiveness with the gay community even in the face of internalized homophobia. This suggests that men with higher levels of internalized homophobia may benefit from a sense of cohesiveness because it exposes them to gay-affirmative values and norms that counter their negative self-regard. It is a sad irony, however, that internalized homophobia is also related to *less* affiliation with the gay community. Only after gay people begin to reduce self-directed antigay attitudes in coming out— often alone—can they begin to affiliate with the gay community and benefit from the ameliorative sense of cohesiveness in combating the negative effects of internalized homophobia.

We have also suggested that internalized homophobia plays a role in AIDS-related risk-taking behavior. This finding has not been consistently reported by other investigators (Sandfort, 1995), suggesting that the relationship may be complex and that a variety of intervening processes might be at work under different circumstances. For example, Herek and Glunt (1995) have suggested that internalized homophobia is associated with efficacy and barriers to safe sex, which, in turn, are related to risk-taking behavior. Our categorization of risk identified a subgroup of gay and bisexual men (we investigated the young, but older men may be similarly affected) who appear to have greater adjustment problems. We have suggested another possible mechanism for the association between internalized homophobia and risk-taking behavior. Men with higher levels of internalized homophobia may have more adjustment problems in general—related to intimacy, sexual behavior, and acceptance of their homosexuality. These mental health problems, along with anxiety about AIDS and depressive symptoms, may lead to escapist behaviors, especially the use of alcohol and drugs during sex, and may result in high-risk behavior (Folkman, Chesney, Pollack, & Phillips, 1992; Kelly, Murphy, Bahr, et al., 1993).

Throughout our presentation, it has been tempting for us to suggest that the detected associations of internalized homophobia and distress (and other correlates we have discussed) are due to the causal role of internalized homophobia. But, of course, the associations reported here do not, on their own, confirm such a causal role. A plausible alternative explanation is that the causal relationship is reversed; that is, the men's distress caused them to direct antigay attitudes toward themselves, leading to the observed higher levels of internalized homophobia. We cannot rule out this explanation, but the causal role of internalized homophobia receives credence from two sources. First, its plausibility is supported by the clinical and theoretical writings discussed in the first part of this chapter. Second, we used different outcomes to examine the correlates of internalized homophobia, and the results from all of these associations converge. We have shown that internalized homophobia is related to demoralization, guilt, suicide ideation, AIDS-related traumatic stress response, sex problems, relationships and intimacy, adjustment to experiences of antigay prejudice, and AIDS-related risk-taking behavior. Although it is possible that each of these types of distress causes internalized homophobia, a more parsimonious explanation is that internalized homophobia has a causal role in all of them. Nevertheless, causal relationships are rarely that simple—these two alternative explanations are not mutually exclusive. Most likely, internalized homophobia is both *cause* and *effect* in the relationships we have described. It is likely that men with higher levels of distress are more susceptible to societal antigay attitudes, and that after such attitudes are internalized, internalized homophobia further increases the level of distress. A more thorough investigation of causality is necessary to untangle these associations.

The study of internalized homophobia raises ethical concerns. It may be erroneously interpreted to suggest that homosexuals are more disturbed than heterosexuals (Gonsiorek, 1991). Because of the long history of stigmatization of lesbians, gay men, and bisexual people by mental health professionals (Bayer, 1981), gay-affirmative psychologists have concentrated their efforts on demonstrating that homosexuals are as well adjusted and as mentally healthy as heterosexuals (e.g., Freedman, 1971; Hooker, 1957; Marmor, 1980b). As a result, gay-affirmative psychologists have been reluctant to describe mental health problems among lesbians, gay men, and bisexual people, probably for fear that it would be misconstrued to support the view that homosexuality itself is a manifestation of emotional maladjustment. But these issues should not be confused. Although it is clear that homosexuality itself is not indicative of psychopathology, lesbian, gay, and bisexual people may suffer mental health effects because of the stress related to their minority status in society (Gonsiorek, 1991; Meyer, 1995). We believe that it is the responsibility of gay-affirmative psychologists to identify socially induced stressful conditions such as internalized homophobia because, as Pearlin (1982) has noted, "the eventual control of disease caused by stress depends on understanding the social etiology of the stress" (p. 368).

Our findings have important public health implications for prevention and treatment. The role of internalized homophobia in mental health suggests the need for intervention at the social level to reduce antigay attitudes and prejudice, and at the individual level to help lesbian, gay, and bisexual people to develop healthy sexual identities.

Comprehensive social preventive efforts to reduce homophobia may include enactment of appropriate legislation, reform of the criminal justice system, and widespread establishment of community education programs (Berrill & Herek, 1992). Individually based interventions should include gay-affirmative psychotherapies that are sensitive to issues of socialization, coming out, and internalized homophobia in the treatment of gay people. Addressing internalized homophobia is of particular significance among populations of gay and bisexual men who have not yet moved far along the coming-out process toward securing a supportive environment. Gay youth constitute one such population that may be at particular risk for suicidal ideation and behavior (Rotheram-Borus & Fernandez, 1995). Prevention among gay and lesbian youths must, therefore, address the issue of internalized homophobia. A supportive environment at schools and at after-school activities may help ward off negative self-attribution and internalized homophobia (see D'Augelli, Chapter 9, this volume).

The provision of gay-affirmative therapy and counseling is especially crucial, as potentially damaging reparative or conversion treatments, which seek to reverse the sexual orientation of homosexually oriented people, are reemerging (Haldeman, 1991; Martin, 1984). The danger in such therapies is that the psychotherapist will reinforce the patient's internalized homophobia and low self-regard. Such therapeutic approaches may be particularly harmful for gay and bisexual men who have higher levels of internalized homophobia—the group that is most likely to seek such therapies. As our data indicate, these are the men who are most vulnerable to psychological distress and suicidal ideation and behavior.

Our findings about the association between internalized homophobia and AIDS-related risk-taking behavior point to the need to address these issues in the design of AIDS prevention programs. AIDS prevention programs have developed sophisticated psychological models that address risk-taking behavior, but few have been aimed at helping the subset of gay and bisexual men who seem to suffer from significant adjustment problems (Kelly, Murphy, Sikkema, & Kalichman, 1993). In addressing mental health, such programs should assess men's adjustment to a homosexual identity and internalized homophobia in addition to addressing problems with alcohol and drug use.

Note

1. This does not mean that this type of risk management is enough. For example, asking sex partners about their HIV status may not be sufficient for managing risk, because some men may not know they are infected or may not disclose it if they are.

References

Allport, G. W. (1954). *The nature of prejudice.* Reading, MA: Addison-Wesley.
American Psychiatric Association. (1980). *Diagnostic and statistical manual of mental disorders* (3rd ed.). Washington, DC: Author.
American Psychiatric Association. (1987). *Diagnostic and statistical manual of mental disorders* (3rd ed., rev.). Washington, DC: Author.
Bayer, R. (1981). *Homosexuality and American psychiatry: The politics of diagnosis.* New York: Basic Books.

Berrill, K. T., & Herek, G. M. (1992). Primary and secondary victimization in antigay hate crimes: Official response and public policy. In G. M. Herek & K. T. Berrill (Eds.), *Hate crimes: Confronting violence against lesbians and gay men* (pp. 289-305). Newbury Park, CA: Sage.

Berzon, B. (1988). *Permanent partners: Building gay and lesbian relationships that last*. New York: Dutton.

Brooks, V. R. (1981). *Minority stress and lesbian women*. Lexington, MA: Lexington.

Cabaj, R. P. (1988). Homosexuality and neurosis: Considerations for psychotherapy. *Journal of Homosexuality, 15*(1-2), 13-23.

Cass, V. C. (1984). Homosexual identity formation: Testing a theoretical model. *Journal of Sex Research, 20,* 143-167.

Cohen, C., & Stein, T. (1986). Reconceptualizing individual psychotherapy with gay men and lesbians. In C. Cohen & T. Stein (Eds.), *Psychotherapy with lesbians and gay men*. New York: Plenum.

Cohen, P., & Cohen, J. (1984). The clinician's illusion. *Archives of General Psychiatry, 41,* 1178-1182.

Coleman, E. (1982). Developmental stages of the coming out process. *Journal of Homosexuality, 7*(2-3), 31-43.

Crocker, J., & Major, B. (1989). Social stigma and self-esteem: The self-protective properties of stigma. *Psychological Bulletin, 96,* 608-630.

Dean, L. (1996). *Summary of measures: The Longitudinal AIDS Impact Project* (Tech. Rep. No. 6, 02:96). New York: Columbia School of Public Health, Division of Sociomedical Sciences, AIDS Research Unit.

Dean, L., & Meyer, I. H. (1995). HIV prevalence and sexual behavior in a cohort of young New York City gay men (aged 18-24). *Journal of Acquired Immune Deficiency Syndromes, 8,* 208-211.

Dean, L., Wu, S., & Martin, J. L. (1992). Trends in violence and discrimination against gay men in New York City: 1984-1990. In G. M. Herek & K. T. Berrill (Eds.), *Hate crimes: Confronting violence against lesbians and gay men* (pp. 46-64). Newbury Park, CA: Sage.

de Monteflores, C., & Schultz, S. J. (1978). Coming out: Similarities and differences for lesbians and gay men. *Journal of Social Issues, 34*(3), 59-72.

Dohrenwend, B. P., Shrout, P. E., Egri, G., & Mendelsohn, F. S. (1980). Nonspecific psychological distress and other dimensions of psychopathology: Measures for use in the general population. *Archives of General Psychiatry, 37,* 1229-1236.

Duberman, M. (1991). *Cures: A gay man's odyssey*. New York: Plume.

Folkman, S., Chesney, M. A., Pollack, L., & Phillips, C. (1992). Stress, coping, and high-risk sexual behavior. *Health Psychology, 11,* 218-222.

Forstein, M. (1988). Homophobia: An overview. *Psychiatric Annals, 18*(1), 33-36.

Freedman, M. (1971). *Homosexuality and psychological functioning*. Belmont, CA: Brooks/ Cole.

Garnets, L. D., Herek, G. M., & Levy, B. (1990). Violence and victimization of lesbians and gay men: Mental health consequences. *Journal of Interpersonal Violence, 5,* 366-383.

Garnets, L. D., & Kimmel, D. C. (1991). Lesbian and gay male dimensions in the psychological study of human diversity. In L. D. Garnets, J. M. Jones, D. C. Kimmel, S. Sue, & C. Tavris (Eds.), *Psychological perspectives on human diversity in America* (pp. 137-192). Washington, DC: American Psychological Association.

Goffman, E. (1963). *Stigma: Notes on the management of spoiled identity*. New York: Simon & Schuster.

Gonsiorek, J. C. (1988). Mental health issues of gay and lesbian adolescents. *Journal of Adolescent Health Care, 9,* 114-122.

Gonsiorek, J. C. (1991). The empirical basis for the demise of the illness model of homosexuality. In J. C. Gonsiorek & J. D. Weinrich (Eds.), *Homosexuality: Research implications for public policy* (pp. 115-136). Newbury Park, CA: Sage.

Haldeman, D. C. (1991). Sexual orientation conversion therapy for gay men and lesbians: A scientific examination. In J. C. Gonsiorek & J. D. Weinrich (Eds.), *Homosexuality: Research implications for public policy* (pp. 149-160). Newbury Park, CA: Sage.

Hanley-Hackenbruck, P. (1988). "Coming out" and psychotherapy. *Psychiatric Annals, 18*(1), 29-32.

Harry, J. (1986). Sampling gay men. *Journal of Sex Research, 22*, 21-34.

Herek, G. M. (1986). The social psychology of homophobia: Toward a practical theory. *New York University Review of Law and Social Change, 16*, 923-934.

Herek, G. M. (1992). The social context of hate crimes: Notes on cultural heterosexism. In G. M. Herek & K. T. Berrill (Eds.), *Hate crimes: Confronting violence against lesbians and gay men* (pp. 89-104). Newbury Park, CA: Sage.

Herek, G. M., & Glunt, E. K. (1995). Identity and community among gay and bisexual men in the AIDS era: Preliminary findings from the Sacramento Men's Health Study. In G. M. Herek & B. Greene (Eds.), *AIDS, identity, and community: The HIV epidemic and lesbian and gay men* (pp. 55-84). Thousand Oaks, CA: Sage.

Hetrick, E. S., & Martin, D. A. (1984). Ego-dystonic homosexuality: A developmental view. In E. S. Hetrick & T. S. Stein (Eds.), *Innovations in psychotherapy with homosexuals* (pp. 2-21). Washington, DC: American Psychiatric Association Press.

Hooker, E. (1957). The adjustment of the male overt homosexual. *Journal of Projective Techniques, 21*, 18-31.

Isay, R. A. (1989). *Being homosexual: Gay men and their development.* New York: Farrar, Straus & Giroux.

Kelly, J. A., Murphy, D. A., Bahr, R. G., Koob, J. J., Morgan, M. G., Kalichman, S. C., Stevenson, Y. L., Brasfield, T. L., Bernstein, B. M., & St. Lawrence, J. S. (1993). Factors associated with severity of depression and high-risk sexual behavior among persons diagnosed with human immunodeficiency virus (HIV) infection. *Health Psychology, 12*, 215-219.

Kelly, J. A., Murphy, D. A., Sikkema, K. J., & Kalichman, S. C. (1993). Psychological interventions to prevent HIV infection are urgently needed: New priorities for behavioral research in the second decade of AIDS. *American Psychologist, 48*, 1023-1034.

Lazarus, R. S., & Folkman S. (1984). *Stress, appraisal, and coping.* New York: Springer.

Link, B. G. (1987). Understanding labeling effects in the area of mental disorders: An assessment of the effects of expectations of rejection. *American Sociological Review, 52*, 96-112.

Malyon, A. K. (1982). Psychotherapeutic implications of internalized homophobia in gay men. *Journal of Homosexuality, 7*(2-3), 59-69.

Marmor, J. (1980a). Epilogue: Homosexuality and the issue of mental illness. In J. Marmor (Ed.), *Homosexual behavior: A modern reappraisal* (pp. 391-401). New York: Basic Books.

Marmor, J. (Ed.). (1980b). *Homosexual behavior: A modern reappraisal.* New York: Basic Books.

Martin, D. (1984). The emperor's new clothes: Modern attempts to change sexual orientation. In E. S. Hetrick & T. S. Stein (Eds.), *Innovations in psychotherapy with homosexuals* (pp. 23-58). Washington, DC: American Psychiatric Association Press.

Martin, J. L., & Dean, L. (1990). Developing a community sample of gay men for an epidemiologic study of AIDS. *American Behavioral Scientist, 33*, 546-561.

McCombs, M. (1992, February 25). The state of the gay union. *Advocate.*

McDonald, G. J. (1982). Individual differences in the coming out process for gay men: Implications for theoretical models. *Journal of Homosexuality, 8*(1), 47-60.

McHenry, S., & Johnson, J. (1993). Homophobia in the therapist and gay or lesbian client: Conscious and unconscious collisions in self-hate. *Psychotherapy, 30*, 141-151.

Merton, R. K. (1957). *Social theory and social structure.* New York: Free Press.

Meyer, I. H. (1993). Prejudice and pride: Minority stress and mental health in gay men (Doctoral dissertation, Columbia University, 1993). *Dissertation Abstracts International, 54*, 12B, 6499.

Meyer, I. H. (1995). Minority stress and mental health in gay men. *Journal of Health and Social Behavior, 36*, 38-56.

Meyer, I. H. (in press). Sampling gay men: Random digit dialing versus recruitment through gay activity sources. *Journal of Homosexuality.*

Meyer, I. H., & Dean, L. (1995). Patterns of sexual behavior and risk taking among young New York City gay men. *AIDS Education and Prevention, 7*(Suppl.), 13-23.

Nicholson, W. D., & Long, B. C. (1990). Self-esteem, social support, internalized homophobia, and coping strategies of HIV+ gay men. *Journal of Consulting and Clinical Psychology, 58*, 873-876.

Nungesser, L. G. (1983). *Homosexual acts, actors, and identities.* New York: Praeger.

Pearlin, L. I. (1982). The social context of stress. In L. Goldberger & S. Breznits (Eds.), *Handbook of stress: Theoretical and clinical aspects.* New York: Academic Press.

Peterson, J. L., & Marin, G. (1988). Issues in the prevention of AIDS among black and Hispanic men. *American Psychologist, 43*, 871-877.

Rotheram-Borus, M. J., & Fernandez, I. (1995). Sexual orientation and developmental challenges experienced by gay and lesbian youths. *Suicide and Life-Threatening Behavior, 25*(Suppl.), 26-34.

Sandfort, T. G. M. (1995). HIV/AIDS prevention and the impact of attitudes toward homosexuality and bisexuality. In G. M. Herek & B. Greene (Eds.), *AIDS, identity, and community: The HIV epidemic and lesbians and gay men* (pp. 32-54). Thousand Oaks, CA: Sage.

Shidlo, A. (1994). Internalized homophobia: Conceptual and empirical issues in measurement. In B. Greene & G. M. Herek (Eds.), *Lesbian and gay psychology: Theory, research, and clinical applications* (pp. 176-205). Thousand Oaks, CA: Sage.

Sophie, J. (1987). Internalized homophobia and lesbian identity. *Journal of Homosexuality, 14*(1-2), 53-65.

Spitzer, R. L. (1981). The diagnostic status of homosexuality in DSM-III: A reformulation of the issues. *American Journal of Psychiatry, 138*, 210-215.

Stein, T. S., & Cohen, C. J. (1984). Psychotherapy with gay men and lesbians: An examination of homophobia, coming out, and identity. In E. S. Hetrick & T. S. Stein (Eds.), *Innovations in psychotherapy with homosexuals* (pp. 59-73). Washington, DC: American Psychiatric Association Press.

Thoits, P. (1985). Self-labeling processes in mental illness: The role of emotional deviance. *American Journal of Sociology, 91*, 221-249.

Troiden, R. R. (1989). The formation of homosexual identities. *Journal of Homosexuality, 17*(1-2), 43-73.

Warren, C. (1980). Homosexuality and stigma. In J. Marmor (Ed.), *Homosexual behavior: A modern reappraisal* (pp. 123-141). New York: Basic Books.

Weinberg, G. (1972). *Society and the healthy homosexual.* New York: St. Martin's.

Weinberg, M. S., & Williams, C. (1974). *Male homosexuals: Their problems and adaptations.* New York: Oxford University Press.

Weston, K. (1991). *Families we choose: Lesbians, gays, kinship.* New York: Columbia University Press.

Wolcott, D. L., Namir, S., Fawzy, F. I., Gottlieb, M. S., & Mitsuyasu, R. T. (1986). Illness concerns, attitudes toward homosexuality, and social support in gay men with AIDS. *General Hospital Psychiatry, 8*, 395-403.

9

Developmental Implications of Victimization of Lesbian, Gay, and Bisexual Youths

ANTHONY R. D'AUGELLI

Studies of bias-related violence that document victimization based on sexual orientation generally provide information about different types of incidents that have occurred to the lesbian, gay, and bisexual people sampled within time frames that vary in their specificity and duration. An analysis of the cumulative experience of being targeted over the course of one's life for unpleasant events ranging from hostile verbal comments to murderous assaults must minimally account for the frequency of events and for the particular kinds of sexual orientation victimization (SOV) experienced: Fifty homophobic comments are surely worse than one; and one vicious assault is more likely to be traumatizing than fifty common epithets.

But many other factors must be ascertained as well to arrive at an understanding of the psychological impact of SOV. Theories of the impact of violence on victims suggest that the characteristics of the person victimized as well as the characteristics of the victimizer (or victimizers), the actions that occurred, and the meanings and consequences of the event for the victim will determine whether someone else's action is experienced as trivial, traumatic, or transformative (Frieze, Hymer, & Greenberg, 1987; Janoff-Bulman & Frieze, 1983; McCann, Sakheim, & Abrahamson, 1988). The age of the victim at the time of the attack is one important factor in the impact of the victimization.

In this chapter, I review current research about SOV directed toward lesbian, gay, and bisexual youths. In contrast to lesbian, gay, and bisexual adults, youths are more likely to be victimized, and the psychological consequences of their victimization may be more severe. There are several reasons youths are more often victimized. First, adolescents in general are at greater risk of experiencing violence than are adults (Hammond & Yung, 1993; U.S. House of Representatives, 1989; Whitaker & Bastian, 1991). Second, lesbian, gay, and bisexual youths are more subject to violence because of their presence in settings in which SOV is most prevalent, such as lesbian/gay-identified neighborhoods in urban areas. Within these neighborhoods, they are more likely to attend social activities than are older lesbian, gay, and bisexual people. Third, lesbian, gay, and bisexual youths are victimized because of their association with the HIV epidemic (Herek & Glunt, 1988). Finally, lesbian, gay, and bisexual youths are victimized as a result of backlash resulting from the greater visibility of lesbian, gay, and bisexual people in society (Berrill, 1990; Hunter, 1990).

With increasing social acceptance of same-sex sexual orientation, more lesbian, gay, and bisexual youths are aware of their sexual orientation at earlier ages, have language to articulate their identities, disclose their identities ("come out") to others earlier, and find greater support from similar youths and from their families (Herdt, 1989; Savin-Williams, 1990, 1995). These factors create a strong personal identity from which to make their lives known to others. In contrast to earlier cohorts, in which shame about sexual orientation interfered with public acknowledgment, contemporary lesbian, gay, and bisexual youths develop in a context of lesbian, gay, and bisexual pride. Thus, lesbian, gay, and bisexual youths are more assertive about their identities and more confrontational than are members of prior generations (Leck, 1994; Schulman, 1994; Signorile, 1993). Their increased assertiveness, however, often puts them in direct conflict with others, including family and peers, as well as with traditional social institutions such as "the family," organized religion, and, most important, schools (Rofes, 1989, 1994). Contemporary youths' affirmative stance provides the personal resilience and the social support required to buffer the many forms of victimization that can follow open assertion of lesbian, gay, or bisexual identity. Nonetheless, the combination of earlier acknowledgment of sexual identity and earlier exposure to different kinds of victimization makes this generation of lesbian, gay, and bisexual youths vulnerable to psychological risks unknown to earlier cohorts. These risks are exacerbated by the HIV epidemic, which has had a profound impact on how lesbian, gay, and bisexual youths develop (Rotheram-Borus, Hunter, & Rosario, 1995).

Developmental Challenges for Lesbian, Gay, and Bisexual Youths

The amplified social vulnerability to victimization of lesbian, gay, and bisexual youths results from the distinctive character of their adolescent years (Savin-Williams, 1994, 1995). The physiological, psychological, and social changes related to pubertal development are difficult for many adolescents, but lesbian, gay, and bisexual youths face even more difficult challenges in developing a positive sexual identity in proximal (parents, family, peers, teachers) and distal (neighborhood, community) environments that are generally conditioned by heterosexist assumptions.

Although no research based on representative samples has explicitly focused on sexual orientation prior to puberty, the conclusion of recent studies is that personal awareness of same-sex erotic feelings often occurs in early adolescence and becomes increasingly crystallized at puberty, spurred in part by advances in cognitive development (D'Augelli & Hershberger, 1993; Herdt & Boxer, 1993; Savin-Williams, 1990). It is entirely possible that same-sex orientation evolves following the same developmental pattern as gender development, but its expression in early childhood is so severely sanctioned that its further elaboration is inhibited, suppressed until feelings reemerge at puberty or later.

The later same-sex feelings emerge, the more extensive has been the person's exposure to (and psychological commitment to) heterosexual socialization expectations. Research suggests, for example, that unconventional gender-related behavior (usually called *gender nonconformity*) in young boys is met with greater sanctions than is nonconventionality in young girls (Archer, 1984; Katz & Ksansnak, 1994), perhaps because girls' exceptional behavior mimics conventional "masculine" characteristics. Indeed, early childhood discouragement of emotional attachments to the same sex may be the first SOV experienced by all youths, regardless of their later sexual identity. The "appropriate" heteroerotic scripts for the development of sexual attachments are established implicitly, but the inappropriateness of homoerotic attachments is communicated explicitly when they occur in early childhood. Not only do parents discourage boys from fantasies and play in which they "marry" other boys, but teachers do as well. Homosociability is the only acceptable way to express same-sex interests, but there are clear social scripts for its expression. For boys, sports participation is the socially sanctioned script for ritualized (and thus controlled) same-sex affection. For girls, traditional female sex role development contains same-sex affection in a way that diffuses its erotic elements.

By the end of elementary school, children in American society have learned that heterosexuality is natural and that homoeroticism is shameful. Indeed, the same behaviors that researchers on adult SOV call "verbal attacks" (e.g., "You're a fag" or "You're *so* gay!") are normative childhood banter, seldom subject to adult sanction. Unfortunately, these adult-validated comments are sometimes directed to children with emerging homoerotic attachments. Such comments are also often provoked by unconventional gender-related behavior. Retrospective accounts of lesbians and gay men often include vivid memories of others' punitive responses to early signs of an emerging same-sex orientation, generally cued by their acting like the opposite sex (see, for example, Brimmer, 1995; Due, 1995). Many of these early incidents are traced to family sanctioning at particular ages—ordinarily when children enter preschool or elementary school. As children's behavior patterns become less fluid with age, parents presume the future stability of the patterns. A socially stigmatized pattern of gender atypicality raises parental concern—not only for a child who might be taunted by peers, but also for the family, whose "product" reflects upon them. Thus, a confluence of concern and anticipatory shame leads parents to monitor and forcefully extinguish "nonconforming" behavior, especially in boys. In most children, the behavioral patterns that are associated with negative reactions will be suppressed and alternatives attempted; feelings will be relabeled, repressed, or denied. Children who manifest extremely atypical gender-related behavior take on psychosocial careers as "sissy boys" or "tomboys."

The biological processes of puberty accelerate the intensity of same-sex orientation, while the increasingly demanding heterosexual social pressures of adolescence preclude its expression. The tension between physiological drives (which propel the eroticizing of others and of social bonds) and the channeling of eroticism into heterosexual social scripts (which mark objects for eroticizing) makes early adolescence, the teenage years, and young adulthood turbulent developmental periods, for if eroticism becomes decreasingly pansexual in the first decade of life, the heterosexual master script becomes increasingly powerful in the second decade. During the second decade of life, the expression of repressed and underdeveloped homoerotic feelings is inevitable and conflictual for all. How the homoerotic/heteroerotic tension is resolved during this part of life strongly predicts adult sexual orientation self-identification.

Positive resolution of the developmental dilemma of puberty by an age-appropriate expression and exploration of homoerotic social and sexual bonds does not typically occur for lesbian, gay, and bisexual youths because of stigmatization. For most lesbian, gay, and bisexual youths, the risks associated with expressing their feelings are learned vicariously as they observe penalties that open lesbian, gay, and bisexual youths and adults experience. Young adults who are lesbian or gay commonly remember that they maintained secrecy during their high school years because they knew what would happen at home or in school. But their reflections may be colored by the experiences of adulthood. It is unlikely that the processes of social perusal, reflection, decision making, and action occurred *at the time in the same way* they are remembered in adulthood. This silent victimization is nearly universal for those youths who are aware that they are interested in their own sex. Even applying the labels to oneself has costs—particularly given the prevalence of myths about lesbian, gay, and bisexual life that youths with such feelings may have internalized. Thus, if *developmental opportunity loss* is the first type of victimization lesbian, gay, and bisexual youths experience, *self-doubt induced by cultural heterosexism* is the second. We know from retrospective reports the negative consequences for youths of years of denial—constriction of affect, escalating social vigilance, turning away of social opportunities, and inauthentic heterosexual role playing (Hetrick & Martin, 1988; Martin, 1982; Remafedi, 1987c). Unfortunately, we have no reliable empirical information on the adult consequences of living the years of one's adolescence and early adulthood in uncertainty, fear, and alienation from self.

Self-acknowledgment of homoerotic feelings, itself the end point of a complex developmental process, instigates other processes of identity consolidation that are fundamentally social. Coming out to oneself usually leads to disclosure to someone else. Ordinarily, telling another person for the first time is experienced as extremely difficult, and this disclosure may follow self-awareness and self-labeling by many years. This first disclosure then creates momentum for more disclosures. There are multiple, overlapping processes involved in removing others' presumptions of heterosexuality, such as telling family (parents, siblings, extended family), friends (ranging from casual acquaintances to close friends), and important others in one's social network (such as coworkers, religious leaders, teachers, and coaches). These disclosure processes facilitate an exiting from heterosexual identity and its lifelong social expectations.

Exits from cultural heterosexuality are stressful both for the person who has been socialized within a heterosexual model and for her or his social network, whose previously unchallenged expectations are violated. Coming out to others initiates a lifetime of complex challenges—opportunities as well as problems—associated with the public knowledge of homoerotic interests. Indeed, if the silent victimization prior to disclosure to someone else exacts its costs, public openness about homoerotic orientation sets up the possibility of a lifetime of untoward events, ranging from religious condemnation to employment discrimination (Badgett, 1995). Indeed, public acknowledgment—even to friends and family—is an admission of criminal status in the states that retain anti-sodomy statutes. And, under current Department of Defense regulations, the verbal admission of same-sex orientation requires evidence that homosexual behavior *has not* occurred and *will not* occur to avoid separation from military service. This *institutional victimization* is the third form of victimization that lesbian, gay, and bisexual people must cope with.

Past writing about coming out has not focused on chronological age at disclosure as a crucial individual difference variable. Yet coming to terms with one's sexual orientation and the many complex dilemmas involved is considerably different for a 14-year-old than it is for a 24-year-old or a 34-year-old, for example. We have only begun the systematic process of understanding identity development for lesbian, gay, and bisexual youths, and we are surely conditioned by an "adultocentric" model wherein ways in which adult lesbian, gay, and bisexual people of earlier cohorts have developed are presumed to be relevant for teenagers, who occupy a very different and rapidly changing cultural space. Extrapolation of thinking about lesbian, gay, and bisexual adults to youths is similarly difficult. Not only do we have less information about such victimization compared with the victimization of lesbian, gay, and bisexual adults, but we know little about how youths successfully cope with victimization of different kinds.

Normative Victimization of
Lesbian, Gay, and Bisexual Youths

Many stressors in the lives of lesbian, gay, and bisexual youths occur only because of their sexual orientation. This kind of victimization—which makes heterosexuality normal and homoeroticism deviant—shapes how lesbian, gay, and bisexual youths develop. In this section, I will review three common cultural experiences that have developmental consequences for lesbian, gay, and bisexual youths: marginalization, coping with familial responses to disclosure of sexual orientation, and the impact of HIV/AIDS.

Marginalization

In contrast to heterosexual youths, lesbian, gay, and bisexual youths have few opportunities to explore their developing identities without risk. The earliest phenomenological experience of a young lesbian, gay male, or bisexual person is a sense of difference. This sense of "otherness" results from isolation from those with similar feelings and from messages that homoerotic feelings are shameworthy. Feeling different (and often not being able to understand the feeling), these youths withdraw from others or try to act "straight," with varying degrees of success. This process widens the gap between private identity and public identity and intensifies social vigilance, lest others figure out one's "true" identity. That homoerotic identity is socially stigmatized is shown by the results of a recent study of sexual harassment in high school, which found that being called "gay" by others was deemed the most upsetting form of sexual harassment (American Association of University Women, 1993).

During the initial period of recognition and labeling of homoerotic feelings, most lesbian, gay, and bisexual youths have little support from peers. In fact, the development of a supportive peer network occurs very slowly for most lesbian, gay, and bisexual youths. An intense fear of rejection by heterosexual peers is commonplace. A recent national survey of males 15 to 19 years of age found that few (12%) felt they could have a gay friend and that most (89%) considered sex between males to be "disgusting" (Marsiglio, 1993). Many lesbian, gay, and bisexual youths become dependent on small networks of friends who know of their sexual orientation. Having a small network of knowing friends while hiding one's sexuality from everyone else (including parents, siblings, and teachers) reinforces marginality and can increase stress. Without the opportunity to discuss their feelings, lesbian, gay, and bisexual youths may further internalize the negative views of society.

The internalization of a devalued marginality can erode coping efforts. Thus, it comes as no surprise that all available research points to a higher than expected frequency of problem behavior among many lesbian, gay, and bisexual youths. Savin-Williams's (1994) review found these major problem areas: (a) Lesbian, gay, and bisexual youths have school problems because of harassment from other students, leading to excessive absences, poor academic performance, and dropping out; (b) lesbian, gay, and bisexual youths run away from home, and some end up homeless; (c) many gay and bisexual male youths engage in conduct problems that bring them into contact with authorities; and (d) lesbian, gay, and bisexual youths abuse alcohol, drugs, and other substances to cope with daily stressors and with facing the future as a member of a stigmatized group.

Coping With Familial Responses to Disclosure of Sexual Orientation

Many problems of lesbian, gay, and bisexual youths are exacerbated by the lack of parental, sibling, and extended family support. The presumption of heterosexuality leaves families unprepared for homoeroticism, and youths' understanding that disclosure will not be greeted enthusiastically maximizes secrecy. Whereas most youths from historically disenfranchised groups rely on family support in the face of victimization based on their stigmatized identity, lesbian, gay, and bisexual youths often cannot. Indeed, if they are victimized, lesbian, gay, and bisexual youths often hesitate to tell their families because of fear of disclosure of their sexual orientation. Youths who reside at home or who are dependent upon their families for food, shelter, and financial support are even less likely to risk rejection if they are attacked than are other youths.

Fears of lesbian, gay, and bisexual youths about family reactions to disclosure of their sexual orientation seem justified. Research on parental reactions to disclosure of sexual orientation reveals considerable upset among parents, many of whom respond negatively at first (Strommen, 1989). Remafedi (1987b) found that 43% of a sample of gay male adolescents reported strong negative reactions from parents about their sexual orientation. Rotheram-Borus, Hunter, and Rosario (1994) found that youths experienced coming out to parents and siblings, being discovered as gay by parents or siblings, telling friends or being discovered by friends, and being ridiculed for being gay as the most common gay-related stressors. Using an adult gay male sample, Cramer and Roach (1988) found that 55% of the men's mothers and 42% of their fathers had initially negative responses. Robinson, Walters, and Skeen (1989) sampled parents of lesbian and gay adults through a national support group for parents and found that many reported initial sadness, regret, and depression, as well as fear for their children's well-being. Boxer, Cook, and Herdt (1991) studied parents of lesbian, gay, and bisexual youths aged 21 and younger, and found that more youths had disclosed to their mothers than to their fathers. Of the lesbian youths, 63% had disclosed to mothers and 37% to fathers; of the males, 54% had disclosed to mothers and 28% to fathers. Parents reported considerable family disruption after the initial disclosure. Herdt and Boxer (1993) found that most youths first disclose their orientation to friends, with more males finding this difficult than females. D'Augelli, Hershberger, and Pilkington (in press) found that three quarters of the youths in their study who lived at home had told their parents about their sexual orientation. Those who had disclosed received mixed acceptance; half of youths' mothers were accepting, but only one quarter of their fathers were. Other research has found that those youths who have secure relationships with their families may experience increased closeness over time following disclosure (Holtzen, Kenny, & Mahalik, 1995).

The Impact of HIV/AIDS

Feelings of marginality and conflicts with family appear to be nearly universal experiences of growing up as a lesbian, gay, or bisexual person. The historical anomaly of the HIV/AIDS epidemic augments these common stressors with challenges unknown prior to the early 1980s (Cranston, 1991; Rotheram-Borus et al., 1995). Issues related to HIV/AIDS are now major normative stressors in the lives of lesbian, gay, and bisexual youths. The most troublesome conflict occurs at the intersection of HIV risk and the expression of homoeroticism though sexual behavior. Male youths who have unsafe sex with other males (receptive anal intercourse without a condom and, at a considerably lower level of risk, receptive oral sex with ingestion) risk HIV infection regardless of their self-identification. Sexual identity depends upon sexual behavior; the psychological experience of sexual behavior helps to confirm self-identification or helps to resolve ambiguity. For young males who wish to engage in sexual activity with other males, fear of HIV infection may be an overpowering obstacle. How a young gay or bisexual male calculates his risk (or avoids the calculation) depends on many factors, another example of a highly critical life challenge for youths already burdened with intense dilemmas.

Recent studies have documented seroprevalence rates for HIV among urban young gay men varying from 7% to 12%, and unprotected intercourse rates of 10% to 40% (Davies et al., 1992; Dean & Meyer, 1995; Lemp et al., 1994; Meyer & Dean, 1995; Remafedi, 1994; Rotheram-Borus, Rosario, et al., 1994; Silvestre et al., 1993; Stall et al., 1992). Hoover et al. (1991) have estimated that seronegative 20-year-old urban gay males have a 20% chance of seroconversion before age 25. It is a developmental requirement that a young gay or bisexual male know how to negotiate a sexual experience with a new partner, yet such a process requires considerable social skill, especially assertiveness. For many gay and bisexual male youths, however, such negotiations are difficult (Grossman, 1994).

A related concern is HIV risk among young lesbians and bisexual females. A recent study by Cochran and Mays (1996) found a low HIV prevalence rate (0.5%) in two samples of 18- to 24-year-old bisexual and lesbian women. More than one fourth of the sample reported heterosexual intercourse in the previous year. Of bisexually identified women, 10% had had sex with a gay male partner within the year. Of the entire sample, 2.8% reported having had sex with a gay male partner within the past 3 months. The women who had had sex with gay men were those in the younger part of the sample, and many were teenagers. As Cochran and Mays also found that heterosexual sexual behavior was associated with having a sexually transmitted disease, further exploration of the relationship between young lesbians' and bisexual women's sexual behavior and HIV risk is clearly important.

It is beyond the scope of this chapter to review the history of HIV/AIDS and its impact on lesbian, gay, and bisexual youths. However, several comments are warranted. Historically, many gay and bisexual men became infected with HIV at least 10 years before they displayed symptoms. The infections occurred for some when they were teenagers or in their early 20s. In contrast to the generation who became adults (21+) in 1980, the generation now approaching 20 years of age was less than 10 years old when the first cases of AIDS were reported in 1981. They became teenagers and young adults during the HIV/AIDS epidemic. For many, coming to an awareness of their own identity occurred amidst enormous cultural controversy about the relationship of homoeroticism to AIDS. Their adolescence was also lived at a time when lesbian and gay people were more visible than ever before. Many were instructed about the existence of gay men within the context of AIDS education in schools. Whereas some of this socialization may have been helpful, the implicit message conflated sexual orientation and sexual behavior: Being gay involves risk for AIDS. The burden of feeling that one's sexual orientation puts one at risk for a potentially lethal infection (even though it is one's sexual and drug-using behaviors and the serostatuses of one's sexual partners that create the literal risk) is a special stress that HIV/AIDS has superimposed on lesbian, gay, and bisexual youth development.

Bias- and Hate-Motivated Attacks on Lesbian, Gay, and Bisexual Youths

The fourth type of victimization experienced by lesbian, gay, and bisexual people takes the form of *direct attacks* in which the attackers know, suspect, or presume that their targets are lesbian, gay, or bisexual.

Research suggests that young lesbian, gay, and bisexual people are often the victims of assaults (D'Augelli & Dark, 1995; Dean, Wu, & Martin, 1992). Dean et al. (1992) have shown that young gay men (aged 18 to 24) in New York are attacked more frequently than are older men. Victimization was found to be highest among women ages 18 to 24 in the National Lesbian and Gay Health Foundation study; 29% reported physical abuse, 50% reported rape and sexual assault, and 18% reported incest (Bradford, Ryan, & Rothblum, 1994). Violence directed at open lesbian, gay, and bisexual college and university students has also been documented (D'Augelli, 1992; Evans & D'Augelli, 1995). In Comstock's (1991) analysis of victimization patterns among college students, 22% reported having been chased or followed; 15% had had objects thrown at them; 4% had been punched, hit, kicked, or beaten; 11% had been the targets of vandalism or arson; 3% had been spat upon; and 1% had been assaulted with a weapon. Comstock concluded that lesbian, gay, and bisexual students are victimized at a rate four times higher than the rate reported by the general college student population. In a study of New

York City lesbian, gay, and bisexual youths from a social services agency, 41% had suffered from physical attacks, nearly half of which were provoked by the youths' sexual orientation (Hunter, 1990).

Lesbian, gay, and bisexual youths appear to be the victims of childhood physical or sexual abuse more frequently than do heterosexual youths, although direct comparisons between studies of lesbian, gay, and bisexual youths and youths in general (see Finkelhor & Dziuba-Leatherman, 1994) are difficult. Boney-McCoy and Finkelhor (1995) reported that 2.6% of females and 1.9% of males in a national telephone sample of 10- to 16-year-olds said they were physically attacked by their parents. In addition, 15.3% of female youths and 5.9% of male youths reported past sexual assault. In contrast, Bradford et al. (1994) reported that 24% of their sample of 1,925 lesbians had been harshly beaten or physically abused while growing up, 21% reported rape or sexual molestation in childhood, and 19% reported childhood incest. Of 1,001 adult gay and bisexual males attending sexually transmitted disease clinics, Doll and her colleagues (1992) found that 37% said they had been encouraged or forced to have sexual contact (mostly with older men) before age 19. Using the same sample, Barthalow et al. (1994) reported a significant association between past sexual abuse and current depression, suicidality, risky sexual behavior, and HIV-positive serostatus.

Attacks Within the Family

The home is often not a safe haven for lesbian, gay, and bisexual youths, especially if they tell their families about themselves. Many parents believe that they are responsible for their offspring's sexual orientation, a belief that puts the family and the youths in conflict that may lead to abuse and violence (Hunter & Schaecher, 1987). For many youths, their families' religious commitments set the stage for rejections of different kinds, ranging from begrudging acknowledgment to forceful ejection from the household. In community surveys of antilesbian/antigay abuse by relatives, 19% to 41% of respondents had experienced verbal insults or threats, and 4% to 7% had encountered physical violence (Berrill, 1990). In a study of lesbian and gay youths at a New York City social service agency dedicated to their needs, Hunter (1990) found that 61% of the violence youths reported as occurring because of their sexual orientation had happened at home. One fourth said that fear of future victimization at home affected their openness about their sexual orientation. Pilkington and D'Augelli (1995) found that more than one third of their lesbian, gay, and bisexual youth sample had been verbally abused by a family member, and 10% were physically assaulted by a family member because of their sexual orientation. Of those youths in this study who were still living at home, one quarter of the males and one third of the females who had disclosed their sexual orientation said that their mothers were verbally abusive; fathers were reported to be verbally abusive by 20% of the disclosed youths (D'Augelli et al., in press). Disclosed lesbian youths living at home were physically attacked by their parents (10% by mothers, 5% by fathers) more often than were disclosed male youths (3% by mothers, 2% by fathers). Many reported fear of verbal or physical abuse at home. Harry (1989a) found that gay males were more likely to be physically abused during adolescence than were heterosexual males, especially if they had histories of childhood femininity and poor relationships with their fathers. The National Lesbian and Gay Health Foundation survey found that 70% of all women beaten or abused as children were attacked by unspecified male relatives; 45% were attacked by female relatives (Bradford et al., 1994). Of those women raped or sexually attacked as children, 31% were attacked by male relatives and 45% by other males they knew. Of those who ever experienced incest (19% of the total sample), 34% of the perpetrators were brothers, 28% were fathers, 27% were uncles, and 18% were cousins.

Attacks in Community Settings

In addition to familial conflicts and violence, lesbian, gay, and bisexual youths who are open about their sexual orientation (or who are assumed to be lesbian or gay) face verbal harassment and physical attacks in community settings. More than half of the gay male youths in Remafedi's (1987a) study reported peer verbal abuse, and nearly one third reported physical assaults. Nearly 40% of the male youths in Remafedi, Farrow, and Deisher's (1991) study said that they had experienced physical violence. In the Bradford et al. (1994) study, 52% of the young lesbians said that they had been verbally attacked, and 6% said that they had been physically attacked. Pilkington and D'Augelli (1995) found that 80% of the lesbian, gay, and bisexual youths in their study reported verbal abuse based on their sexual orientation; 48% reported that such abuse had occurred more than twice. Gay male youths reported significantly more verbal abuse. Of the total group, 44% had been threatened with physical violence; 23% had had personal property damaged; 33% had had objects thrown at them; 30% had been chased, 16% more than once; and 13% had been spat upon. As for more serious attacks, 17% had been assaulted (punched, kicked, or beaten); 10% had been assaulted with a weapon; and 22% reported sexual assault. More than half of the male youths in Remafedi's (1987c) study reported peer verbal abuse, and nearly one third (30%) reported physical assault. Nearly 40% of the male youths in the Remafedi et al. (1991) study said that they had experienced physical violence. Physical attacks by family members, peers, or strangers were reported by 41% of the lesbian and gay youths surveyed by Hunter (1990), with nearly half of the attacks attributable to sexual orientation. In a study of gay male youths drawn from the same social service agency used by Hunter (1990), Rotheram-Borus, Rosario, and Koopman (1991) found that 27% reported physical assault, 14% reported rape or sexual assault, and 55% said that they had been ridiculed by someone because of their sexual orientation. In the National Lesbian and Gay Health Foundation study, 52% of the total sample of women said that they had been verbally attacked, and 6% said that they had been physically attacked (Bradford et al., 1994). Nearly half (44%) of another sample of lesbian and gay youths said that they were either physically or emotionally abused, with sexual orientation the primary reason for the abuse (Hammelman, 1993).

Attacks in Schools

In addition to familial conflicts and victimization in the community, open lesbian, gay, and bisexual youths face verbal harassment and physical attacks in schools. Because young people spend so much time in schools, and because of the relationship between academic achievement and later accomplishments, these settings are of crucial importance to our understanding of lesbian, gay, and bisexual youths' transitions into early adulthood. Many school problems of lesbian, gay, and bisexual students, such as poor academic performance, truancy, and dropping out of school, are direct or indirect results of verbal and physical abuse perpetrated by peers or others in schools (Uribe & Harbeck, 1991). Up to half of lesbian and gay male adults report having experienced some form of victimization in school (Berrill, 1990). Gross, Aurand, and Adessa (1988) found that 50% of a sample of gay men reported victimization in junior high school and 59% in high school; of lesbians sampled, 12% were victimized in junior high school and 21% in high school. These findings were corroborated in a later survey (Gross & Aurand, 1992). In 1991, 37% of lesbians and gay men surveyed by the National Gay and Lesbian Task Force Policy Institute (1994) reported experiencing harassment, threats, or actual violence in junior and senior high school. A survey of New York State junior and senior high school students showed that nearly one third witnessed acts of violence directed at students or teachers thought to be lesbian or gay (White, 1988). In the Pilkington and D'Augelli (1995) study, 31% of the youths feared verbal abuse at school, and 26% feared physical abuse at school.

The Impact of Victimization on Mental Health

The four forms of SOV that I have described—developmental opportunity loss, self-doubt, institutional victimization, and direct attacks—increase adjustment difficulties that can lead to mental health problems for some youths. General population surveys have shown that youths victimized by assaults show more symptoms, posttraumatic stress reactions, and sadness than do youths who are not attacked, and that symptomatology is worse among survivors of sexual assault (Boney-McCoy & Finkelhor, 1995). There is every reason to assume that these relationships are further intensified for lesbian, gay, and bisexual youths. The evidence of significant stressors in this population is compelling. In the Bradford et al. (1994) study, mental health problems were common among 17- to 24-year-old lesbians. Nearly two thirds (62%) had received counseling. The concerns most frequently taken to counselors were family problems, depression, problems in relationships, and anxiety. Remafedi (1987a) found that nearly three quarters of a sample of adolescent gay males had received mental health services. A study of young gay university males revealed many personal and emotional concerns, the most frequently reported of which were dealing with parents about sexual orientation (93% reported it to be a concern), relationship problems, worry about AIDS, anxiety, and depression (D'Augelli, 1991).

The available evidence also suggests a disproportionately high incidence of suicide attempts among lesbian, gay, and bisexual youths compared with findings for youths in general. Lewinsohn, Rohde, and Seeley (1996) have noted that lifetime suicide attempt rates in studies of high school students range from 6% to 10%. All of the available research on suicide attempts among lesbian, gay, and bisexual youths shows higher rates. An early study of gay male youths found that 31% had made a suicide attempt (Roesler & Deisher, 1972). The first Kinsey report devoted exclusively to homosexuality found that 20% of the gay men studied reported a suicide attempt prior to age 20 (Bell & Weinberg, 1978). A decade later, Hetrick and Martin (1988) found that 21% of their clients at a social service agency for troubled youth had made a suicide attempt. Harry (1989b) concluded that lesbians and gay men are more likely to make suicide attempts at times of conflicts about sexual orientation, especially in adolescence.

Recent empirical studies have come to similar conclusions about elevated risk for suicide among lesbian, gay, and bisexual youths. Remafedi (1987a) found that 34% of his gay male adolescent sample had attempted suicide. In a later study with a larger sample, Remafedi et al. (1991) found that 30% had made a suicide attempt. Those who had attempted suicide were younger, had more feminine gender role concepts, and were more likely to report drug and alcohol abuse. Remafedi et al. found that nearly half of the gay male youths studied reported that their suicide attempts were precipitated by "family problems." Another study of gay male youths found that 23% had attempted suicide at least once, and that 59% evidenced serious suicidal thinking (Schneider, Farberow, & Kruks, 1989). Schneider et al. (1989) found that suicide attempters had not yet established a stable sexual identity, and that attempts occurred most often before youths acknowledged their sexual identity to others. They also found that early awareness of sexual orientation was associated with suicide attempts. Of the young women in the National Lesbian and Gay Health Foundation survey, only 41% said that they had never contemplated suicide, and about one quarter had made an attempt (Bradford et al., 1994). Herdt and Boxer (1993) found that 29% of lesbian, gay, and bisexual youths in a Chicago youth support group program had made a suicide attempt. More than half (53%) of the lesbian youths reported suicide attempts, compared with 20% of the gay male youths. In the D'Augelli and Hershberger (1993) study, 42% of the 194 youths reported a past suicide attempt. Attempters were aware of their sexual attractions at an earlier age, were more open about themselves, had lower self-esteem, and showed more current symptoms. Attempters were also more often victimized than were nonattempters. The strongest correlations with past suicide attempts were the loss of friends due to sexual orientation and low self-esteem (Hershberger, Pilkington, & D'Augelli, 1997).

Many lesbian, gay, and bisexual youths—whether in school or not—cope with the challenges of victimization on their own, or with the help of a small network of others whose confidence is predictable. Some, especially those who are seriously hurt as a result of an assault, may have no choice but to turn to others, such as parents, teachers, or religious leaders, who may be unaccepting of their sexual orientation. For some youths, attacks lead to the precipitous disclosure of their sexual orientation. For others, a fragile equilibrium in which neither they nor their families have confronted the issue of sexual orientation may be shattered by victimization (Boxer et al., 1991). Thus, youths may experience additional difficulties in the process of seeking help after being attacked, whether the victimization is routine mistreatment or a direct physical attack. Some lesbian, gay, and bisexual adults experience increased vulnerability, intensified internalized homophobia, depression, guilt, and self-blame as a consequence of victimization (Garnets, Herek, & Levy, 1990). Herek, Gillis, Cogan, and Glunt (1997) found that lesbian, gay, and bisexual adult victims of antilesbian/antigay bias crimes were more psychologically distressed than were victims of other kinds of crimes. An extension of this research to lesbian, gay, and bisexual youths is very much needed. It may be hypothesized that negative reactions to victimization based on sexual orientation would be more common among lesbian, gay, and bisexual youths than among adults, especially for those youths who have low self-esteem, who have little family support, and who have not found support in lesbian, gay, and bisexual community settings.

Research Questions

The first generation of research about victimization directed to lesbian, gay, and bisexual youths has been concerned with simple documentation. In a general sense, we know that lesbian, gay, and bisexual young people are verbally insulted and physically hurt; that they appear to be harmed more often than older lesbian, gay, and bisexual people and more often than heterosexual youths; and that they are not free from fear of victimization in their homes, communities, or schools. In families, in communities, and in schools, youths engage in varying degrees of contortion of self to avoid becoming the target of others' hostility. Greater openness—whether by being "identifiable," by telling others about oneself, by being "outed" by others, or by appearing to be lesbian or gay—may lead to more victimization. Honesty may not be the best policy, especially for a young lesbian, gay, or bisexual person living at home with family members who have strong homophobic views. Although there is much left to be learned about victimization of lesbian, gay, and bisexual youths, we know enough about some of the developmental implications of victimization to suggest interventions (D'Augelli, 1993, 1996).

The next generation of research on this topic must address the details. The set of questions ahead differs if one emphasizes patterns of victimization or mechanisms that explain how different kinds of SOV promote or interfere with developmental advancement to adulthood. Studying younger populations compresses the time frame for recall of past experiences, allowing greater accuracy and reflection about victimization. For instance, one could study youths who have recently come out and learn of their experiences prior to their disclosure. From this group, details of early development could be learned, so that we might begin to articulate a developmental model of sexual orientation as well as understand victimization that occurs in childhood. Research on youths who begin to tell others is crucial for identifying the stimuli that provoke victimization based on sexual orientation. Is physical appearance relevant? Can telling one untrustworthy high school peer set into motion a chain of events that leads to attacks? Do certain personality characteristics (sociability, assertiveness, and so on) lead to attacks? Do certain characteristics diminish the chance of attacks? Or is the nature of youths' proximal social environments—the heterosexism of families, schools, neighborhoods—at the core of victimization patterns? This contextualization of victimization may also help disentangle victimization based on other characteristics, such as gender, racial/ethnic background, and socioeconomic status, from attacks related to youths' sexual orientation.

Research on victimized youths must extend its purview over time to encompass developmental sequelae. There are no longitudinal data on lesbian, gay, and bisexual youths that detail patterns of SOV. Which SOVs are perceived as distressing is an important question, as is how lesbian, gay, and bisexual youth networks may help to "neutralize" SOV by warning about typical attacks and suggesting how to cope with them.

Linking patterns of SOV to later adjustment indicators will help us to know how well youths respond to SOV. The coping mechanisms that lesbian, gay, and bisexual youths use to deal with different kinds of victimization must be detailed. Most lesbian, gay, and bisexual youths cope effectively with victimization and become well-adjusted adults. However, when SOV is associated with distress, it is crucial to know the mediating emotional conditions involved. Little is known about how variability in crucial factors such as prior mental health status, personal characteristics (especially self-esteem and coping skills), support from family and friends, and involvement with helping resources of different kinds (especially those affirming youths' sexual orientation) might buffer the impacts of verbal and physical abuse.

Conclusions

Based on a reading of the available research literature, some general predictions are possible about the future needs of lesbian, gay, and bisexual youths. More youths will be disclosing their sexual orientation to others, and at earlier ages. The junior and senior high school years will become times during which more youths will self-label in a positive way than in past generations. As youths self-label earlier, they will experience greater vulnerability too. The increased cultural visibility of lesbian, gay, and bisexual people will stimulate more negative reactions from heterosexuals. As youths experience more conflict, more of them will seek social support. Some will seek help as a result of the psychological consequences of persistent verbal harassment, and some will need help recovering from physical assaults. More youths will also self-identify as lesbian, gay, and bisexual during their college years, as this is often the first time that parental scrutiny is significantly diminished.

Contemporary lesbian, gay, and bisexual youths, if given access to helping resources such as lesbian, gay, and bisexual peer support and other affirming helping resources, will do well in meeting the challenges of developing into well-functioning lesbian, gay, and bisexual adults. The ideology of "queer" affirmation provides youths with an invigorating model for enhancing personal resilience and developing group solidarity. It is crucial to avoid stereotyping lesbian, gay, and bisexual youths as passive and helpless victims. In fact, youths have provided a visible challenge to older lesbian, gay, and bisexual people to demand fair treatment in society. Yet young lesbian, gay, and bisexual people should not be romanticized. Many lesbian, gay, and bisexual youths have problems, and these problems should not be minimized. The challenges unique to lesbian, gay, and bisexual youths are mostly caused by cultural and institutional victimization as well as direct attacks. Both systemic victimization and direct attacks must be eliminated. Personal and social identities can develop only in safe and supportive social circumstances. Developmental delays and dysfunctions in the processes of identity development are more likely to occur in hostile and heterosexist environments. In hostile contexts, internalized homophobia and social inhibition prevent the development of self-esteem and social integration. And for some lesbian, gay, and bisexual youths, diminished self-esteem and loneliness may lead to despair. Until we know which youths move toward adulthood with resilience and which slide toward self-erasure, which conditions encourage resourcefulness and which deplete it, it is crucial that we consider lesbian, gay, and bisexual young people to be potential targets of victimization who are in need of protection and support.

References

American Association of University Women. (1993). *Hostile hallways: The AAUW survey on sexual harassment in America's schools*. Washington, DC: Author.

Archer, J. (1984). Gender roles as developmental pathways. *British Journal of Social Psychology, 23,* 245-256.

Badgett, M. V. L. (1995). The wage effects of sexual orientation discrimination. *Industrial and Labor Relations Review, 48,* 726-739.

Barthalow, B. N., Doll, L. S., Joy, D., Douglas, J. M., Bolan, G., Harrison, J. S., Moss, P. M., & McKirnan, D. (1994). Emotional, behavioral, and HIV risks associated with sexual abuse among homosexual and bisexual men. *Child Abuse & Neglect, 18,* 753-767.

Bell, A. P., & Weinberg, M. S. (1978). *Homosexualities: A study of diversity among men and women*. New York: Simon & Schuster.

Berrill, K. T. (1990). Anti-gay violence and victimization in the United States: An overview. *Journal of Interpersonal Violence, 5,* 274-294.

Boney-McCoy, S., & Finkelhor, D. (1995). Psychosocial sequelae of violent victimization in a national youth sample. *Journal of Consulting and Clinical Psychology, 63,* 726-736.

Boxer, A. M., Cook, J. A., & Herdt, G. (1991). Double jeopardy: Identity transitions and parent-child relations among gay and lesbian youth. In K. Pillemer & K. McCartney (Eds.), *Parent-child relations throughout life* (pp. 59-92). Hillsdale, NJ: Lawrence Erlbaum.

Bradford, J., Ryan, C., & Rothblum, E. D. (1994). National Lesbian Health Care Survey: Implications for mental health care. *Journal of Consulting and Clinical Psychology, 62,* 228-242.

Brimmer, L. D. (1995). *Being different: Lambda youths speak out*. New York: Franklin Watts.

Cochran, S. D., & Mays, V. M. (1996). Prevalence of HIV-related sexual risk behaviors among young 18- to 24-year-old lesbian and bisexual women. *Women's Health: Research on Gender, Behavior, and Policy, 2*(1-2), 75-89.

Comstock, G. D. (1991). *Violence against lesbians and gay men.* New York: Columbia University Press.

Cramer, D. W., & Roach, A. J. (1988). Coming out to Mom and Dad: A study of gay males and their relationships with their parents. *Journal of Homosexuality, 15*(3-4), 79-92.

Cranston, K. (1991). HIV education for gay, lesbian, and bisexual youth: Personal risk, personal power, and the community of conscience. *Journal of Homosexuality, 22*(3-4), 247-259.

D'Augelli, A. R. (1991). Gay men in college: Identity processes and adaptations. *Journal of College Student Development, 32,* 140-146.

D'Augelli, A. R. (1992). Lesbian and gay male undergraduates' experiences of harassment and fear on campus. *Journal of Interpersonal Violence, 7,* 383-395.

D'Augelli, A. R. (1993). Preventing mental health problems among lesbian and gay college students. *Journal of Primary Prevention, 13*(4), 1-17.

D'Augelli, A. R. (1996). Enhancing the development of lesbian, gay, and bisexual youths. In E. D. Rothblum & L. Bond (Eds.), *Prevention of heterosexism and homophobia* (pp. 124-150). Thousand Oaks, CA: Sage.

D'Augelli, A. R., & Dark, L. J. (1995). Vulnerable populations: Lesbian, gay, and bisexual youth. In L. D. Eron, J. H. Gentry, & P. Schlegel (Eds.), *Reason to hope: A psychosocial perspective on violence and youth* (pp. 177-196). Washington, DC: American Psychological Association.

D'Augelli, A. R., & Hershberger, S. L. (1993). Lesbian, gay, and bisexual youths in community settings: Personal challenges and mental health problems. *American Journal of Community Psychology, 21,* 421-448.

D'Augelli, A. R., Hershberger, S. L., & Pilkington, N. W. (in press). Lesbian, gay, and bisexual youths and their families: Disclosure of sexual orientation and its consequences. *American Journal of Orthopsychiatry.*

Davies, P. M., Weatherburn, P., Hunt, A. J., Hickson, F. C. I., McManus, T. J., & Coxon, A. P. M. (1992). The sexual behavior of young gay men in England and Wales. *AIDS Care, 4,* 259-272.

Dean, L., & Meyer, I. H. (1995). HIV prevalence and sexual behavior in a cohort of New York City gay men (aged 18-24). *Journal of Acquired Immune Deficiency Syndromes, 8,* 208-211.

Dean, L., Wu, S., & Martin, J. L. (1992). Trends in violence and discrimination against gay men in New York City: 1984-1990. In G. M. Herek & K. T. Berrill (Eds.), *Hate crimes: Confronting violence against lesbians and gay men* (pp. 46-64). Newbury Park, CA: Sage.

Doll, L. S., Joy, D., Barthalow, B. N., Harrison, J. S., Bolan, G., Douglas, J. M., Saltzman, L. E., Moss, P. M., & Delgado, W. (1992). Self-reported childhood and adolescent sexual abuse among adult homosexual and bisexual men. *Child Abuse & Neglect, 16,* 855-864.

Due, L. (1995). *Joining the tribe: Growing up gay and lesbian in the 90's.* Garden City, NY: Anchor.

Evans, N. J., & D'Augelli, A. R. (1995). Lesbians, gay men, and bisexual people in college. In R. C. Savin-Williams & K. M. Cohen (Eds.), *The lives of lesbians, gays, and bisexuals* (pp. 201-226). New York: Harcourt Brace Jovanovich.

Finkelhor, D., & Dziuba-Leatherman, J. (1994). Victimization of children. *American Psychologist, 49,* 173-183.

Frieze, T. H., Hymer, S., & Greenberg, M. S. (1987). Describing the crime victim: Psychological reactions to victimization. *Professional Psychology, 18,* 299-315.

Garnets, L. D., Herek, G. M., & Levy, B. (1990). Violence and victimization of lesbians and gay men: Mental health consequences. *Journal of Interpersonal Violence, 5,* 366-383.

Gross, L., & Aurand, S. K. (1992). *Discrimination and violence against lesbian women and gay men in Philadelphia and the Commonwealth of Pennsylvania.* Philadelphia: Philadelphia Lesbian and Gay Task Force.

Gross, L., Aurand, S. K., & Adessa, R. (1988). *Violence and discrimination against lesbian and gay people in Philadelphia and the Commonwealth of Pennsylvania.* Philadelphia: Philadelphia Lesbian and Gay Task Force.

Grossman, A. H. (1994). Homophobia: A cofactor of HIV disease in gay and lesbian youth. *Journal of the Association of Nurses in AIDS Care, 5,* 39-43.

Hammelman, T. L. (1993). Gay and lesbian youth: Contributing factors to serious attempts or considerations of suicide. *Journal of Gay and Lesbian Psychotherapy, 2,* 77-89.

Hammond, W. R., & Yung, B. (1993). Psychology's role in the public health response to assaultive violence among African American men. *American Psychologist, 48,* 142-154.

Harry, J. (1989a). Parental physical abuse and sexual orientation. *Archives of Sexual Behavior, 18,* 251-261.

Harry, J. (1989b). Sexual identity issues. In *Report of the Secretary's Task Force on Youth Suicide* (DHHS Publication No. ADM 89-1622, Vol. 2, pp. 131-142). Washington, DC: Government Printing Office.

Herdt, G. H. (1989). Gay and lesbian youth: Emergent identities and cultural scenes at home and abroad. *Journal of Homosexuality, 17*(1-2), 1-42.

Herdt, G. H., & Boxer, A. M. (1993). *Children of Horizons: How gay and lesbian teens are leading a new way out of the closet.* Boston: Beacon.

Herek, G. M., Gillis, J. R., Cogan, J. C., & Glunt, E. K. (1997). Hate crime victimization among lesbian, gay, and bisexual adults: Prevalence, psychological correlates, and methodological issues. *Journal of Interpersonal Violence, 12,* 195-215.

Herek, G. M., & Glunt, E. K. (1988). An epidemic of stigma: Public reactions to AIDS. *American Psychologist, 43,* 886-891.

Hershberger, S. L., Pilkington, N. W., & D'Augelli, A. R. (1997). Predictors of suicidality among gay, lesbian, and bisexual youths. *Journal of Adolescent Research, 12,* 477-497.

Hetrick, E. S., & Martin, A. D. (1988). The stigmatization of the gay and lesbian adolescent. *Journal of Homosexuality, 15*(1-2), 163-183.

Holtzen, D. W., Kenny, M. E., & Mahalik, J. R. (1995). Contributions of parental attachment to gay and lesbian disclosure to parents and dysfunctional cognitive processes. *Journal of Counseling Psychology, 42,* 350-355.

Hoover, D. R., Munoz, A., Carey, V., Chmiel, J. S., Taylor, J. M. G., Margoloic, J. B., Kingsley, L., & Vermund, S. H. (1991). Estimating the 1978-1990 and future spread of HIV-1 in subgroups of homosexual men. *American Journal of Epidemiology, 134,* 1190-1205.

Hunter, J. (1990). Violence against lesbian and gay male youths. *Journal of Interpersonal Violence, 5,* 295-300.

Hunter, J., & Schaecher, R. (1987). Stresses on lesbian and gay adolescents in schools. *Social Work in Education, 9,* 180-190.

Janoff-Bulman, R., & Frieze, I. H. (1983). A theoretical perspective for understanding reactions to victimization. *Journal of Social Issues, 39*(2), 1-17.

Katz, P. A., & Ksansnak, K. R. (1994). Developmental aspects of gender role flexibility and traditionality in middle childhood and adolescence. *Developmental Psychology, 30,* 272-282.

Leck, G. (1994). Politics of adolescent sexual identity and queer responses. *High School Journal, 77,* 186-192.

Lemp, G. F., Hirozawa, A. M., Givertz, D., Nieri, G. N., Anderson, L., Lindegren, M. L., Janssen, R. S., & Katz, M. (1994). Seroprevalence of HIV and risk behaviors among young homosexual and bisexual men. *Journal of the American Medical Association, 272,* 449-454.

Lewinsohn, P. M., Rohde, P., & Seeley, J. R. (1996). Adolescent suicide ideation and attempts: Prevalence, risk factors, and clinical implications. *Clinical Psychology: Science and Practice, 3,* 25-46.

Marsiglio, W. (1993). Attitudes towards homosexual activity and gays as friends: A national survey of heterosexual 15- to 19-year-old males. *Journal of Sex Research, 30,* 12-17.

Martin, A. D. (1982). Learning to hide: The socialization of the gay adolescent. *Adolescent Psychiatry, 10,* 52-65.

McCann, I. L., Sakheim, D., & Abrahamson, D. (1988). Trauma and victimization: A model of psychological adaptation. *Counseling Psychologist, 16,* 531-594.

Meyer, I. H., & Dean, L. (1995). Patterns of sexual behavior and risk taking among young New York City gay men. *AIDS Education and Prevention, 7*(Suppl.), 13-23.

National Gay and Lesbian Task Force Policy Institute. (1994). *Anti-gay/lesbian violence, victimization, and defamation in 1993.* Washington, DC: Author.

Pilkington, N. W., & D'Augelli, A. R. (1995). Victimization of lesbian, gay, and bisexual youth in community settings. *Journal of Community Psychology, 23,* 33-56.

Remafedi, G. (1987a). Adolescent homosexuality: Psychosocial and medical implications. *Pediatrics, 79,* 331-337.

Remafedi, G. (1987b). Homosexual youth: A challenge to contemporary society. *Journal of the American Medical Association, 258,* 222-225.

Remafedi, G. (1987c). Male homosexuality: The adolescent's perspective. *Pediatrics, 79,* 326-330.

Remafedi, G. (1994). Predictors of unprotected intercourse among gay and bisexual youths: Knowledge, beliefs, and behavior. *Pediatrics, 94,* 163-168.

Remafedi, G., Farrow, J. A., & Deisher, R. W. (1991). Risk factors for attempted suicide in gay and bisexual youth. *Pediatrics, 87,* 869-875.

Robinson, B. E., Walters, L. H., & Skeen, P. (1989). Response of parents to learning that their child is homosexual and concern over AIDS: A national survey. *Journal of Homosexuality, 18*(1-2), 59-80.

Roesler, T., & Deisher, R. W. (1972). Youthful male homosexuality. *Journal of the American Medical Association, 219,* 1018-1023.

Rofes, E. E. (1989). Opening up the classroom closet: Responding to the educational needs of gay and lesbian youth. *Harvard Educational Review, 59,* 444-453.

Rofes, E. E. (1994). Making our schools safe for sissies. *High School Journal, 77,* 37-40.

Rotheram-Borus, M. J., Hunter, J., & Rosario, M. (1994). Suicidal behavior and gay-related stress among gay and bisexual male adolescents. *Journal of Adolescent Research, 9,* 498-508.

Rotheram-Borus, M. J., Hunter, J., & Rosario, M. (1995). Coming out as lesbian or gay in the era of AIDS. In G. M. Herek & B. Greene (Eds.), *AIDS, identity, and community: The HIV epidemic and lesbians and gay men* (pp. 150-168). Thousand Oaks, CA: Sage.

Rotheram-Borus, M. J., Rosario, M., & Koopman, C. (1991). Minority youth at high risk: Gay males and runaways. In M. E. Colten & S. Gore (Eds.), *Adolescent stress: Causes and consequences* (pp. 181-200). New York: Aldine de Gruyter.

Rotheram-Borus, M. J., Rosario, M., Meyer-Bahlburg, H. F. L., Koopman, C., Dopkins, S. C., & Davies, M. (1994). Sexual and substance use acts of gay and bisexual male adolescents in New York City. *Journal of Sex Research, 31,* 47-57.

Savin-Williams, R. C. (1990). *Gay and lesbian youth: Expressions of identity.* Washington, DC: Hemisphere.

Savin-Williams, R. C. (1994). Verbal and physical abuse as stressors in the lives of lesbian, gay male, and bisexual youths: Associations with school problems, running away, substance abuse, prostitution, and suicide. *Journal of Consulting and Clinical Psychology, 62,* 261-269.

Savin-Williams, R. C. (1995). Lesbian, gay male, and bisexual adolescents. In A. R. D'Augelli & C. J. Patterson (Eds.), *Lesbian, gay, and bisexual identities across the lifespan* (pp. 165-189). New York: Oxford University Press.

Schneider, S. G., Farberow, N. L., & Kruks, G. N. (1989). Suicidal behavior in adolescent and young adult gay men. *Suicidal and Life-Threatening Behavior, 19,* 381-394.

Schulman, S. (1994). *My American history: Lesbian and gay life during the Reagan/Bush years.* New York: Routledge.

Signorile, M. (1993). *Queer in America: Sex, the media, and the closets of power.* New York: Random House.

Silvestre, A. J., Kingsley, L. A., Wehman, P., Dappen, R., Ho, M., & Rinaldo, C. R. (1993). Changes in HIV rates and sexual behavior among homosexual men, 1984 to 1988. *American Journal of Public Health, 83,* 578-580.

Stall, R., Barrett, D., Bye, L., Catania, J., Frutchey, C., Hennessey, J., Lemp, G., & Paul, J. (1992). A comparison of younger and older gay men's HIV risk-taking behaviors: The Communication Technology 1989 Cross-Sectional Survey. *Journal of Acquired Immune Deficiency Syndromes, 5,* 682-687.

Strommen, E. F. (1989). Hidden branches and growing pains: Homosexuality and the family tree. *Marriage and Family Review, 14,* 9-34.

Uribe, V., & Harbeck, K. M. (1991). Addressing the needs of lesbian, gay, and bisexual youth: The origins of Project 10 and school-based intervention. *Journal of Homosexuality, 22*(3-4), 9-28.

U.S. House of Representatives, Select Committee on Children, Youth, and Families. (1989). *Down these mean streets: Violence by and against America's children.* Washington, DC: Government Printing Office.

Whitaker, C. J., & Bastian, L. D. (1991, May). *Teenage victims* (Tech. Rep. No. 128129). Washington, DC: U.S. Department of Justice, Office of Justice Programs, Bureau of Justice Statistics National Crime Survey.

White, D. H. (1988). *Governor's Task Force on Bias-Related Violence: Final report.* Albany, NY: Governor's Office.

10

The Postmodern Family

An Examination of the Psychosocial and Legal Perspectives of Gay and Lesbian Parenting

ANDREW McLEOD

ISIAAH CRAWFORD

An emerging appreciation of the plurality of postmodern culture has prompted an investigation into the various forms that families assume. No aspect of this investigation has produced as much controversy as the issue of gays and lesbians raising children. The question of whether gay men and lesbians are fit parents is currently being tackled in the legal as well as academic arenas. As detailed below, academic research has consistently indicated that gay parents and their children do not differ significantly from the norm. However, court decisions in child custody cases have sent mixed messages regarding the legal protection of gays' and lesbians' parental rights.

The variance in court rulings regarding child custody can be explained partly by the fact that research findings are often not integrated into the judicial decision-making process. Even when courts consider the research, questions are frequently raised regarding its validity. All microscopes are pointed toward gay and lesbian parents, as their sexual orientation seems to be considered a critical variable in determining the suitability of a family environment for a child's healthy development. However, a broader analysis of the dominant belief systems influencing this investigation is needed to elucidate the attitudes and presumptions that obscure the issue.

Although parenting by lesbians and gay men is not a new phenomenon, lesbian mothers and gay fathers have become increasingly more open about their sexual orientation (Ricketts & Achtenberg, 1990). Gays and lesbians also have an increasing number of options to become parents. In the past, most gay men and women with children probably had them as the result of heterosexual unions. Today, however, many are pursuing such options as foster care, adoption, surrogacy, and donor sperm insemination. The number of gay parents is difficult to estimate because so many of them are forced to conceal their orientation due to fear of discrimination. In 1990, one author estimated that there were 1 to 5 million lesbian mothers and 1 to 3 million gay fathers in the United States (Gottman, 1990).

Although gays and lesbians now have broadened avenues through which they may become parents, they are precluded overall from the legal parental rights granted to heterosexuals. The general assumption that gay and lesbian parents have adverse effects on the psychological and social development of their children is a major force underlying judicial decision making in custody litigation (Patterson, 1992; Ricketts & Achtenberg, 1990). For example, the states of Florida and New Hampshire have enacted legislation that prohibits gays and lesbians from qualifying as foster or adoptive parents (Leiter, 1997). In other states, foster care and adoption agencies do not have particular policies singling out gays and lesbians as unfit, but they frequently make it extremely difficult for gays and lesbians to become parents (Ricketts & Achtenberg, 1990). Many gay parents are also denied custody of or visitation with their biological children (Patterson, 1992).

As legal issues pertaining to gay and lesbian parents have received more national attention, state courts have been divided in determining gays' and lesbians' rights in custody cases. According to the National Center for Lesbian Rights, eight state supreme courts have ruled that a homosexual parent should not automatically be denied custody, whereas five others have ruled in the opposite direction (Cohn, 1995). This issue has not been addressed by the U.S. Supreme Court.

The Courts and Scientific Data

The courts have used a variety of approaches in determining custody in cases involving lesbian or gay parents. Some judges have taken the stance, for example, that although homosexuality, by itself, does not necessarily render a parent unfit, a homosexual relationship in the child's home creates an unsuitable environment for the child (Rosenblum, 1991). When custody has been granted to gay parents in this instance, it has usually been with the stipulation that they not live with a partner or associate with other homosexuals (Ali, 1989). In other cases, gay and lesbian parents have been denied custody of a child on the basis of their sexual orientation per se, because the child was presumed to face heightened stigma as a consequence of the parent's sexual orientation (Ali, 1989; Ronner, 1995) or was expected to be negatively affected in the development of sexual orientation or gender identity (Shapiro, 1996). A thorough discussion of the legal merits of these rulings is beyond the scope of the present chapter (for reviews, see Ali, 1989; Rosenblum, 1991; Shapiro, 1996). However, we briefly review social and behavioral science data relevant to these and other questions that have been raised about lesbians and gay men as parents.

The Child's Best Interests

The children of gay parents do not differ from children of heterosexual parents in overall social or psychological adjustment (Gottman, 1990; Kirkpatrick, Smith, & Roy, 1981; Miller, 1979; Patterson, 1992). On the question of stigmatization, Green, Mandel, Hotvedt, Gray, and Smith (1986) found no differences in the ways that homosexual and heterosexual mothers rated the social skills and popularity of their children among their peers. The children in this study also did not evidence differences in their own ratings of their popularity among same-sex and opposite-sex peers. This study is limited by the use of self-report measures, which may be confounded by a desire to present oneself in a favorable light. Other research indicates that although children of gay mothers rarely recall facing harassment from their peers, adolescents are more likely to receive negative messages concerning their parents' homosexuality (Cramer, 1986).

The notion that gay parents might influence their children's psychosexual development and, essentially, make them gay is based on the assumption that homosexuality is an undesirable and conditioned pattern of behavior. While not necessarily endorsing this premise, empirical research has nevertheless consistently indicated that children of gay parents are no more likely to be gay than are children of heterosexual parents (Bigner & Bozett, 1990; Cramer, 1986; Gottman, 1990; Patterson, 1992). A longitudinal study conducted in the United Kingdom by Golombok and Tasker (1996) found no significant differences in sexual attraction or self-labeled sexual orientation between adult children (M = 23.5 years) of lesbian and heterosexual mothers, although significantly more children raised by lesbian mothers reported having had sexual relationships with others of the same sex (all of the children reported having had at least one sexual relationship with a person of the opposite sex). In a study of 82 adult sons of gay fathers (Bailey, Bobrow, Wolfe, & Mikach, 1995), data about sexual orientation were available for 75; of these, 68 (91%) were heterosexual. Similarly, empirical evidence indicates that children of gay parents do not differ from children of heterosexual parents on the basis of gender identity and gender role behavior, as well as social and psychological adjustment (Gottman, 1990; Green et al., 1986; Kirkpatrick et al., 1981; Patterson, 1992).

Fitness of Lesbian and Gay Parents

The notion that gays and lesbians are unfit to be parents is not supported by empirical evidence (Bigner & Bozett, 1990; Bigner & Jacobsen, 1992; Gottman, 1990; Harris & Turner, 1986; Patterson, 1992; Ricketts & Achtenberg, 1990). Research has consistently demonstrated that the parenting abilities and child-rearing practices of gay and lesbian parents are similar to those of heterosexual parents (see Patterson, 1992, for a review). In addition, both gay and heterosexual parents report relatively few serious problems and overall positive relationships with their children (Harris & Turner, 1986). Several gay parents also have reported that their sexual orientation has been a strengthening experience for their children (Harris & Turner, 1986; Patterson, 1992). For example, gay parents in one study maintained that the honesty and openness surrounding their sexual orientation allowed for greater interpersonal intimacy between them and their children (Bigner & Bozett, 1990). It has also been argued that children of gay parents may be able to approach their own sexuality with greater acceptance, to develop greater empathy for others, and to have tolerance for alternative viewpoints (Patterson, 1992).

In response to the belief that lesbian couples do not create safe homes for their children, recent research has compared lesbian mothers who have conceived through artificial insemination with married heterosexual parents. Results from this study demonstrated that both groups exhibit similarly satisfying relationships with their partners (Flaks, Ficher, Masterpasqua, & Joseph, 1995). The quality of the spousal relationships of lesbian mothers was also comparable to the established norms of married couples. Further analyses of data from this sample indicated that lesbian mothers were as knowledgeable about effective parenting skills as were their heterosexual counterparts, could identify critical issues in child-care situations, and could formulate appropriate solutions to the problems they encountered. Lesbian mothers demonstrated not only the ability to create an environment with a stable spousal relationship, but also the knowledge necessary to execute effective parenting skills.

Similarly, gay fathers' parenting styles and attitudes toward fathering have been found to be more similar to than different from those of non-gay fathers (Bigner & Jacobsen, 1992). Research indicates that there are no differences between homosexual and heterosexual fathers with regard to degree of involvement with children's activities, intimacy with children, problem solving, provision of recreational activities, encouragement of child autonomy, and the manner in which problems of child rearing are handled (Bigner & Bozett, 1990; Bigner & Jacobsen, 1992; Harris & Turner, 1986; Miller, 1979). From their review of the literature, Bigner and Bozett (1990) concluded that gay fathers not only have positive relationships with their children, they also try harder than nongay fathers to create stable homes and maintain more positive relationships with their children.

Heterosexuals' Attitudes Toward Gay Parenting

A 1992 *Newsweek*/Gallup poll evidenced a split between the growing acceptance of homosexuals in today's political climate and continued support for legal obstructions that limit gays' and lesbians' parental rights ("Gays Under Fire," 1992). In that poll, 78% of respondents believed that homosexuals should be afforded the same rights as heterosexuals in job opportunities. Moreover, substantial majorities approved of gay spouses receiving economic benefits such as health insurance (67% approved) and inheritance rights (70% approved). But as the survey questions came closer to measuring attitudes toward a gay family unit, opinion became more conservative. A total of 61% of respondents disapproved of legally sanctioning gay spouses' adoption rights, and 58% disapproved of legally sanctioned gay marriages. Attitudes appeared to be split between support for gays' and lesbians' individual rights and the rejection of gay families (see Strand, Chapter 6, this volume).

Negative assumptions about gays and lesbians seem to influence heterosexuals' perceptions of the parenting abilities of gays and lesbians and the psychological well-being of their children. For example, in a study of undergraduates' attitudes toward gay parenting, a gay male couple was viewed as being less emotionally stable, having poorer parenting potential, and creating a more dangerous home when compared with a heterosexual couple (Crawford & Solliday, 1996). In an attempt to explicate these assumptions, we conducted a study that empirically demonstrated that heterosexuals' attitudes toward gay and lesbian parents and their children may be rooted within the notion that gay parents influence their children's psychosexual development and essentially make them gay (McLeod, Crawford, & Zechmeister, 1997).

Our study examined undergraduates' attitudes toward gay fathers and their children by comparing participants' evaluations of vignettes depicting either a gay male couple or a heterosexual couple and their adopted son. Each couple and their adopted child were portrayed in the midst of ambiguous and mild family discord. Participants rated the couples along several dimensions, including parenting ability, the degree to which the child's distress was attributed to the parental relationship, the extent to which reassigning custody to the grandparents was beneficial for the child, the quality of the child's peer relationships, and the perceived overall distress that the child was experiencing, as well as the degree of distress related to confusion regarding the child's gender role, gender identity, and sexual orientation. In order to determine the variables that may have contributed to participants' perceptions of gay fathers and their adopted son, we also assessed religiosity, political conservatism, and adherence to gay male stereotypes.

Results indicated that although participants did not view any differences in the overall parenting ability of the gay and heterosexual couples, comparisons of the ratings of the heterosexual father to his gay counterpart indicated that the gay father was actually perceived as more loving toward his son and as spending a greater quality of time with him. However, custody reassignment was rated as more beneficial for the son raised by gay fathers, and a trend indicated that the child's perceived problems were related to the parental relationship more when the parents were described as gay. This apparent contradiction may be explained by the finding that the boy raised by gay fathers was viewed as experiencing a greater level of identity distress, which was attributed to confusion regarding his sexual orientation and male identity.

An analysis of the ratings of the gay family unit revealed that assumptions pertaining to the child's identity distress and the benefit of custody reassignment were significantly predicted by the participants' stereotype of gay men as effeminate, above and beyond the participants' political conservatism and religious attendance. In contrast to studies reviewed by DeCrescenzo (1984)—which found that gays were frequently stereotyped as sexually promiscuous, impulsive, and inclined to abuse a child sexually (see also Simon, Chapter 4, this volume)—our study found these stereotypes to be more common for heterosexual men. However, these heterosexual male stereotypes were not significantly related to differences in the ratings of the heterosexual fathers. Despite the heterosexual male stereotypes and the higher rating of the gay father compared with his heterosexual counterpart, this study demonstrated that the more effeminate gay men were perceived to be, the more likely it was that participants viewed the child as experiencing sexual and gender identity distress and benefiting from custody reassignment.

Family Values

The predominant belief that parental homosexuality is an important predictor of a child's psychological well-being seems to be contingent upon the belief that gay parents violate traditional gender roles. Empirical research indicates that many heterosexuals who hold negative attitudes toward gays and lesbians subscribe to an implicit inversion theory through which homosexuals are perceived as being more like the opposite sex (Kite & Deaux, 1987). Negative attitudes toward gays and lesbians are also mediated by adherence to traditional ideologies of gender (Herek, 1984, 1988; Kerns & Fine, 1994; Kurdek, 1988; Stark, 1991; see Kite & Whitley, Chapter 3, this volume). Moreover, traditional notions of the family that build upon or define gender roles are also significant predictors of negative attitudes toward gays and lesbians (Herek, 1988). Because antigay sentiments are also predicated on the perception that gays and lesbians hold value systems that are different from those of the dominant culture (Haddock, Zanna, & Esses, 1993; see also Haddock & Zanna, Chapter 5, this volume), it becomes increasingly clear that the presumed cross-gender behavior of gays and lesbians may exclude them from what has become known as "family values" in our culture.

Not only may the perceived violation of traditional gender and family ideologies contribute to the ascription of an "antifamily" status to gays and lesbians, but the categorization of people as homosexual may also tend to give precedence to sexual orientation as a defining aspect of an individual's overall value system. More than heterosexual relationships, the perception of gay and lesbian relationships tends to be reduced to sexual identity and ultimately sexual behavior (Weston, 1991). Highlighting sexual behavior as the central feature of an identity or relationship tends to overshadow other personal qualities, such as intimacy and love (Weston, 1991). For example, Testa, Kinder, and Ironson (1987) found that homosexual couples were perceived to be less in love and less satisfied with their relationships than were heterosexual couples presented with identical information. Lacking the validation of marriage, gay and lesbian relationships also may be more likely to be viewed in terms of a sexual freedom and individualism that preclude the kinship ties, responsibility, and affection normally associated with family (Weston, 1991).

The dominant view of gay and lesbian relationships as nonprocreative and primarily sexual in nature casts gays and lesbians even further from the domain of kinship. The notion of family in North American culture has been predominantly constructed around biological ties or blood relationships and seems to place greater value on these ties. However, several scientific and sociological changes surrounding parenting options (i.e., artificial insemination, surrogacy, and adoption) have changed the face of the typical family. In addition to an increasing divorce rate, these options contribute to more single-parent families and extended stepfamilies. The emerging recognition and validation of gay relationships is just one of several factors broadening the perspective of what constitutes family. To capture the nature of these changes, Weston (1991) has described a continuum of ideological transformations from *biological* to *chosen* families, with heterosexual families more often associated with the former and gay families with the latter. In this postmodern sociopolitical climate, the dominant culture contends with the fact that the notion of family is expanding beyond biological ties to incorporate the element of choice in the construction of family. Gays' and lesbians' chosen families face the challenge of having to validate their relationships as conducive to the kinship associated with the biological family.

The overall perception of gays and lesbians as violating what has traditionally been associated with family may be mobilized by an underlying commitment to a system constructed around gender, sexuality, and family. Characteristics that have been found in individuals who hold negative attitudes toward gays and lesbians include authoritarianism (Haddock et al., 1993) and a moral reasoning based on rules and regulations (Kurdek, 1988). Based on these findings, Kurdek (1988) has suggested that negative attitudes toward gays and lesbians may stem from an overall need for regulations that uphold the conventional social order. Examination of negative attitudes toward gay and lesbian parents has revealed that the needed conventional social order seems to be based on rules regarding traditional notions of a gender-sexuality-family system.

Adherence to a traditional gender-sexuality-family order means that conventional rules regarding heterosexuality and clearly defined gender roles are perceived as necessary for a healthy family environment. Because this constellation is made up of interlocking spheres of gender, sexuality, and family, a violation in one part of the order may undermine the entire order. The person who relies on conventional rules of social order may need to conceptualize a potential contradiction in a manner that would present less ambiguity. For example, Storms (1978) found that feminine heterosexual men were liked less than masculine heterosexual men, but feminine homosexual men were liked more than masculine homosexual men. Perhaps heterosexuals who adhere to conventional rules that fuse heterosexuality with masculinity in their view of men resent having these rules disconfirmed (Storms, 1978). From this perspective, homosexuality may be kept from threatening the social order of a gender-sexuality-family system through the imposition of a cross-gender stereotype and a subsequent nonfamily status onto gays and lesbians.

Because gays and lesbians may be viewed as nonreproductive as well as violating the social order of gender and family, they may be seen as less than family by those who observe the dominant standard of a "biological" family and its gender-sexuality-family system. Believing that gay and lesbian parents will make their children gay (and hence cross-gendered) helps maintain adherence to the traditional gender-sexuality-family perspective by protecting it from the contradiction that gay parents may, after all, be reproductive by raising "normal" children. Thus, perceiving gays and lesbians as consistently violating the rules about gender, sexuality, and family keeps those who have a need for rules regarding social order from having to face the ambiguity of contradictions.

Rigid adherence to a conventional gender-sexuality-family order may be explained by the psychological needs it fulfills. Herek (1986) has contended that these attitudes serve the purpose of meeting psychological needs that are relevant to one's self-concept, thereby allowing individuals to establish their identity. In this way, antigay attitudes can be symbolic, "expressing abstract ideological concepts that are closely linked to one's own notion of self and to one's social networks and reference groups" (Herek, 1984, p. 8). In a North American society founded on the principle of a nuclear family that requires a heterosexual couple and specific male and female parental roles, believing that gays and lesbians are unfit to be parents can symbolically express a feeling that exalted values are being violated, and can thereby function to affirm those values (Herek, 1986). Espousing and publicly endorsing antigay values may serve the psychological need to reaffirm one's commitment to socially acceptable family values. It may also serve the purpose of affirming one's identification as a respectable and moral parent and an advocate for the nuclear family committed to one's prescribed gender role and sexuality. Given the considerable benefits of supporting one's sense of self as what one wishes to perceive oneself to be, the symbolic attitude of hostility to gay parenting would understandably solicit strong support.

Conclusion

The legal system and psychological research continue to debate the pertinence of parental sexual orientation in the creation of a healthy family environment. Rules about gender and sexuality have traditionally served as the infrastructure of the family, and when people are perceived to violate these rules, they are often stigmatized as antifamily. This prevailing attitude inspires the presumption that gays and lesbians are not fit to be parents. Consequently, research that does not support this supposition is often met with skepticism and resistance. This phenomenon is comparable to Abramowitz's (1978) notion of a *heartpothesis*, where, in the face of substantial empirical disconfirmation, scholars and scientists cling to a conviction. In contrast to hypotheses, which are rendered mortal by empirical fact, heart-potheses are immune to data. Whereas research is customarily conducted to corroborate or refute hypotheses, tests of heart-potheses often have a surreptitious political or social function, that of granting scientific status to personal beliefs (Abramowitz, 1978).

The postmodern family is challenged by heart-potheses and must bear the burden of dismantling them by encouraging the implementation of nonbiased social science research that addresses the myths surrounding gay and lesbian people. In addition, it must demand that the legal system discontinue its policy of dismissing the findings of this research. In failing to do so, the judiciary renders gay and lesbian families vulnerable to the prejudices of society.

References

Abramowitz, S. I. (1978). Splitting data from theory on the Black patient-White therapist relationship. *American Psychologist, 33,* 957-958.

Ali, S. (1989). Homosexual parenting: Child custody and adoption. *UC Davis Law Review, 22,* 1009-1038.

Bailey, M. J., Bobrow, D., Wolfe, M., & Mikach, S. (1995). Sexual orientation of adult sons of gay fathers. *Developmental Psychology, 31,* 124-129.

Bigner, J. J., & Bozett, F. W. (1990). Parenting by gay fathers. In F. W. Bozett & M. B. Sussman (Eds.), *Homosexuality and family relations* (pp. 155-176). New York: Harrington Park.

Bigner, J. J., & Jacobsen, R. B. (1992). Adult responses to child behavior and attitudes toward fathering: Gay and nongay fathers. *Journal of Homosexuality, 23*(3), 99-112.

Cohn, D. (1995, May 9). Courts send mixed messages in custody cases. *Washington Post,* p. B7.

Cramer, D. (1986). Gay parents and their children: A review of research and practical implications. *Journal of Counseling and Development, 64,* 504-507.

Crawford, I., & Solliday, E. (1996). The attitudes of undergraduate college students toward gay parenting. *Journal of Homosexuality, 30*(4), 63-77.

DeCrescenzo, T. A. (1984). Homophobia: A study of the attitudes of mental health professionals toward homosexuality. In R. Schoenberg, R. S. Goldberg, & D. A. Shore (Eds.), *Homosexuality and social work* (pp. 115-135). New York: Haworth.

Flaks, D. K., Ficher, I., Masterpasqua, F., & Joseph, G. (1995). Lesbians choosing motherhood: A comparative study of lesbian and heterosexual parents and their children. *Developmental Psychology, 31,* 105-114.

Gays under fire. (1992, September 14). *Newsweek,* pp. 35-40.

Golombok, S., & Tasker, F. (1996). Do parents influence the sexual orientation of their children? Findings from a longitudinal study of lesbian families. *Developmental Psychology, 32,* 3-11.

Gottman, J. S. (1990). Children of gay and lesbian parents. In F. W. Bozett & M. B. Sussman (Eds.), *Homosexuality and family relations* (pp. 177-196). New York: Harrington Park.

Green, R., Mandel, J. B., Hotvedt, M. E., Gray, J., & Smith, L. (1986). Lesbian mothers and their children: A comparison with solo parent heterosexual mothers and their children. *Archives of Sexual Behavior, 15,* 167-184.

Haddock, G., Zanna, M. P., & Esses, V. M. (1993). Assessing the structure of prejudicial attitudes: The case of attitudes toward homosexuals. *Journal of Personality and Social Psychology, 65,* 1105-1118.

Harris, M. B., & Turner, P. H. (1986). Gay and lesbian parents. *Journal of Homosexuality, 12*(2), 101-113.

Herek, G. M. (1984). Beyond "homophobia": A social psychological perspective on attitudes toward lesbians and gay men. *Journal of Homosexuality, 10*(1-2), 1-21.

Herek, G. M. (1986). On heterosexual masculinity. *American Behavioral Scientist, 29,* 563-577.

Herek, G. M. (1988). Heterosexuals' attitudes toward lesbians and gay men: Correlates and gender differences. *Journal of Sex Research, 25,* 451-477.

Kerns, J. G., & Fine, M. A. (1994). The relation between gender and negative attitudes toward gay men and lesbians: Do gender role attitudes mediate this relation? *Sex Roles, 31,* 297-307.

Kirkpatrick, M., Smith, C., & Roy, R. (1981). Lesbian mothers and their children: A comparative survey. *American Journal of Orthopsychiatry, 51,* 545-551.

Kite, M. E., & Deaux, K. (1987). Gender belief systems: Homosexuality and the implicit inversion theory. *Psychology of Women Quarterly, 11,* 83-96.

Kurdek, L. A. (1988). Correlates of negative attitudes toward homosexuals in heterosexual college students. *Sex Roles, 18,* 727-738.

Leiter, R. A. (Ed.). (1997). *National survey of state laws.* Detroit, MI: Gale Research.

McLeod, A., Crawford, I., & Zechmeister, J. (1997). *Heterosexuals' attitudes toward gay fathers and their children.* Manuscript submitted for publication.

Miller, B. (1979). Gay fathers and their children. *Family Coordinator, 28,* 544-552.

Patterson, C. J. (1992). Children of lesbian and gay parents. *Child Development, 63,* 1025-1042.

Ricketts, W., & Achtenberg, R. (1990). Adoption and foster parenting for lesbian and gay men: Creating new traditions in family. In F. W. Bozett & M. B. Sussman (Eds.), *Homosexuality and family relations* (pp. 83-118). New York: Harrington Park.

Ronner, A. (1995). Bottoms v. Bottoms [444 S.E. 2d 276 (Va. 1994)]: The lesbian mother and the judicial perpetuation of damaging stereotypes. *Yale Journal of Law and Feminism, 7,* 341-373.

Rosenblum, D. M. (1991). Custody rights of gay and lesbian parents. *Villanova Law Review, 36,* 1665-1696.

Shapiro, J. (1996). Custody and conduct: How the law fails lesbian and gay parents and their children. *Indiana Law Journal, 71,* 623-671.

Stark, L. P. (1991). Traditional gender role beliefs and individual outcomes: An exploratory analysis. *Sex Roles, 24,* 639-650.

Storms, M. D. (1978). Attitudes toward homosexuality and femininity in men. *Journal of Homosexuality, 3,* 257-263.

Testa, R. J., Kinder, B. N., & Ironson, G. (1987). Heterosexual bias in the perception of loving relationships of gay males and lesbians. *Journal of Sex Research, 23,* 163-172.

Weston, K. (1991). *The families we choose.* New York: Columbia University Press.

11

Bad Science in the Service of Stigma
A Critique of the Cameron Group's Survey Studies

GREGORY M. HEREK

Psychologist Paul Cameron and his research group have argued that homosexuals threaten public health (e.g., Cameron, Proctor, Coburn, & Forde, 1985), social order (Cameron, Cameron, & Proctor, 1989), and the well-being of children (Cameron & Cameron, 1996a, 1996b; Cameron et al., 1986). Their conclusions are generally at odds with other published research, and, as explained below, objective indexes show that their work has had no apparent impact on scientific research on sexual orientation. Outside the world of science and academia, however, their reports have been taken more seriously.

For example, their statistics were quoted extensively by proponents of Colorado's antigay Amendment 2 (Booth, 1992; Bull & Gallagher, 1996; Herman, 1997). In a position statement distributed by Colorado for Family Values, the Cameron group's data were directly cited to support a variety of assertions, including that "homosexuals are, statistically, about 18 times more likely to engage in sexual practices with minors than are heterosexuals" and that homosexuals "perpetrate more than ⅓ of all reported child molestations" (Marco, 1991, p. 8). Their influence apparently extended to the Colorado attorney general, Gale Norton, who was reported to have paid Cameron a large consulting fee to assist in preparing the state's case defending the constitutionality of Amendment 2 (Bull & Gallagher, 1996; Pietrzyk, 1994).

The Cameron group's work also has been used in the public policy arena at the federal level. In 1985, for example, Cameron was hired by then-Representative William Dannemeyer (R-CA) as a consultant on AIDS (Cimons, 1985; "Public Financing of Hate," 1985). In 1993, their research was used by the Pentagon's Military Working Group, which provided recommendations concerning President Clinton's plan to eliminate restrictions on military service by openly gay personnel (Bull & Gallagher, 1996; Otjen, 1994).

In addition, *The Gay Agenda*—a church-produced video that featured sensationalist footage of lewd behavior in gay pride parades (Colker, 1993)—included statistics that, although not attributed to the Cameron group, were identical to those reported in Cameron et al.'s (1989) Table 1 ("Tape's Statistics," 1993). The video was widely distributed throughout the United States (Colker, 1993; Herman, 1997) and, according to a court deposition by Lieutenant General John P. Otjen (1994), was used by the Military Working Group as a source of information about homosexuality.

Although Paul Cameron has been criticized in the popular press (Fettner, 1985; Pietrzyk, 1994; Walter, 1985), extensive scientific critiques of his group's research have not been widely available. Those that have been published have been brief (Boor, 1988a, 1988b; Duncan, 1988; Gonsiorek & Weinrich, 1991; Weinrich, 1988) or were published in obscure journals (Brown & Cole, 1985). The scientific community's relative inattention to the Cameron group's work is perhaps not surprising, given the poor quality of the latter's data and the low prestige of the journals in which it has appeared. Most scientists appear to have simply ignored it.

Lacking training in research methods and statistics, however, nonscientists may not be equipped to subject the Cameron group's results to the rigorous scrutiny that they warrant. Consequently, nonscientists may mistakenly assume that the Cameron group's papers must be basically sound because they included lengthy bibliographies, reported many statistics, and were published in academic journals. Unfortunately, they may fail to recognize that the mere presence of bibliographic references does not guarantee an assertion's accuracy or validity, that statistics can easily be generated from faulty data, and that academic journals vary widely in their quality and their criteria for accepting papers for publication.

The first part of this chapter critically reviews the principal source of data for the Cameron group's publications, their 1983-1984 surveys conducted in eight U.S. municipalities. Between 1985 and 1996, the group published seven articles based on this data set (Cameron & Cameron, 1995, 1996a, 1996b; Cameron, Cameron, & Proctor, 1988; Cameron et al., 1985, 1986, 1989). Six serious errors are identified in the Cameron group's sampling techniques, survey methodology, and interpretation of results. The presence of even one of these errors would be sufficient to cast serious doubts on the legitimacy of any study's results. In combination, they make the data virtually meaningless. The latter section of the chapter uses objective indicators to show that the Cameron group's survey results have had no discernible impact on scientific research. They have been published in journals with extremely low levels of professional prestige and scientific impact, and have been cited in only a handful of other research articles, most of which criticized their methodology. It is concluded that the Cameron group's surveys are an example of bad science that has been used to perpetuate the stigma historically associated with homosexuality.

The Cameron Group's Surveys

The Cameron group conducted their main survey in seven cities and towns in 1983 (Cameron et al., 1985, 1986). Subsequently, Cameron et al. (1988) combined additional data from a 1984 Dallas (Texas) sample with the 1983 data set. Most subsequent papers reported data from the combined samples (Cameron & Cameron, 1995, 1996a, 1996b). This section examines in detail the methods used in conducting those surveys. Issues related to sampling are considered first, followed by other methodological aspects of the survey.[1]

The Sample

In most empirical research, every member of the population of interest cannot be directly observed. Instead, inferences are made about the larger population using data collected from a subset, or *sample*, of that population. Samples are of two kinds. In a *probability sample*, all population elements (e.g., persons, households) have some opportunity of being included, and the mathematical probability can be calculated that any one of them will be selected. Consequently, data from a probability sample can be used to make generalizations about the population from which the sample was drawn provided that the sample was properly designed and executed, had an adequate response rate, and was sufficiently large. In a *convenience sample*, by contrast, population elements are selected on the basis of their availability (e.g., because they volunteered), with the consequence that an unknown portion of the population is excluded (e.g., those who did not volunteer). Because some members of the population have no chance of being sampled, the extent to which a convenience sample—regardless of its size—actually represents the entire population cannot be known.

Many strategies can be used to create a probability sample. Each starts with a *sampling frame*, which can be thought of as a list of all elements in the population of interest (e.g., names of individuals, telephone numbers, house addresses, census tracts). The sampling frame defines the population from which the sample is drawn and to which the sample data will be generalized. Probably the most familiar type of probability sample is the *simple random sample*, for which all elements in the sampling frame have an equal chance of selection and sampling is done in a single stage with each element selected independently (rather than, for example, in clusters). Somewhat more common than simple random samples are *systematic samples*, which are drawn by starting at a randomly selected element in the sampling frame and then taking every nth element (e.g., starting at a random location in a telephone book and then taking every 100th name). In yet another approach, *cluster sampling*, a researcher selects the sample in stages, first selecting groups of elements, or clusters (e.g., city blocks, census tracts, schools), and then selecting individual elements from each cluster (e.g., randomly or by systematic sampling).

Because probability samples can be recruited in a variety of ways, researchers are expected to provide enough information about their methods in their published reports so that other scientists can replicate their procedures. However, details about sampling methodology have been sketchy or entirely absent from the Cameron group's published papers. They simply characterized their approach as "conventional one-wave systematic area cluster sampling" (e.g., Cameron et al., 1986, p. 328), without further elaboration. They provided no information, for example, about what units were used for clustering (census tracts? city blocks?), how many clusters were selected, what proportion of addresses within each cluster was included in the sample, or how homogeneous the households within the clusters were on relevant variables (e.g., educational level, age).

The researchers' failure to describe their procedures means that the adequacy of their methods in this regard cannot be evaluated. Even if we assume that their study design met minimal requirements for recruiting a probability sample, however, three serious errors related to sampling issues are readily evident from their published reports.

Error 1:
Despite Their Characterizations
of It, the Sample Was Not National

The Cameron group claimed that theirs was a "national" sample (e.g., Cameron et al., 1988, p. 211, abstract), and they have repeatedly used their data to make generalizations about the entire population (e.g., "We found that about 2% of U.S. males claimed to be homosexual and about another 2% claimed to be bisexual in 1983"; Cameron, 1988, p. 867). However, the initial sampling frame consisted of only seven municipalities (Bennett, Nebraska; Denver, Colorado; Los Angeles, California; Louisville, Kentucky; Omaha, Nebraska; Rochester, New York; Washington, D.C.). Data from an eighth city (Dallas, Texas) were added later. By sampling only these cities and towns—whose selection appears to have been arbitrary[2]—the Cameron group systematically excluded all U.S. adults who resided elsewhere when the study was conducted. Even if the study were otherwise flawless, therefore, valid conclusions about the entire U.S. adult population could not be drawn from this sample. At best, the findings could be generalized only to the populations of the eight municipalities.

Error 2:
The Response Rate Was Unacceptably Low

Although not representative of the entire U.S. population, accurate descriptions of sexual attitudes and behaviors in the eight municipalities in the early 1980s might have been useful in their own right. However, the Cameron group's results cannot be considered representative of even the specific municipalities because the vast majority of their sample did not complete the survey. Appreciating the importance of this criticism requires an understanding of the concept of response rate.

Once a sample is selected, an attempt is made to collect data (e.g., through interviews or questionnaires) from all of its members. In practice, researchers never obtain responses from 100% of the sample. Some sample members inevitably are traveling, hospitalized, incarcerated, away at school, or in the military. Others cannot be contacted because of their work schedules, community involvements, or social lives. Others simply refuse to participate in the study, even after the best efforts of the researcher to persuade them otherwise.

Each type of nonparticipation biases the final sample, usually in unknown ways. In the 1980 General Social Survey (GSS), for example, those who refused to be interviewed were later found to be more likely than others to be married, middle-income, and over 30 years of age, whereas those who were excluded from the survey because they were never at home were less likely to be married and more likely to live alone (Smith, 1983). The importance of intensive efforts at recontacting sample members who are difficult to reach (e.g., because they are rarely at home) was apparent in that GSS respondents who required multiple contact attempts before an interview was completed (the "hard-to-gets") differed significantly from other respondents in their labor force participation, socioeconomic status, age, marital status, number of children, health, and sex (Smith, 1983).

The *response rate* describes the extent to which the final data set includes all sample members. It is calculated as the number of people with whom interviews are completed ("completes") divided by the total number of people or households in the entire sample, including those who refused to participate and those who were not at home (see Equation 1).

$$\text{Response Rate} = \left(\frac{\text{Completes}}{\text{Completes} + \text{Refusals} + \text{Not at Homes} + \text{Others}} \right) \qquad [1]$$

Whether data are collected through face-to-face interviews, telephone interviews, or mail-in surveys, a high response rate is extremely important when results will be generalized to a larger population. The lower the response rate, the greater the sample bias. Fowler (1984), for example, warned that data from mail-in surveys with return rates of "20 or 30 percent, which are not uncommon for mail surveys that are not followed up effectively, usually look nothing at all like the sampled populations" (p. 49). This is because "people who have a particular interest in the subject matter or the research itself are more likely to return mail questionnaires than those who are less interested" (p. 49).

The Cameron group never reported their true response rate in their published papers. Instead, for their initial, seven-municipality sample, Cameron et al. (1985) reported a "compliance rate" of 43.5% (p. 293), by which they apparently meant that 43.5% of the respondents who were given a survey subsequently completed and returned it. Although this figure is no substitute for the response rate, it has some utility, once the Cameron group's arithmetic errors are corrected (using their own approach, the compliance rate should have been calculated at 47.5%).[3] It indicates that a majority (52.5%) of those who were contacted and invited to participate did not complete a questionnaire. Those who refused to participate differed from those who completed the questionnaire in important ways (Cameron et al., 1985). They tended to be older and male, whereas people who returned the questionnaire were disproportionately young, highly educated, and White (Cameron & Cameron, 1996a).

The compliance rate, however, is inadequate for evaluating sample bias because it excludes the substantial number of households in the sample that were never contacted at all—the "not-at-homes" (Cameron et al., 1985, p. 292).[4] Substituting data from the Cameron group's published papers into Equation 1, the response rate can be computed as the number of completed surveys (4,340) divided by the total number of valid households initially selected for the target sample (18,418—which is the sum of the reported number of respondents contacted, including refusals [9,129], plus the reported not-at-homes [9,289]). Thus, the approximate response rate for the seven-municipality study was 4,340/18,418 = 23.6%.[5]

When they first reported the data from the Dallas sample, Cameron et al. (1988) once again provided only a "compliance rate," in this case 57.7% (p. 212). Using their reported data (Cameron et al., 1988) and Equation 1, the response rate for the Dallas survey was as follows:

$$\left(\frac{842}{1460 + 2609}\right) = 20.69\% \qquad [2]^6$$

Combining the Dallas data with the 1983 survey data yields an overall response rate across the eight municipalities of approximately 23%.[7]

Thus, completed surveys were successfully obtained from less than one fourth of the sample households. The residents of three out of every four households that should have been in the study never participated because they directly refused, accepted a survey form but never returned it, or were never contacted.

Although survey researchers do not have an absolute standard for what constitutes an acceptable response rate, a rate of 23% is clearly inadequate. In this regard, it is instructive to consider survey research norms in the early 1980s, when the Cameron group's data were collected. Smith (1983) cited telephone and face-to-face interview studies to posit that a response rate of 75% (or, as he phrased it, a *nonresponse* rate of 0.25) was "typical for good, state-of-the-art surveys" (p. 387). Around the same time, Fowler (1984) observed that academic survey organizations could usually achieve response rates in the 75% range, although some types of samples (e.g., central-city samples, random-digit dialing telephone samples) were likely to have lower rates. In a passage that is particularly relevant to the present discussion, Fowler also noted:

> One occasionally will see reports of mail surveys in which 5 to 20 percent of the sample responded. In such instances, the final sample has little relationship to the original sampling process. Those responding are essentially self-selected. It is very unlikely that such procedures will provide any credible statistics about the characteristics of the population as a whole. (p. 48)

This characterization fits the Cameron group's surveys, which had barely more than a 20% response rate. Even if their initial sampling frame and methodology might have potentially yielded an appropriately representative sample of the households in the eight municipalities, the execution was such that the sample cannot be considered "random" (e.g., Cameron & Cameron, 1996b, p. 765). Rather, the Cameron group's efforts ultimately resulted in what was essentially a convenience sample. Consequently, their conclusions, at best, cannot be generalized to any group other than the respondents themselves (and, as argued below, there are many reasons to believe that the data do not even provide a valid description of the sample members). The extent to which they describe the entire U.S. population—or even the populations of the eight municipalities sampled—cannot be known.[8]

Cameron and Cameron (1988) conceded this point when, in response to similar criticisms (Boor, 1988a, 1988b; Duncan, 1988), they asserted that theirs was "a 'national random sample' in the usual, rather imprecise, sense of the term employed in the social sciences" (p. 490). Whatever imprecise sense the Camerons had in mind, professional survey researchers do *not* use phrases such as *national random sample* carelessly or imprecisely (e.g., Fowler, 1984; Sudman, 1976).

Cameron and Cameron (1988) tried to salvage their data and defend their practice of generalizing from a sample that, by their own admission, they had incorrectly characterized as national and random by claiming that they observed "usually reasonable agreement" between data reported from other studies and response patterns to some of their questions. However, the adequacy of a sample is judged first by the method through which respondents were included in it. Data from a badly executed sample may manifest some response patterns that resemble those observed in well-designed studies with probability samples, but that fact does not make the former sample representative (e.g. Sudman, 1976).[9]

Error 3:
Subsamples Were Too Small to
Permit Reliable Analyses

The use of appropriate sampling methods and an adequate response rate are necessary for a representative sample, but not sufficient. In addition, the sample size must be evaluated. All other things being equal, smaller samples (e.g., those with fewer than 1,000 respondents) have greater *sampling error* than do larger samples. To understand the notion of sampling error, it is helpful to recall that data from a sample provide merely an estimate of the true proportion of the population that has a particular characteristic. If 100 different samples are drawn from the same sampling frame, they could potentially result in 100 different patterns of responses to the same question. These patterns, however, would converge around the true pattern in the population.

The sampling error is a number that describes the precision of an estimate from any one of those samples. It is usually expressed as a margin of error associated with a statistical level of confidence. For example, a presidential preference poll may report that the incumbent is favored by 51% of the voters, with a margin of error of plus or minus 3 points at a confidence level of 95%. This means that if the same survey were conducted with 100 different samples of voters, 95 of them would be expected to show the incumbent favored by between 48% and 54% of the voters (51% ± 3%).

The margin of error due to sampling decreases as sample size increases, to a point. For most purposes, samples of between 1,000 and

2,000 respondents have a sufficiently small margin of error that larger samples are not cost-effective. However, if subgroups are to be examined, a larger sample may be necessary because the margin of error for each subgroup is determined by the number of people in it. For example, although a national survey with a probability sample of 1,000 adults has a margin of error of roughly 1 to 3 percentage points (using a 95% confidence interval),[10] analyses of responses from the African Americans in that sample (who would probably number about 100) would have a margin of error of roughly 4 to 10 points (for further explanation of sampling theory and procedures, see Bradburn & Sudman, 1988; Fowler, 1984; Schuman & Kalton, 1985; Sudman, 1976).

If the Cameron group's combined 1983-1984 sample had been a random national sample, its size ($N = 5,182$ people) would have permitted estimates of population characteristics with only a small margin of error. For example, if 5% of the sample reported that they were homosexual, the margin of error associated with this estimate would be approximately one percentage point (at the 99% confidence interval); that is, we could be 99% confident that the true proportion of the populations of Los Angeles, Dallas, Omaha, and the other municipalities included in the sample was at least[11] 4% to 6% homosexual (i.e., 5% ± 1%), disregarding for the moment the other limitations inherent in the survey's methodology (see the discussion of validity, below).

This is not to say that the same margin of error applies to the Cameron group's sample. Their sampling method employed clustering, which can produce higher sampling errors than a simple random sample, depending on the size of the final clusters and the amount of homogeneity in relevant variables within the clusters (e.g., Fowler, 1984; Sudman, 1976), neither of which can be determined from the information provided by the Cameron group in their published papers. Because the low response rate rules out the possibility of making any population estimates on the basis of their data, however, this point is moot.

Yet even if none of these problems were present, reliable estimates could *not* be made on the basis of extremely small subgroups, as the Cameron group purported to do in several papers. For example, Cameron and Cameron (1996a) identified 17 respondents from the combined 1983-1984 samples who claimed to have a homosexual parent. The questionnaire responses of this subsample were scrutinized for various negative experiences, such as reporting incestuous relations with a parent (5 reported such incest). From these data, Cameron and Cameron

(1996b) concluded that 29% (5/17) of children of a homosexual parent have incestuous relations with a parent, compared with 0.6% of the children of heterosexuals, and that "having a homosexual parent(s) appears to increase the risk of incest with a parent by a factor of about 50" (p. 772).

Even if data from their sample could be generalized (which, as shown above, is not the case) and if all of the self-reports were valid (an assumption that is questioned below), making estimates from a subsample of 17 has an unacceptably large margin of sampling error. In a simple random sample of 17, the margin of error due to sampling (with a confidence level of 99%) would be plus or minus 33 percentage points.[12] In the Cameron group's cluster sample, the margin of error would probably be even higher. Thus, the confidence interval surrounding the Cameron group's proportion of 29% would range from at least –4% to +62%. This is such a wide margin of error that it is meaningless. Moreover, because the confidence interval includes zero, the Cameron group cannot legitimately conclude that the *true* number of children of homosexual parents (in the eight municipalities sampled) who were victims of parental incest was actually different from zero.

Validity

The three major errors discussed to this point are sufficiently serious to negate any claims the Cameron group has made about the representativeness of their sample. Their findings simply cannot be generalized legitimately to a larger population. Such a statement, however, can also be made about the vast majority of published psychological studies (although the authors of most such studies have neither incorrectly characterized their samples as random nor made sweeping generalizations about the general population on the basis of their data). Is it possible that the Cameron group's studies, although not based on a representative sample, still offer valuable insights about sexual orientation and behavior?

In order for the Cameron group's results to be useful in this sense, their questionnaire and the procedures they used to collect data would have to be valid. The *validity* of a method (e.g., a survey questionnaire) refers to how accurately it measures what it is supposed to measure. If survey items are so complex or ambiguous that different respondents interpret them differently, for example, their validity is compromised. Validity is also threatened if respondents do not provide accurate or honest answers, because of either their inability to do so (e.g., due to memory problems) or their unwillingness to answer truthfully (e.g., because the researchers communicated their biases or expectations to the respondents).

The following sections address the potential error and bias introduced into the results by the wording and format of questionnaire items, intentional misstatements by respondents, the apparent lack of quality control in the interview process, and the communication of researchers' biases to respondents.

Error 4:
The Validity of the Questionnaire Items Is Doubtful

Formulating valid survey questions is an art as well as a science. The best questions are those that are understood easily and interpreted uniformly by all respondents, regardless of their education or other background factors. Participants in a questionnaire study provide inaccurate responses for two principal reasons: They are unable to do so or they are unwilling to do so. Both problems are likely to have affected responses to the Cameron group's surveys.

Validity problems resulting from respondents' inability to provide accurate information. According to Cameron et al. (1986), their self-administered questionnaire consisted of 550 items and required approximately 75 minutes to complete. It included a large number of questions that dealt with highly sensitive aspects of sexuality, many of them presented in an extremely complicated format. This procedure raises concerns about respondent fatigue and item difficulty.

By the time they reach the later stages of a very long task (such as filling out a questionnaire for more than an hour), respondents tire. They often become careless in their responses or skip questions entirely in their hurry to finish. One way to assess whether respondent fatigue created problems in a long questionnaire is to include consistency checks: Items from an early section of the questionnaire are repeated in a later part (either in identical form or alternatively phrased) so that the reliability of responses can be checked. The Cameron group did not report any systematic checks for the internal consistency of questionnaire responses, although in one paper they noted discrepancies between responses to some of the survey items about early sexual experiences, commenting, "Alas, we live in an imperfect universe" (Cameron et al., 1986, p. 334).

Another problem results from the use of highly complex questions. One of the first rules of writing items for self-administered questionnaires is to keep them as simple and brief as possible (e.g., Sheatsley, 1983). The Cameron group's questionnaire, however, contained questions that not only covered sensitive topics but also required respondents to read a large number of alternatives and follow intricate instructions. One section, for example, required respondents to read a list of 36 categories of persons (e.g., "my female grade school teacher," "my male jr/sr high school teacher," "my female physician/psychologist/counselor," "my male [camp, Y, Scout] counselor," "a foster-mother"), then to note the age at which "this person (these people) made *serious sexual advances* to me," then to note the age at which "this person (these people) had (experienced) *physical sexual relations* with me," and then to provide a number to complete the following sentence: "Added together, I had sexual relations with _____ different ones" (in each category) (Cameron et al., 1986; Institute for the Scientific Investigation of Sexuality [ISIS], 1984b, emphasis in original). Another item, which followed a question about the respondent's sexual orientation, asked, "Why do you think you became this way?" It was followed by 44 alternatives, the first of which included "I was seduced by a homosexual adult," "I had childhood homosexual experiences with an adult," and "I failed at heterosexuality" (Cameron & Cameron, 1996b; ISIS, 1984b). Many respondents probably found such tasks confusing (because of their length and complexity) or alienating (because of their content). In addition, it is likely that many respondents did not read these long lists of response alternatives carefully and completely.

A related problem is that the questionnaire used language that was probably difficult for many respondents to understand. In one section, for example, respondents were asked how old they were when they first experienced each of a series of sexual acts, including "fondling/manipulating a female's genitals/vagina," "urinating or defecating on a male," "performing anal sex (penis/finger/hand into anus) on a male," and "performing oral/genital sex on a female" (ISIS, 1984b). Terms such as *defecating, urinating, genitals, anus, penis,* and *vagina* may not have been understood by some respondents, especially those with poor reading skills and those who knew only slang terms for these concepts (Catania, Gibson, Chitwood, & Coates, 1990). Whether such problems led to underreporting or overreporting of various experiences cannot be known from the Cameron group's data.

Validity problems resulting from intentional misrepresentations by respondents. Another threat to validity occurs when respondents purposely lie or hide the truth. Self-report measures are necessarily based on the assumption that respondents do their best to provide truthful answers. In some cases, however, people do not wish to divulge sensitive information about themselves, as in self-reports of finances and information about behavior that is stigmatized, illegal, or potentially embarrassing. In other cases, they intentionally give false answers out of a mischievous or malicious motivation.

In the Cameron group's survey, most questionnaire items focused on highly personal and sensitive sexual issues. Recognizing the inherent difficulty in obtaining honest answers to such questions, experienced survey researchers use a variety of techniques to overcome respondents' reluctance to reveal sensitive information or respond accurately. Perhaps the most important of these is establishing rapport with respondents, assuring them that their privacy will be preserved, and convincing them that providing accurate information serves an important and useful purpose (Sudman & Bradburn, 1985). In addition, sensitive items are typically located in the latter part of the questionnaire, so that rapport and an appropriate context will have been established before they are asked (Sudman & Bradburn, 1985).

The Cameron group appears not to have used such procedures. One indication is that the questions posed early in the survey asked about the respondent's sexual orientation ("If you ever had a divorce, did it involve your partner being bi- or homosexual? [no/yes]" and "If you ever had a divorce, did it involve your being bi- or homosexual? [no/yes]"; ISIS, 1984b). Another indication that the Cameron group failed to present the study in a credible and sensitive manner is the fact that their interviewers apparently were reported to local police authorities on several occasions—"at least once in every city" (Cameron et al., 1985, p. 297). Indeed, the local newspaper in one of the cities in the study quoted a police officer who had advised a neighbor not to fill out the questionnaire: "I looked at the thing and it's kind of raunchy. But there's nothing illegal about it" (Flanery, 1983, p. 1).

Moreover, contradictory information in the Cameron group's published reports makes it unclear whether respondents could reasonably believe that their answers were anonymous. Throughout their reports, the Cameron group described the questionnaire as anonymous and reported that it was returned in a sealed envelope. Cameron and Cameron (1996b) stated that "we guaranteed respondents no identifiers and that the interviewer would not know responses" (p. 761). Cameron et al. (1989), however, reported that "postquestionnaire inquiry with selected respondents indicated that many homosexuals did not count persons contacted in an orgy or restroom type setting as 'partners' " (p. 1175). For the latter statement to be true, the researchers had to know which respondents to select for the postquestionnaire inquiry in order to reach "many homosexuals" who had participated in orgies or sex in rest rooms (there were too few such individuals to have been detected simply through a small number of randomly targeted follow-up interviews). How the supposedly anonymous questionnaire answers (e.g., self-reports of sexual orientation and sexual activities) were linked to specific respondents was not reported. Apparently, however, respondents' anonymity was not absolute, a factor likely to discourage some respondents from divulging sensitive information about themselves.

Given these problems, it is not surprising that many members of the sample simply refused to participate. Others, however, probably completed the questionnaire but provided bogus answers. In one critique of the survey, published as a letter to the editor of the *Nebraska Medical Journal* shortly after the Cameron group's first report appeared in that journal, Brown and Cole (1985) raised this concern:

> How do we know the respondents were not faking their responses? Unfortunately some people enjoy having a bit of fun with researchers and do not respond truthfully. Perhaps a sizeable number of respondents were having "fun" with these researchers. Any sensible person who has seen this questionnaire, which asks quite personal questions about "unusual practices" would question the sincerity, if not the truthfulness, of persons responding. (pp. 411-412)

Suppose, for example, that some respondents did indeed provide systematically untrue responses with the mischievous intention of creating a profile of an individual who routinely engages in what might be considered outrageous sexual behavior. They probably would have overstated their general level of sexual activity, reported routine participation in multiple unconventional sexual acts, and indicated an unusual sexual history (e.g., incest with multiple family members). Because the

Cameron group based many conclusions on extremely small subsets of their sample, if as few as two dozen people out of 5,182 (less than one half of 1% of the combined sample) faked their responses in this manner, they would have accounted for a substantial portion of reports of such activities.[13]

The impact of such mischief makers is maximized in samples with otherwise low response rates, like that of the Cameron group, because such samples tend to exclude respondents who provide dispassionate, honest answers that would offset the influence of individuals who purposely provide false data. Because they lacked systematic checks on the validity of responses to their questionnaire, and because interviewers did not directly observe respondents while they completed the questionnaire, the Cameron group could not determine how many of their respondents fit this pattern.

In summary, the length, format, and content of the questionnaire—as well as the manner in which it was administered and the researchers' apparent failure to create a credible context for eliciting highly sensitive information—raise serious concerns about its validity, none of which were addressed in the Cameron group's published papers.

Error 5:
The Interviewers May Have Been Biased
and May Not Have Followed Uniform Procedures

Because the goal of survey research is to identify commonalities and differences on specific variables (e.g., opinions, behaviors), every effort must be made to eliminate extraneous variation in responses. For this reason, professional survey organizations carefully train and monitor their interviewers in the field to ensure that they strictly follow standardized procedures and communicate an unbiased and nonjudgmental attitude to participants (e.g., Prewitt, 1983). Experimental studies have convincingly shown that the expectations of the individuals who collect the data can influence participants' responses (e.g., Rosenthal, 1966; Rosenthal & Rosnow, 1969). To avoid systematic biases from interviewers' personal values or expectations, researchers typically employ field staff who are generally unaware of the study's hypotheses and who are carefully trained to communicate a nonjudgmental and respectful attitude to all respondents. These considerations are especially important in surveys that involve sensitive information.

It is not apparent that adequate quality control procedures were followed by the Cameron group. Apart from briefly noting that "almost all interviewers were 30- to 45-year old females" (Cameron & Cameron, 1995, p. 612), the Cameron group never provided information about the characteristics, qualifications, and training of people who collected their data. It is reasonable to assume that the surveys were *not* conducted by a professional survey organization. Otherwise, the published reports most likely would have noted this fact. The Cameron group's reports provided no information about how interviewers were trained or supervised in the field. For example, it is not clear if a supervisor recontacted a portion of the respondents to check that an interviewer had indeed visited their homes (and did not falsely report having done so, or did not complete the questionnaire himself or herself), a standard quality control practice.

A more serious concern is that high-level members of the research team apparently were directly involved in data collection. This conclusion is suggested by a 1984 pamphlet distributed by the Institute for the Scientific Investigation of Sexuality, which listed Paul Cameron as the organization's chairperson.[14] The pamphlet reported results from the Cameron group's 1983 survey (which the pamphlet characterized as having been conducted by ISIS) and related the following anecdote:

> Among the questions to which respondents replied was one regarding whether "you have ever deliberately killed?" One young homosexual in Omaha who replied affirmatively gave the ultimate answer when he provided his phone and social security numbers and plea to "keep him in mind if we wanted anyone killed." His metallic eyes and spring steel sneer as he assured us of his sincerity are not readily forgotten. (ISIS, 1984a)

The quoted material is significant because it suggests that the author of the pamphlet—perhaps Cameron himself—was directly involved in data collection for the 1983 survey. This is problematic because the authors of the study had clear expectations about the results (which, as noted in the next section, were communicated to the public while data collection was in progress). They also had strong biases about sexual orientation, revealed in their public statements indicating antipathy toward homosexuality at the time the surveys were conducted (e.g., Cameron, 1982, 1983; "Quarantine of Gays," 1984). Even if they made an honest effort to avoid communicating these biases to respondents, it is unlikely that they could have successfully done so if they directly participated in data collection.

Error 6:
The Cameron Group's Biases Were Publicized
to Potential Respondents While Data Were Being Collected

One of the principal challenges inherent in social research is that the individuals who are being studied can become aware of the researcher's expectations or goals, which can alter their behavior. For this reason, researchers do not communicate their expectations or hypotheses in advance to research participants. Nor do they bias participants' responses by suggesting that a particular answer is more correct or desirable than others.

Contrary to this well-established norm, Paul Cameron publicly disclosed the survey's goals and his own political agenda in the local newspaper of at least one surveyed city (Omaha) while data collection was in process (Flanery, 1983). In that front-page interview, he was reported to have characterized the survey as providing "ammunition for those who want laws adopted banning homosexual acts throughout the United States" and was quoted as saying that the survey's sponsors were "betting that (the survey results will show) that the kinds of sexual patterns suggested in the Judeo-Christian philosophy are more valid than the Playboy philosophy" (p. 1).

Whether or not similar publicity directly linked to the survey appeared in other target cities during data collection is not known. While data collection was in progress, however, Cameron received national attention for his calls to quarantine gays (Cameron, 1983), which included public remarks in Houston while the Dallas survey was being conducted ("Quarantine of Gays," 1984).

Such publicity must be assumed to have biased the sample composition and the responses of those who elected to participate, at least in Omaha, which constituted approximately 19% of the final sample. After reading or hearing about the front-page item in Omaha's only daily newspaper, many potential respondents probably decided not to participate, whereas others may have given false answers to the researchers because they perceived that the survey had political or religious—rather than scientific—aims.

Conclusions About the Study Methods

The six criticisms detailed above are summarized in Table 11.1. As noted earlier, an empirical study manifesting even one of these weaknesses would be considered seriously flawed. In combination, the multiple methodological problems evident in the Cameron group's surveys mean that their results cannot even be considered a valid description of the specific group of individuals who returned the survey questionnaire. Because the data are essentially meaningless, it is not surprising that they have been virtually ignored by the scientific community. The following section addresses this issue.

Scientific Impact of the Cameron Group's Studies

Science is a collective enterprise. Published research papers can be considered scientifically significant to the extent that they influence the thinking and research of other scientists and have an impact on the formulation of new research questions and the design of future studies. Based on this rationale, research studies are often evaluated, in part, according to the prestige of the scientific journals in which they are published and the extent to which they are subsequently cited in the scientific literature by other researchers and professional colleagues (e.g., Seglen, 1994).

Objective measures are available for both of these criteria, using data published regularly in the *Social Sciences Citation Index* (*SSCI*) and the *Journal Citation Reports* (*JCR*) (e.g., Institute for Scientific Information [ISI], 1994). The *SSCI* is a quarterly publication that lists, alphabetically by author, all articles that have been cited in scientific journals during the given time period and the bibliographic references for the articles that have cited them. The *JCR* compiles data from the *SSCI* to report an *impact factor* for individual academic journals. The impact factor describes the average frequency with which articles in a particular journal are cited. It is computed as the number of times any article from that journal is cited during the first 2 years following its publication divided by the total number of articles published in that journal during the time period (ISI, 1994). To provide a simplified example: Suppose that a particular journal published 25 articles in 1990, and those 25 articles were

Table 11.1 Six Major Errors in the Cameron Group's Survey Reports and Their Implications

Source of Error	Consequences
1. Sample restricted to eight municipalities	The sample was not national as characterized; findings cannot be generalized beyond the eight municipalities.
2. Unacceptably low response rate	The sample is essentially a convenience sample; it cannot be considered representative of a larger population.
3. Extremely small subsamples	Analyses of subgroups (e.g., respondents reporting gay parents) have such a large margin of error that they are meaningless.
4. Doubtful validity of questionnaire items	Results are suspect because many respondents probably had difficulty understanding the questions or intentionally gave false answers.
5. Possibly biased interviewers; lack of quality control	May have influenced who participated and how participants responded to questions.
6. Researchers' biases publicized during data collection	May have influenced who participated and how participants responded to questions.

subsequently cited a combined total of 125 times between 1990 and 1992. The journal's impact factor for 1990 would be 125/25 or 5.0.

Although the impact factor has limitations, it is widely used by librarians, information scientists, and researchers from a variety of disciplines as an objective indicator of what Nisonger (1994) has described as "some amorphous positive attribute that is often called quality, value, or impact" (p. 448; for use of the impact factor score in evaluating psychology journals, see Feingold, 1989; Rotton, Levitt, & Foos, 1993).

Tables 11.2 and 11.3 report the impact factors for five of the six journals in which the Cameron group has published its survey reports and other papers, along with those of other selected social science journals for comparison purposes. (The *Nebraska Medical Journal*, in which Cameron et al., 1985, first published their survey results, could not be included because it was not among the nearly 1,500 journals listed in the *JCR*.) Four of the Cameron group's publication outlets—*Journal of Psychology, Journal of Psychology and Theology, Omega,* and *Psychological Reports*—were categorized as general psychology journals in the *JCR* (Garfield, 1994, 1995). They are listed in Table 11.2, along with examples of some of the top- and

Table 11.2 Impact Scores and Ranks Within Categories for Selected General
Psychology Journals in 1994 and 1995

Journal	1994 Impact	1994 Rank	1995 Impact	1995 Rank
Examples of high-ranked journals				
Psychological Review	7.187	1/97	5.058	5/84
Psychological Bulletin	6.697	3/97	6.966	1/84
American Psychologist	4.209	4/97	5.304	4/84
Examples of low-ranked journals				
Studia Psychologica	0.029	97/97	0.130	73/84
New Zealand Journal of Psychology	0.238	71/97	0.000	84/84
Outlets for Cameron group's research				
Journal of Psychology and Theology	0.296	61/97	0.066	81/84
Psychological Reports	0.242	69/97	0.295	53/84
Journal of Psychology	0.158	82/97	0.338	48/84
Omega: Journal of Death and Dying	0.153	83/97	0.187	67/84

SOURCE: *SSCI Journal Citation Reports*, 1994 and 1995.
NOTE: In 1994, 97 journals were ranked in the General Psychology category; 84 were ranked in that category in 1995.

bottom-ranked journals in that category for 1994 and 1995. *Adolescence* was categorized as a developmental psychology journal in the *JCR*, and is listed in Table 11.3 along with examples of top- and bottom-ranked journals in that category for 1994 and 1995. In addition to impact factors, Tables 11.2 and 11.3 list the numerical ranks for journals within their respective categories for 1994 and 1995 (Garfield, 1994, 1995).

Focusing first on the top rows of Table 11.2, the average number of citations for a paper published in the highest-ranked journals (*Psychological Review* in 1994, *Psychological Bulletin* in 1995) was approximately seven. In other words, articles published in these journals were cited, on average, seven times in the 2 years after their initial publication. Table 11.3 shows that two of the top-ranked developmental psychology journals (*Child Development* and *Developmental Psychology*) had impact scores in 1994 and 1995 that ranged from approximately 2.1 to 3.2. For the lowest-ranked journals in both tables, the impact factor was less than 0.24.

All of the journals used by the Cameron group were in the lower half of the rankings—in many cases, near the bottom. For those journals, the

Table 11.3 Impact Scores and Ranks Within Categories for Selected Developmental Psychology Journals in 1994 and 1995

	1994		1995	
Journal	Impact	Rank	Impact	Rank
Examples of high-ranked journals				
Child Development	2.320	2/32	3.190	1/36
Developmental Psychology	2.058	3/32	2.332	5/36
Examples of low-ranked journals				
Journal of Genetic Psychology	0.216	31/32	0.160	36/36
Praxis der Kinderpsychologie und Kinderpsychiatrie	0.176	32/32	0.227	35/36
Outlet for Cameron group's research				
Adolescence	0.312	30/32	0.314	33/36

SOURCE: *SSCI Journal Citation Reports,* 1994 and 1995.
NOTE: In 1994, 32 journals were ranked in the Developmental Psychology category; 36 were ranked in that category in 1995.

impact factors were substantially less than 1.0, meaning that the average article published in them was not cited at all in the 2 years after its initial publication.

Put another way, none of the Cameron group's research reports have been published in highly respected, scientifically rigorous, and highly influential psychological journals, such as those in the top half of the *JCR* rankings for 1994 or 1995. Instead, most of their survey papers (four of seven) appeared in *Psychological Reports,* which was ranked 69th (of 97 journals) for impact in 1994 and 53rd (of 84) in 1995. Other approaches to ranking the prestige and significance of journals have similarly ranked *Psychological Reports* at a low level in comparison with other psychology journals. Moreover, these rankings have shown a fair degree of consistency over the years. In the late 1980s, for example, Feingold (1989) ranked journals using both *SSCI* impact factors and number of citations to that journal in related American Psychological Association-sponsored journals (which are usually considered to have high impact and high prestige). He reported that *Psychological Reports* was one of the least-cited psychology journals. Approximately a decade earlier, using 1977 *SSCI* impact ratings, Buffardi and Nichols (1981) ranked *Psychological Reports* 90th out of 99 psychology journals (see also Rotton et al., 1993).

According to *JCR*, *Psychological Reports* was the third-largest journal for which statistics were collected, publishing 510 articles in 1994 and 504 articles in 1995 (Garfield, 1994, 1995). That it publishes a large number of papers is consistent with earlier reports that *Psychological Reports* has a substantially lower rejection rate than is typical for psychology journals (Buffardi & Nichols, 1981; Markle & Rinn, 1977; Rotton et al., 1993). *Psychological Reports* is also unlike the vast majority of psychology and social science journals in that it requires a fee from contributing authors; in 1996, the fee was $27.50 per page for longer articles ("Psychological Reports," 1996). In 1977, approximately 5% of psychology journals charged such fees (Markle & Rinn, 1977). No current list comparable to that compiled by Markle and Rinn (1977) is available, but the practice of charging a per page fee or requiring purchase of preprinted copies of an article remains rare. Such fees are not charged by the high-prestige psychology journals (e.g., those published by the American Psychological Association).

As shown in Tables 11.2 and 11.3, the other journals in which the Cameron group has published had similarly low impact ranks in 1994 and 1995. As with *Psychological Reports*, these ratings have been consistently low over time. Using 1977 *SSCI* impact ratings to rank 99 psychology journals, for example, Buffardi and Nichols (1981) ranked the *Journal of Psychology* 79th. *Adolescence*, which Cameron himself once labeled as obscure (Cameron, n.d.), was ranked 98th.[15]

Thus, the Cameron group has published all of its survey reports in academic journals with low prestige and, at least in the case of *Psychological Reports*, with a low rejection rate and a publication fee required from authors. Given the multiple, serious methodological flaws detailed in the first section of this chapter, it is reasonable to conclude that the Cameron group's papers would have been rejected by more prestigious scientific journals. This observation is not intended to disparage all of the articles published by *Psychological Reports* and the other journals used by the Cameron group. However, the present critique demonstrates that the papers published in those journals do not always meet high scientific standards. Therefore, they must be critically evaluated by the reader on a case-by-case basis.

In itself, showing that they were published in low-prestige journals does not demonstrate that the Cameron group's papers had no scientific impact. Indeed, the frequency with which any given article is cited

Table 11.4 Citation Frequencies for Cameron Group's Survey Reports, 1985-1995

Paper (Topic)	Cited in Same Journal	Cited in Another Journal	Total Citations
Cameron et al., 1985 (diseases)	0	1	1
Cameron et al., 1986 (child molestation)	0	1	1
Cameron et al., 1988 (armed forces)	3 (2)	1	4 (3)
Cameron et al., 1989 (public health)	0	0	0
Cameron & Cameron, 1995 (incest)	1	0	1

SOURCE: *Social Sciences Citation Index.*
NOTE: For each entry, the first number indicates the total number of citations to the article. For entries greater than 1, the number in parentheses indicates how many different authors cited the paper. Because papers published after 1995 could not have registered any citations in the *SSCI* by the time this chapter went to press, they are omitted from the table. Self-citations are not included in this table.

is probably based more on the article's qualities than on the journal in which it is published (Seglen, 1994). It is reasonable to ask, therefore, whether the Cameron group's papers had an impact on scientific thought and research, even though they appeared in low-prestige journals.

Based on data from the *SSCI*, Table 11.4 shows the frequency with which five papers published by the Cameron group reporting data from the 1983-1984 surveys were cited in the scientific literature through August 1996 (the latest information available as this chapter went to press). The remaining survey papers (Cameron & Cameron, 1996a, 1996b) are not included in the table because they had not been in print long enough to show any citations in the *SSCI*. Self-citations—that is, citations by the Cameron group of their own work—are excluded.

As shown in Table 11.4, the survey reports were cited in scientific journals a total of seven times by a total of six different authors. Four citations appeared in the same journal as the cited paper (*Psychological Reports* in all four cases); all four were brief letters or articles that disputed the Cameron group's conclusions (Boor, 1988a, 1988b; Duncan, 1988; Herron & Herron, 1996). Of the three remaining papers, one merely cited a Cameron group report in its comprehensive meta-analysis of all published studies of heterosexuals' attitudes toward homosexuality (Whitley & Kite, 1995) and the other two (Schmidt, Krasnik, Brendstrup,

Zoffman, & Larsen, 1989; Wellman, 1993) cited the Cameron group's research only in their discussion sections, indicating that the Cameron group data did not constitute a starting point for the research.[16]

Thus, behavioral and social scientists have virtually ignored the Cameron group's surveys. Other than the Cameron group itself, no researchers cited the survey papers as a source of ideas for new research on sexual orientation, and none cited the surveys in support of the Cameron group's assertions about the dangers to society posed by homosexuals. Were it not for the sensationalist uses to which they have been put by the Cameron group, the survey data would probably be totally unknown to the U.S. public.[17]

Conclusion

Data from the Cameron group's survey studies do not provide a valid description of the U.S. adult population, nor of the populations of the eight municipalities that they sampled. The response rate was unacceptably low and, for their analyses of subgroups in the data set, the margin of error was unacceptably large. The doubtful validity of the survey questions and the lack of quality control during data collection further vitiate the studies. Finally, public expressions of the researchers' biases during data collection had an unknown—but possibly substantial— impact on the findings.

Any one of these problems would raise extremely serious doubts about the quality of the data. In combination, they reduce the studies' scientific credibility so substantially that the data should best be ignored. Indeed, except for criticisms and a few passing mentions, the survey studies have been ignored by serious researchers. Unfortunately, the data have had a more substantial impact in the public arena, where they have been used to promote stigma and to foster unfounded stereotypes of lesbians and gay men as predatory, dangerous, and diseased.

Responding to previous criticisms, many of them similar to those discussed here, Cameron and Cameron (1988) stated, "We believe our results are 'close to target' or 'true' in the usual sense of the word in the discipline" and challenged their critics to "spend their nickel and demonstrate otherwise" (p. 490). Fortunately, the scientific enterprise is not based on the results of a single study. Instead, empirical research is always evaluated in comparison to the findings reported by other scientists. A thorough review of the scientific literature relevant to the conclusions drawn by the Cameron group is beyond the scope of this chapter. It is appropriate to note briefly, however, that the general consensus among researchers—apart from the Cameron group—is that the children of gay and lesbian parents do not manifest psychological or social detriments compared with the children of heterosexual parents (e.g., Patterson, 1992, 1994), that homosexuals have no greater propensity than heterosexuals to molest children (e.g., Groth & Birnbaum, 1978; Herek, 1991; Jenny, Roesler, & Poyer, 1994), and that sexual orientation per se is unrelated to psychological health (American Psychological Association, 1975; Gonsiorek, 1991).

Paul Cameron and his colleagues are certainly entitled to their belief that "homosexual practitioners engage in pathology and generate personal and social pathology as a consequence" (Cameron & Cameron, 1988). That assertion, however, should be recognized as a statement of their personal values and beliefs, not empirical fact. Accepting the Cameron group's survey studies as a valid source of empirical data ultimately demeans the social and behavioral sciences by fostering the perception that they are driven by ideological concerns rather than a quest for truth and accuracy. Instead, the Cameron group's reports should be dismissed as an example of bad science in the service of anti-gay stereotypes and stigma.

Notes

1. For a more detailed—but easily accessible—discussion of the points raised here, readers are referred to Bradburn and Sudman (1988). For a more technical discussion, see Biemer, Groves, Lyberg, Mathiowetz, and Sudman (1991), Bradburn (1983), Lessler (1984), and Turner and Martin (1984).

2. Cameron et al. (1989) reported that five cities were selected to represent high (Los Angeles, Washington), intermediate (Denver, Louisville), and low (Omaha) "levels of homosexual activity as indexed by published homosexual guides to sexual opportunities" (p. 1168). No details about the selection process (e.g., which guides were consulted; definitions of high, intermediate, and low levels of homosexual activity) were provided, nor was any rationale offered for selecting those specific cities from among others in the same category. No rationale was offered for selecting Bennett, Nebraska, and Rochester, New York, which, despite being described as pilot study sites (e.g., Cameron et al., 1985, 1986), were nevertheless included in the final data set (see note 9). Whatever the rationale, the sample could—at best—represent only the households in those eight cities (including Dallas) and towns.

3. Using Cameron et al.'s (1985) own data and procedures, 47.5% equals the number of returned surveys (4,340) divided by the sum of the following: the number of completed surveys (4,340) *plus* the number of rejections (3,363) plus the mail-in surveys that were distributed but never returned (which can be computed as 1,426, using the published data). I was able to replicate the Cameron group's erroneous figure of 43.5% by counting the completed mailed-in surveys twice in the denominator. After two papers reported the compliance rate as 43.5% (Cameron et al., 1985, 1986), Cameron et al. (1988), without explanation, reported it as 47.5%. The latter figure does not accurately describe the sample's response rate, but at least it is arithmetically correct.

4. The Cameron group apparently made only one attempt to contact each household. Not-at-homes and "locations that were considered too dangerous to ensure the safety of the interviewers were skipped" (Cameron & Cameron, 1996a, pp. 605-606). As a result, the not-at-homes constituted an unusually large portion of their sample—approximately 53%—compared with surveys conducted by professional survey research organizations (e.g., not-at-homes constituted only 3.4% of the 1980 GSS sample [Smith, 1983] and 1.9% of the Laumann, Gagnon, Michael, & Michael [1994] sample). Thus, the Cameron group's not-at-homes included individuals who would have been reached—perhaps with only one or two callbacks—by professional survey researchers.

5. This figure is only approximate because, consistent with their overall lack of methodological detail, none of the published reports by the Cameron group indicated whether the not-at-homes included ineligible addresses (e.g., vacant buildings, businesses). Because such addresses are appropriately excluded from calculation of the response rate, Cameron et al.'s response rate may actually have been somewhat higher than 23.6%.

6. In his critique, Boor (1988a) computed Cameron et al.'s (1988) response rate as 20.25%. The discrepancy between Boor's estimate and that provided here results from his inclusion of 89 non-English-speaking individuals in the denominator. Those 89 individuals were not included in the present calculation because it could reasonably be argued that the sampling frame was English-speaking adults, although the Cameron group did not make this point explicit in their published reports.

7. Although the Cameron group has consistently combined data from their Dallas sample with data from the 1983 samples, this procedure may be problematic for two reasons. First, the sampling methods may have differed between the two studies. The researchers reported that they " 'tilted' the [Dallas] sampling frame by oversampling in areas that yielded greater proportions of homosexuals" (Cameron et al., 1988, p. 212). They did not explain how specific areas were selected for oversampling, what proportion of the sample was recruited from the oversampled areas, and whether the data were appropriately weighted to compensate for the oversampling. A second problem with combining the data sets is that the Dallas respondents answered a somewhat different set of questions. The Dallas questionnaire included additional items about homosexuals serving in the military (Cameron et al., 1988) as well as the question "Was a parent homosexual?" (Cameron & Cameron, 1996b, p. 763). The Cameron group never reported where these questions were inserted into the questionnaire. Because survey responses can be affected dramatically by the order in which questions are asked (see, e.g., Schuman & Presser, 1981), the new items in the Dallas questionnaire—depending on their location in the survey— could have caused subsequent questions to be interpreted differently than in the 1983 sample. This concern is not addressed in the Cameron group's publications.

8. Although an extensive critique of the Cameron group's other published papers is beyond the scope of the present chapter, another example of inappropriate generalizations from a biased sample is found in Cameron, Playfair, and Wellum (1994). In that paper, the

Cameron group counted obituaries in various gay community publications and claimed to be able to use them to calculate the average life expectancy for homosexuals. Their conclusion—that homosexual men and women have a shorter life span than heterosexual men and women—provides a textbook example of the perils of using data from a convenience sample to generalize to an entire population. Obviously, an obituary of a noncelebrity appears in a gay community newspaper only if (a) someone notifies the newspaper about the death and (b) the editor decides to print the obituary. By restricting their analysis to obituaries in gay newspapers, the Cameron group systematically excluded from their calculations all homosexual men and women who died during the same time period but whose loved ones did not report their deaths to the gay press.

The inadequacy of this approach is evident from internal inconsistencies within the Cameron group's own data. For example, if the average lesbian life span is similar to that of gay men who do not have AIDS, as the Cameron group claimed ("under 50 years" versus "mid-40s," respectively; Cameron et al., 1994, p. 259), the ratio of lesbian obituaries to gay male obituaries should approximately equal the ratio of gay men to lesbians in the population. The Cameron group's own numbers (e.g., Cameron & Cameron, 1996a, 1996b) put the latter ratio at approximately 1.6 to 1 (or approximately 2.6 to 1 if bisexuals are dropped). (These figures are only approximate because the reported numbers of homosexual and bisexual male and female respondents are not consistent across the Cameron group's papers.) However, the ratio of men to women in their gay obituaries study (Cameron et al., 1994) is quite different: approximately 6 to 1 if AIDS and violent deaths are excluded, 32 to 1 if they are included. Thus, even the Cameron group would have to concede that either (a) the obituaries data do not include a representative sample of lesbians, or (b) population estimates based on their survey data are wrong. An observer with training in research methodology would most likely conclude that both sets of data are fatally flawed.

9. Another flaw in the sample is that data from two small "pilot studies" (Cameron et al., 1986, p. 328) in Bennett (Nebraska) and Rochester (New York) were subsequently included in the final data set. The purpose of a pilot study is to collect preliminary data and identify problems in a study's procedures (e.g., ambiguous items in a questionnaire). Combining the pilot study data with data from the study proper suggests that no changes were made to the study procedures or the questionnaire as a result of the pilot study. If this was the case (an unlikely occurrence, as seasoned survey researchers know), it should have been acknowledged in the Cameron group's reports. In addition, later reports completely omitted mention of the pilot studies and characterized the sample as having been recruited from five cities (e.g., Cameron et al., 1989) or, when the Dallas sample was added, six cities (e.g., Cameron & Cameron, 1996a, 1996b). Although the results apparently still included the pilot study data, this fact was not reported.

10. The margin of error is also affected by how the characteristic in question is distributed throughout the sample. If the hypothetical sample of 1,000 is fairly homogeneous (e.g., 95% have the characteristic and 5% do not), the margin of error is one percentage point. If it is heterogeneous (e.g., 50% versus 50%), the margin of error is three points.

11. In attempts to estimate the number of U.S. adults who are homosexual, researchers have generally described their estimates as a lower bound of the true population proportion (e.g., Laumann et al., 1994; Rogers & Turner, 1991). This assumption is based on the fact that homosexuality is widely stigmatized in the United States and that stigmatized characteristics tend to be underreported in self-reports (Sudman & Bradburn, 1985).

12. In this case, the confidence interval equals .29 ± .33. The standard error was calculated as:

$$\sqrt{\frac{p(1-p)}{n}} = \sqrt{\frac{.29(.71)}{17}} = 0.11$$ [3]

where *p* is the proportion of the sample manifesting the characteristic in question, and *n* is the sample size (e.g., Fowler, 1984, p. 37). The confidence interval for a confidence level of 99% is three standard errors above and below the sample proportion.

13. This conjecture is not intended to deny the reality of problems such as incest and sexual assault, but rather to question how many individuals who have experienced it so extensively are likely to report it in a lengthy survey given to them at their door by a stranger who, in at least one of the cities sampled, had been identified on the front page of the local newspaper as pursuing an antigay religious and political agenda (Flanery, 1983).

14. The pamphlet, titled "Murder, Violence, and Homosexuality" (ISIS, 1984a), featured on its cover a photograph of a blonde Caucasian girl, approximately 10 years old, cowering in a corner, with her hands raised in a defensive, self-protective posture, her face showing clear signs of distress. The photograph also shows the arm and hand of an adult male holding a large hatchet or ax above the girl. The pamphlet begins by warning readers that they are "15 times more apt to be killed by a gay than a heterosexual during a sexual murder spree," that "homosexuals have committed most of the sexual conspiracy murders," that "most victims of sex murders died at the hands of gays," and that "half of all sex murderers are homosexuals" (ISIS, 1984a).

15. In an undated letter circulated in Lincoln, Nebraska, during a 1982 campaign for a gay rights ordinance, Cameron criticized an article by Newton (1978) that was published in *Adolescence*, the same journal in which Cameron and Cameron (1996b) subsequently published results from their survey. Cameron (n.d.) began his remarks about the Newton article as follows: "David Newton, writing in an *obscure* journal, makes a claim that would not be allowed in a *refereed* journal" (p. 1; emphasis added).

16. Schmidt et al. (1989) cited the report by Cameron et al. (1985) that 5.8% of the men in their sample were bisexual or gay. Wellman (1993) cited Cameron et al.'s (1989) "report that well over ⅓ of sexually abused children are boys, and that almost all of these cases involve a male perpetrator" (p. 540). Wellman's characterization was more accurate than that of the Cameron group. In contrast to her precise description of the findings, the Cameron group characterized all male-male sexual assaults as being committed by homosexuals (for a critique, see Herek, 1991).

17. In considering the overall impact of the Cameron group's work on homosexuality, citation counts for their four other papers about homosexuality published through 1996 were also examined. Cameron and Ross (1981) was cited seven times by six different authors in the 15 years since its publication in the *Journal of Psychology and Theology*. Three of the citations occurred in review articles in that same journal that focused exclusively or primarily on papers that had been published in that journal. The remaining four citations occurred in other journals, including one paper that comprehensively cataloged all articles listed in *Psychological Abstracts* between 1979 and 1983 under topic headings related to homosexuality. Cameron (1985) was cited twice by one author; Cameron and Cameron (1988) was cited once; all three citations occurred in other journals (i.e., not the journal in which the Cameron paper was published). Cameron et al. (1994) was never cited. Cameron, Cameron, and Landess (1996) had not been in print long enough to show any *SSCI* citations. In addition to their papers on homosexuality during this time period, the Cameron group also published two papers on topics related to AIDS, neither of which reported original data. Cameron (1987) and Cameron and Playfair (1991) were each subsequently cited in three other published papers (for both articles, one citation occurred in the same journal and two occurred in other journals).

References

American Psychological Association. (1975). Minutes of the Council of Representatives. *American Psychologist, 30,* 633.

Biemer, P. P., Groves, R. M., Lyberg, L. E., Mathiowetz, N. A., & Sudman, S. (1991). *Measurement errors in surveys.* New York: John Wiley.

Boor, M. (1988a). Homosexuals in the armed forces: A reply to Cameron, Cameron, and Proctor. *Psychological Reports, 62,* 488.

Boor, M. (1988b). Homosexuals in the armed forces: A rejoinder to the reply by Cameron and Cameron. *Psychological Reports, 62,* 602.

Booth, M. (1992, September 27). Controversial researcher focus of rights debate. *Denver Post,* p. 6A.

Bradburn, N. M. (1983). Response effects. In P. H. Rossi, J. D. Wright, & A. B. Anderson (Eds.), *Handbook of survey research* (pp. 289-328). New York: Academic Press.

Bradburn, N. M., & Sudman, S. (1988). *Polls and surveys: Understanding what they tell us.* San Francisco: Jossey-Bass.

Brown, R. D., & Cole, J. K. (1985). Letter to the editor. *Nebraska Medical Journal, 70,* 410-414.

Buffardi, L. C., & Nichols, J. A. (1981). Citation impact, acceptance rate, and APA journals. *American Psychologist, 36,* 1453-1456.

Bull, C., & Gallagher, J. (1996). *Perfect enemies: The Religious Right, the gay movement, and the politics of the 1990s.* New York: Crown.

Cameron, P. (1982, January 2). Majority rights will suffer. *Lincoln* [Nebraska] *Star,* p. 8.

Cameron, P. (1983, February 6). Protect public: Quarantine gays (Guest column). *USA Today.*

Cameron, P. (1985). Homosexual molestation of children/sexual interaction of teacher and pupil. *Psychological Reports, 57,* 1227-1236.

Cameron, P. (1987). Corrected statistical analysis suggests casual transmission of AIDS in the African study of the Centers for Disease Control. *Psychological Reports, 60,* 177-178.

Cameron, P. (1988). Letters: Kinsey sex surveys. *Science, 240,* 867.

Cameron, P. (n.d.). Dear community leader [Letter to community leaders in Lincoln, NE, circa December 24, 1981]. (Copy on file with G. M. Herek)

Cameron, P., & Cameron, K. (1988). Reply to Boor and Duncan. *Psychological Reports, 62,* 490.

Cameron, P., & Cameron, K. (1995). Does incest cause homosexuality? *Psychological Reports, 76,* 611-621.

Cameron, P., & Cameron, K. (1996a). Do homosexual teachers pose a risk to pupils? *Journal of Psychology, 130,* 603-613.

Cameron, P., & Cameron, K. (1996b). Homosexual parents. *Adolescence, 31,* 757-776.

Cameron, P., Cameron, K., & Landess, T. (1996). Errors by the American Psychiatric Association, the American Psychological Association, and the National Educational Association in representing homosexuality in amicus briefs about Amendment 2 to the U.S. Supreme Court. *Psychological Reports, 79,* 383-404.

Cameron, P., Cameron, K., & Proctor, K. (1988). Homosexuals in the armed forces. *Psychological Reports, 62,* 211-219.

Cameron, P., Cameron, K., & Proctor, K. (1989). Effect of homosexuality upon public health and social order. *Psychological Reports, 64,* 1167-1179.

Cameron, P., & Playfair, W. L. (1991). AIDS: Intervention works; "education" is questionable. *Psychological Reports, 68,* 467-470.

Cameron, P., Playfair, W. L., & Wellum, S. (1994). The longevity of homosexuals: Before and after the AIDS epidemic. *Omega, 29,* 249-272.

Cameron, P., Proctor, K., Coburn, W., & Forde, N. (1985). Sexual orientation and sexually transmitted diseases. *Nebraska Medical Journal, 70,* 292-299.

Cameron, P., Proctor, K., Coburn, W., Forde, N., Larson, H., & Cameron, K. (1986). Child molestation and homosexuality. *Psychological Reports, 58,* 327-337.

Cameron, P., & Ross, K. P. (1981). Social psychological aspects of the Judeo-Christian stance toward homosexuality. *Journal of Psychology and Theology, 9*(1), 40-57.

Catania, J. A., Gibson, D. R., Chitwood, D. D., & Coates, T. J. (1990). Methodological problems in AIDS behavioral research: Influences on measurement error and participation bias in studies of sexual behavior. *Psychological Bulletin, 108,* 339-362.

Cimons, M. (1985, August 20). Dannemeyer hires AIDS quarantine advocate. *Los Angeles Times,* p. 4.

Colker, D. (1993, February 22). Anti-gay video highlights church's agenda. *Los Angeles Times,* p. A1.

Duncan, D. F. (1988). Homosexuals in the armed forces: A comment on generalizability. *Psychological Reports, 62,* 489.

Feingold, A. (1989). Assessment of journals in social science psychology. *American Psychologist, 44,* 961-964.

Fettner, A. G. (1985, September 23). The evil that men do. *New York Native,* pp. 23-24.

Flanery, J. A. (1983, May 23). Lincoln man: Poll will help oppose gays. *Omaha World Herald,* p. 1.

Fowler, F. J., Jr. (1984). *Survey research methods.* Beverly Hills, CA: Sage.

Garfield, E. (Ed.). (1994). *SSCI Journal Citation Reports: A bibliometric analysis of social science journals in the ISI database.* Philadelphia: Institute for Scientific Information.

Garfield, E. (Ed.). (1995). *SSCI Journal Citation Reports: A bibliometric analysis of social science journals in the ISI database.* Philadelphia: Institute for Scientific Information.

Gonsiorek, J. C. (1991). The empirical basis for the demise of the illness model of homosexuality. In J. C. Gonsiorek & J. D. Weinrich (Eds.), *Homosexuality: Research implications for public policy* (pp. 115-136). Newbury Park, CA: Sage.

Gonsiorek, J. C., & Weinrich, J. D. (1991). The definition and scope of sexual orientation. In J. C. Gonsiorek & J. D. Weinrich (Eds.), *Homosexuality: Research implications for public policy* (pp. 1-12). Newbury Park, CA: Sage.

Groth, A. N., & Birnbaum, H. J. (1978). Adult sexual orientation and attraction to underage persons. *Archives of Sexual Behavior, 7,* 175-181.

Herek, G. M. (1991). Myths about sexual orientation: A lawyer's guide to social science research. *Law and Sexuality, 1,* 133-172.

Herman, D. (1997). *The antigay agenda: Orthodox vision and the Christian Right.* Chicago: University of Chicago Press.

Herron, W. G., & Herron, M. J. (1996). The complexity of sexuality. *Psychological Reports, 78,* 129-130.

Institute for Scientific Information. (1994). *Social sciences citation index.* Philadelphia: Author.

Institute for the Scientific Investigation of Sexuality. (1984a). *Murder, violence, and homosexuality* [Brochure]. Lincoln, NE: Author.

Institute for the Scientific Investigation of Sexuality. (1984b). [Unpublished questionnaire]. Lincoln, NE: Author.

Jenny, C., Roesler, T. A., & Poyer, K. L. (1994). Are children at risk for sexual abuse by homosexuals? *Pediatrics, 94*(1), 41-44.

Laumann, E. O., Gagnon, J. H., Michael, R. T., & Michaels, S. (1994). *The social organization of sexuality: Sexual practices in the United States.* Chicago: University of Chicago Press.

Lessler, J. T. (1984). Measurement error in surveys. In C. F. Turner & E. Martin (Eds.), *Surveying subjective phenomena* (pp. 405-440). New York: Russell Sage Foundation.

Marco, T. (1991). *Special gay rights legislation.* Colorado Springs, CO: Author.

Markle, A., & Rinn, R.C. (1977). *Author's guide to journals in psychology, psychiatry, and social work.* New York: Haworth.

Newton, D. E. (1978). Homosexual behavior and child molestation: A review of the evidence. *Adolescence, 13,* 29-43.

Nisonger, T. E. (1994). A methodological issue concerning the use of *Social Sciences Citation Index Journal Citation Reports* impact factor data for journal ranking. *Library Acquisitions: Practice and Theory, 18,* 447-458.

Otjen, J. P. (1994, February 16). *Deposition of General John P. Otjen in the matter of Cammermeyer v. Aspin et al.* (W. D. Wash. 1994).

Patterson, C. J. (1992). Children of lesbian and gay parents. *Child Development, 63,* 1025-1042.

Patterson, C. J. (1994). Lesbian and gay families. *Current Directions in Psychological Science, 3,* 62-64.

Pietrzyk, M. E. (1994, October 3). Queer science: Paul Cameron, professional sham. *The New Republic,* pp. 10-12.

Prewitt, K. (1983). Management of survey organizations. In P. H. Rossi, J. D. Wright, & A. B. Anderson (Eds.), *Handbook of survey research* (pp. 123-144). New York: Academic Press.

Psychological Reports [journal information]. (1996). *Psychological Reports, 79,* inside cover.

Public financing of hate (Editorial). (1985, August 21). *Los Angeles Times,* p. 4.

Quarantine of gays urged in Houston because of AIDS. (1984, January 4). *San Francisco Chronicle,* p. 25.

Rogers, S. M., & Turner, C. F. (1991). Male-male sexual contact in the USA: Findings from five sample surveys, 1970-1990. *Journal of Sex Research, 28,* 491-519.

Rosenthal, R. (1966). *Experimenter effects in behavioral research.* New York: Appleton-Century-Crofts.

Rosenthal, R., & Rosnow, R. L. (1969). *Artifact in behavioral research.* New York: Academic Press.

Rotton, J., Levitt, M., & Foos, P. (1993). Citation impact, rejection rates, and journal value. *American Psychologist, 48,* 911-912.

Schmidt, K. W., Krasnik, A., Brendstrup, E., Zoffman, H., & Larsen, S. O. (1989). Occurrence of sexual behaviour related to the risk of HIV infection. *Danish Medical Bulletin, 36,* 84-88.

Schuman, H., & Kalton, G. (1985). Survey methods. In G. Lindzey & E. Aronson (Eds.), *Handbook of social psychology* (3rd ed., pp. 635-697). New York: Random House.

Schuman, H., & Presser, S. (1981). *Questions and answers in attitude surveys: Experiments on question form, wording, and context.* New York: Academic Press.

Seglen, P. O. (1994). Causal relationship between article citedness and journal impact. *Journal of the American Society for Information Science, 45,* 1-11.

Sheatsley, P. B. (1983). Questionnaire construction and item writing. In P. H. Rossi, J. D. Wright, & A. B. Anderson (Eds.), *Handbook of survey research* (pp. 195-230). New York: Academic Press.

Smith, T. W. (1983). The hidden 25 percent: An analysis of nonresponse on the 1980 General Social Survey. *Public Opinion Quarterly, 47,* 386-404.

Sudman, S. (1976). *Applied sampling.* New York: Academic Press.

Sudman, S., & Bradburn, N. M. (1985). *Asking questions: A practical guide to questionnaire design.* San Francisco: Jossey-Bass.

Tape's statistics on gay sex practices are disputed. (1993, February 23). *Minneapolis Star Tribune*, p. 4.

Turner, C. F., & Martin, E. (Eds.). (1984). *Surveying subjective phenomena*. New York: Russell Sage Foundation.

Walter, D. (1985, October 29). Paul Cameron. *The Advocate*, pp. 28-33.

Weinrich, J. D. (1988). Re: Sex survey (Letter). *Science, 242*, 16.

Wellman, M. M. (1993). Child sexual abuse and gender differences: Attitudes and prevalence. *Child Abuse & Neglect, 17*, 539-547.

Whitley, B. E., Jr., & Kite, M. E. (1995). Sex differences in attitudes toward homosexuality: A comment on Oliver and Hyde (1993). *Psychological Bulletin, 117*, 146-154.

Index

About the Editor

Gregory M. Herek, Ph.D., is a research psychologist at the University of California, Davis. His empirical research includes studies of heterosexuals' attitudes toward gay men and lesbians, violence against lesbians and gay men, public attitudes concerning the AIDS epidemic, and the impact of AIDS on gay and bisexual men. He has published numerous scholarly articles on these topics. His most recent book is *Out in Force: Sexual Orientation and the Military* (coedited with J. B. Jobe and R. M. Carney, 1996). In 1992, he coedited (with K. T. Berrill) *Hate Crimes: Confronting Violence Against Lesbians and Gay Men*. He is currently writing a book on antigay prejudice. He is a Fellow of the American Psychological Association (APA) and the American Psychological Society (APS). He is the recipient of the 1996 APA Award for Distinguished Contributions to Psychology in the Public Interest. His other awards include the Outstanding Achievement Award from the APA Committee on Lesbian and Gay Concerns (1992) and APA Division 44's annual award for Distinguished Scientific Contributions to Lesbian and Gay Psychology (1989). He is past chair of the APA Committee on Lesbian and Gay Concerns.

Dr. Herek's other professional involvements also have focused on lesbian and gay concerns and AIDS issues. In 1993, he testified on behalf of the APA and five other national professional associations at the U.S. House of Representatives Armed Services Committee hearings on gay people and the U.S. military. In 1986, he testified on behalf of the APA at the House Criminal Justice Subcommittee's hearings on antigay violence. He also has assisted the APA in preparing amicus briefs in court cases challenging the constitutionality of state sodomy laws, child custody for lesbian and gay parents, and military policies excluding lesbians and gay men. In addition, he has served as consultant and expert witness in numerous legal cases involving the civil rights of lesbians and gay men.

About the Contributors

Isiaah Crawford, Ph.D., is Associate Professor and Chair of the Department of Psychology, Loyola University, Chicago. He received his doctoral degree from DePaul University in 1987. His research interests focus on HIV/AIDS prevention and clinical intervention, attitudes toward marginalized group members, and professional practice and training.

Anthony R. D'Augelli, Ph.D., is Professor of Human Development in the Department of Human Development and Family Studies at Pennsylvania State University. A community psychologist, he is coeditor (with Charlotte J. Patterson) of *Lesbian, Gay, and Bisexual Identities Over the Lifespan* (1995) and *Lesbian, Gay, and Bisexual Identities and the Family* (1998). His primary research interests focus on coping processes among lesbian, gay, and bisexual youths.

Laura Dean, M.Ed., is Director of the AIDS Research Unit in the Sociomedical Science Division of the Columbia University School of Public Health. She has been studying the psychosocial impact of AIDS in New York City's gay community since 1984. Currently, she is focusing on the gay primary relationship and its connection to health and behavior.

Joanne DiPlacido, Ph.D., is Assistant Professor of Psychology at Central Connecticut State University. She is also the principal investigator for the Women Loving Women Health Project of CUNY, which is supported by grants from the Lesbian Health Fund of the Gay and Lesbian Medical Association and the Wayne F. Placek Fund of the American

275

Psychological Foundation. Her research interests include minority stress and health; lesbian and bisexual women's health issues; lesbian, gay, and bisexual issues in psychology; lifespan development; and psychosocial factors and chronic illness.

Karen Franklin, Ph.D., is a forensic psychologist and private investigator in Oakland, California. In addition to her doctorate in clinical psychology from the California School of Professional Psychology, she holds an undergraduate degree in journalism. Her major research interest is the intersection between psychology and law.

Geoffrey Haddock, Ph.D., is a Lecturer in Psychology at the University of Exeter in England. He received his doctorate from the University of Waterloo and completed a postdoctoral fellowship at the University of Michigan. His primary research interest is the psychology of attitudes, including the topics of attitude structure and the psychology of prejudice.

Mary E. Kite, Ph.D., is a faculty member of the Department of Psychological Science at Ball State University. She received her doctorate in social psychology from Purdue University in 1987. Her research interests include gender stereotyping, attitudes toward homosexuality, and the academic climate for women. She was recently promoted to the rank of full professor and is currently serving as Graduate Coordinator for her department.

Andrew McLeod is a graduate student in the clinical psychology Ph.D. program at Loyola University, Chicago.

Ilan H. Meyer, Ph.D., is Assistant Professor of Public Health at Columbia School of Public Health and a Project Director at the Harlem Center for Health Promotion and Disease Prevention. He is currently studying mental health problems of gay men and AIDS-related issues in various populations.

Peter M. Nardi, Ph.D., is Professor of Sociology at Pitzer College, one of the Claremont Colleges. He is the coeditor of *Social Perspectives on Lesbian and Gay Studies: A Reader* (1998), *In Changing Times: Gay Men and Lesbians Encounter HIV/AIDS* (1997), and *Growing Up Before Stonewall: Life*

Stories of Some Gay Men (1994), and editor of *Men's Friendships* (1992). He is special features coeditor of *Sexualities*, a new international journal published by Sage Publications, and the book review coeditor for *GLQ: A Journal of Lesbian & Gay Studies*. He is politically active in the gay community, having served as chair of the Sociologists' Lesbian & Gay Caucus of the American Sociological Association, cochair of the Los Angeles Gay Academic Union, and copresident and board member of the Los Angeles chapter of the Gay & Lesbian Alliance Against Defamation (GLAAD). He has also published several op-ed pieces in the *Los Angeles Times* on gay/lesbian issues. He is currently working on a project studying gay men's friendships.

Drury Sherrod, Ph.D., is a social psychologist and a partner in the jury research firm of Mattson & Sherrod, Inc., in Los Angeles. He received his doctoral degree from Stanford University and has taught psychology at the Claremont Colleges, Carnegie-Mellon University, and Hamilton College. He is the author of *Social Psychology* (1984) and numerous articles on jury behavior, gender and friendship, environmental stress, and attribution theory. He has consulted with and conducted pro bono research for the Lambda Legal Defense and Education Fund.

Angela Simon, Ph.D., is Assistant Professor in the Behavioral and Social Sciences Division at El Camino College in Torrance, California. Her research interests include the study of attitudes toward lesbians and gays and the self- and social perception of emotion. Her teaching interests include social psychology, critical thinking, emotion, and gender.

Douglas Alan Strand is a doctoral candidate in the Department of Political Science at the University of California, Berkeley. He has served as a consultant to the American National Election Study (NES), developing and analyzing survey content on the topic of homosexuality in the NES 1993 Pilot Study. His dissertation work investigates public attitudes in the politics of "family values."

Bernard E. Whitley, Jr., Ph.D., is Professor of Psychological Science at Ball State University. He received his doctoral degree in social-personality psychology from the University of Pittsburgh in 1983. His research interests include attitudes toward homosexuality and academic dishonesty. He is the author of *Principles of Research in Behavioral Science (1996)*.

Mark P. Zanna, Ph.D., is Professor of Psychology at the University of Waterloo. He is the editor of *Advances in Experimental Social Psychology* and coeditor of the *Ontario Symposium*. His main research interest is the psychology of attitudes, including the psychology of prejudice.

DATE DUE

MAY 1 9			
DEC 0 9			